CAMPAIGN FINANCE

WHAT EVERYONE NEEDS TO KNOW®

CAMPAIGN FINANCE

WHAT EVERYONE NEEDS TO KNOW®

ROBERT E. MUTCH

OXFORD
UNIVERSITY PRESS

Oxford University Press is a department of the University of Oxford. It furthers the University's objective of excellence in research, scholarship, and education by publishing worldwide. Oxford is a registered trade mark of Oxford University Press in the UK and certain other countries.

"What Everyone Needs to Know" is a registered trademark of Oxford University Press.

Published in the United States of America by Oxford University Press 198 Madison Avenue, New York, NY 10016, United States of America.

© Oxford University Press 2016

Cataloging-in-Publication Data is available at the Library of Congress.
ISBN 978–0–19–027469–6 (hbk.); 978–0–19–027468–9 (pbk.)

1 3 5 7 9 8 6 4 2
Printed by R.R. Donnelley, United States of America

CONTENTS

ACKNOWLEDGMENTS   xiii
INTRODUCTION   xv

1 What is the campaign finance problem?   1

What is the disagreement between supporters and opponents of reform?   1

How big a problem is quid pro quo *corruption?*   2

*Whether the problem is political corruption or political
inequality, campaign finance is about paying for election
campaigns. How much do they cost?*   3

Do elections cost a lot more now than they used to?   4

Is it true that the candidate with the most money always wins?   5

Where do candidates get the money to pay for their campaigns?   5

What is the role of political parties?   6

How has Congress regulated money in elections?   7

What is the state of the Federal Election Campaign Act today?   8

2 Watergate and *Buckley v. Valeo*   10

What was Watergate?   10

What was the campaign finance part of Watergate?   13

How did Congress change campaign finance law after Watergate?   15

Who were Buckley and Valeo?   16

*Why did Senator Buckley and the other challengers think the
1974 reforms were unconstitutional?*   17

How did the circuit court decide Buckley v. Valeo*?*   18

How did the Supreme Court decide Buckley v. Valeo*?*   19

*How did the challengers, the defenders, and the justices deal with
the reform goals of curbing campaign costs, preventing corruption,
and promoting equality?*   21

Why is Buckley v. Valeo *still important today?*   22

3 The rise and fall of public funding   25

How does the Presidential Election Campaign Fund work?   25

*Did Congress come up with the idea of public funding in response
to Watergate?*   26

*What did reformers hope to accomplish by using public funds to
pay for elections?*   27

Why was Senator Long's public funding bill so controversial?   28

*If the income tax checkoff was so controversial in the 1960s,
how did it survive the political battles in Congress?*   29

*What happened to the tax incentives for small contributions
that Congress passed in 1971?*   30

*Why did the public funding program pay for the party conventions
as well as the elections?*   30

Why did Congress repeal public funding for party conventions?   32

How does the public funding program treat minor parties?   33

How does the public funding program treat independents?   33

Did public funding meet its goal of bringing in new, small donors?   35

*Public funding is also supposed to bring in new candidates. Did the
presidential program do that?*   36

*But participation in the tax checkoff had dropped by 2012.
Did the same thing happen with public opinion?*   37

What kinds of public funding programs are the states enacting?   38

Which states subsidize election campaigns?   39

Which cities have public funding programs?   41

How does New York City's public funding program work?   42

How well did the presidential public funding program work?   43

4 Disclosure and the Federal Election Commission   46

What does the FEC do?   47

Why did Congress create the Federal Election Commission?   48

How does the FEC work? Is it like other independent agencies?   49

How well does the current disclosure law work?   51

How does the FEC enforce other parts of the FECA?   54

Why are there so many partisan deadlocks on the FEC?   56

Why has disclosure become so controversial?   57

What are the intimidation charges raised by opponents
of disclosure?   59

5 Political action committees   61

Why do we have PACs? Who created them and why?   61

Why did corporations suddenly begin forming PACs in
the late 1970s?   63

Why did reformers try to curb PACs in the 1980s?   64

Did politicians begin refusing PAC contributions in the 1980s?   66

Were independent expenditures new?   67

What is a connected PAC?   68

How do the five categories of connected PACs differ from
one another?   69

Do business and labor PACs do different things with their money in
elections?   70

What are nonconnected PACs?   71

What do ideological PACs do?   71

What do leadership PACs do?   72

6 Super PACs 75

Where did the super PAC come from? 75

What makes super PACs super? 76

What is a hybrid PAC? 77

Why is coordination between candidates and super PACs a problem? 78

What did Congress do about independent expenditures
after Watergate? 79

How did Citizens United and SpeechNow make coordination between
candidates and super PACs such a big problem? 80

What are the rules against candidates coordinating with super PACs? 82

How close did candidates and super PACs get in 2012? 83

How did the super PAC change the way presidential candidates
run their campaigns? 84

Stephen Colbert formed a super PAC on his Comedy Central
TV show, The Colbert Report. What was that about? 85

Jeb Bush's super PAC did not help him at all. And Hillary Clinton's
super PAC did not help her fend off Bernie Sanders. So how big a
deal are super PACs, really? 87

7 Billionaires 89

There seem to be a lot of billionaire donors these days. Is this new? 89

What is different about megadonors today? 90

How did fundraising by presidential candidates in 2015 differ
from that of previous elections? 91

Jeb Bush was the establishment candidate who raised the most money
from billionaires, but his campaign never got off the ground. So were the
billionaires really all that important? 93

Were billionaires any more important in the Democrats' race? 94

What is the Koch brothers' network? 95

What did the Koch network do in the 2012 and 2014 elections? 97

How are other conservative billionaires becoming active in elections? 98

Are liberal billionaires doing anything similar to what the
Koch brothers are doing? 99

Are individual liberal billionaires building personal political operations,
as rich conservatives are doing? 101

8 Outside money 103

What was soft money? 103

Did both parties raise soft money? 105

How did the nature of soft money change after 1992? 106

What was the McCain-Feingold Act? 108

What is a 527? 109

Did 527s just replace party soft money? 110

What are 501(c) tax-exempt groups? 112

What was Wisconsin Right to Life v. FEC? 113

Was there still a lot of outside money in the 2008 election? 114

How did the FEC weaken disclosure rules for tax-exempt groups? 114

What are 501(c)(4)s? 115

How did Citizens United change the role of 501(c)s in elections? 116

What was the controversy over the IRS's scrutiny of applications
to form social welfare groups? 117

What did the American Bar Association recommend the IRS do
about political activity by nonpolitical groups? 118

9 Corporations, Unions, and Citizens United 121

What can corporations do in elections now that they could not
do before Citizens United? 121

Did Citizens United overturn the Tillman Act's ban on
political contributions? 122

Did the Tillman Act work? Or did corporations keep making
campaign contributions after it banned them? 123

When did corporations and unions begin using their money to influence elections?   124

How did conservatives try to limit labor participation in elections?   125

Why did the Department of Justice challenge the legality of labor PACs in Pipefitters v. United States?   126

What was the issue in First National Bank of Boston v. Bellotti?   127

Why did the Supreme Court give First Amendment rights of political speech to corporations in Citizens United?   129

How big a change did Citizens United *make to the way campaigns are financed?*   130

What about corporate personhood? Did Citizens United *say corporations are people?*   130

Did Citizens United *release a flood of corporate money for independent expenditures?*   131

Citizens United *also permitted unlimited spending by labor unions. Has that happened?*   132

Critics of Citizens United *also said it would let foreign money into U.S. elections. Has that happened?*   133

Is the Republican Party financed by business and the Democratic Party by labor?   134

What about corporate lobbying? Isn't that at least as big a problem as campaign finance?   135

10 Conclusion   137

Why does the future look bright for reform opponents?   137

Is there is any chance for reviving public funding for presidential elections?   138

What about public funding for state and city elections? Is that likely to continue?   138

Will small-donor programs be able to counter the surge of rich donors and democratize campaign finance?   140

Well-financed non-party groups seem to be more active than the parties in recent elections. Are the parties getting weaker?   141

Can the FEC be made to work?   143

Will disclosure survive? 143

There seems to be a lot of support for a constitutional amendment to overturn Citizens United. *Is that likely to happen?* 144

Why are the prospects for reform so poor? 145

The chances of curbing big money in elections would be a lot better if the 5–4 split on the Supreme Court went the other way. How likely is that? 147

CHRONOLOGY **149**
NOTES **163**
GLOSSARY **197**
FURTHER READING **203**
INDEX **205**

ACKNOWLEDGMENTS

This book has been in the back of my mind for some time. I have been writing about the history of campaign finance for more than twenty-five years, and I have more historical research to do. My writing has focused on explaining how we got into our current situation, but not on explaining that situation. Eventually, I started thinking about writing a general introduction to campaign finance, about the basics that people need to know to understand what they read, see, and hear in the news. Last year I decided it was time to organize those thoughts into a book. Bob Bauer, Rick Hasen, Robin Kolodny, Michael Malbin, Dick Pious, Trevor Potter, Ann Ravel, and Paul Ryan commented on chapters and gave me good advice, as did two anonymous reviewers. If some errors still got through, blame me, not them. I had the good fortune to work again with Nancy Toff at Oxford University Press. She immediately liked the idea for this book and pushed me to get it done—quickly.

INTRODUCTION

The 2014 congressional elections cost $3.8 billion. That is a lot of money. But is it more than a congressional election should cost? Or is it just about right? Questions like these are raised in the media after every election, and people read news articles and op-ed columns looking for answers. They do not get good answers, though, because the questions themselves are biased. They cannot be answered objectively because there is no standard measure for how much an election should cost. Yes or no answers only express political opinions.

Liberal pundits worry that money in elections is a problem that keeps getting worse, while conservatives assure us that there is nothing to worry about. This difference of opinion is just one aspect of the long debate over what, if anything, we should do about the way we finance our election campaigns. It is likely that no one on either side of the debate would have spent much time commenting on the $3.8 billion spent in 2014 had it all come from individuals making small contributions. That is because the issue is not how much money was spent but where it came from. The question at the center of the campaign finance debate is where the money *should* come from.

Can we still say we live in a democracy if a few hundred rich families continue to provide increasingly disproportionate shares of campaign funds? Or are those families simply exercising their rights as citizens of a democracy? Should campaign funds come from federal and state government treasuries rather than from private citizens? And if we keep our privately financed system, should we reduce wealth-based political inequality by placing limits on how much people can give and spend? Or would such limits amount to suppressing speech? At root, the debate is about the fundamental political question of how we define democracy and how we want our democracy to work.

That debate began with *Buckley v. Valeo*, the 1976 Supreme Court decision that is the landmark case in campaign finance law. Only campaign finance experts know much about that decision now, but when it was handed down it was almost as controversial as *Citizens United* is today. *Buckley* erected the constitutional framework within which all campaign finance law must be interpreted. Today's debate, and *Citizens United* itself, can be understood only by going back to *Buckley*.

At issue in that case were the post-Watergate reforms. Watergate was a big political scandal that grew out of the 1972 presidential election and eventually caused President Richard M. Nixon to resign. Campaign finance issues—huge sums of money from rich donors, illegal corporate contributions, and the flouting of disclosure laws—were only part of the scandal, but they made front-page news for months.

Congress responded to the Watergate scandal by enacting a comprehensive set of campaign finance reforms. The reforms were an extensive set of amendments to the 1971 Federal Election Campaign Act (FECA). They passed both houses of Congress by large bipartisan majorities, but opponents, led by Senator James Buckley (Cons.-NY), immediately challenged their constitutionality. The Supreme Court upheld most of the reforms, but planted the seeds for decades of controversy by striking down limits on political expenditures.

That controversy may ultimately be a philosophical one about how to define democracy, but in practice it is conducted in terms of laws and regulations, such as 527s, soft money, super PACs, dark money, and 501(c)(4)s. This book seeks to shed light on the campaign finance debate by explaining those laws and regulations.

CAMPAIGN FINANCE

WHAT EVERYONE NEEDS TO KNOW®

1

WHAT IS THE CAMPAIGN FINANCE PROBLEM?

This is the most basic question about campaign finance, and it is where differences of opinion begin. The disagreement is between those who think there is a problem that should be solved by passing reform laws, and those who think that the real problem is reformers who want to regulate a system that works well just as it is. Or was, before Congress passed the 1974 amendments to the Federal Election Campaign Act (FECA).

What is the disagreement between supporters and opponents of reform?

The disagreement goes back to *Buckley v. Valeo*, specifically to the Supreme Court's decision to strike down limits on political expenditures. The 1974 FECA amendments had limits on campaign contributions and expenditures, and it was the battle between supporters and opponents of these limits that were the focus of the case.

The defenders of the FECA argued that the limits strengthened democracy by reducing the undue influence of wealth on elections and public policy. The opponents said the limits weakened democracy by violating First Amendment protections for political speech. The disagreement was between egalitarian and inegalitarian definitions of democracy. The Supreme Court agreed with the inegalitarian definition and struck down the limits as a suppression of speech. The only constitutionally permissible reason to regulate campaign funds, the court said, is to prevent corruption.

The disagreement still is between egalitarian and inegalitarian definitions of democracy; the court's ruling that the egalitarian definition is unconstitutional has not changed that fact. But if supporters of reform hoped to have any success in a courtroom, they had to disguise their argument for equality as an argument against corruption. The only upside to this situation was that preventing corruption is a popular position, at least as long as people do not get too specific as to what they mean by that term. People may not always agree on what constitutes corruption, but everyone is against it. The Supreme Court, though, was specific as to what it meant: *quid pro quo* corruption, which essentially means bribery.

How big a problem is quid pro quo *corruption?*

That depends on whom you ask. The general public seems to think it is a much bigger problem than political scientists and journalists do.

When lobbyist Jack Abramoff pleaded guilty to conspiracy to bribe members of Congress, 77 percent of respondents to a *New York Times*/CBS News poll said that what he did was not an isolated incident but "the way things work in Congress." In a follow-up question, 92 percent said they believed that *all* members of Congress accept bribes at least some of the time. Almost no one who is active on either side of the campaign finance issue would agree with public opinion on this point. Bribery is a crime, and crime is not rampant on Capitol Hill.[1]

But reformers and the general public do agree that money has too much influence in elections and over policymaking in Congress. A 2013 *New York Times*/CBS News poll reported 85 percent of respondents saying that Congress served "special interests," not their constituents, and three-fourths of respondents to a 2014 CBS News poll said that the wealthy had more influence in elections than other Americans.[2]

The difference is that much of the public seems to think that the problem is a political system corrupted by illegal acts of bribery, while reformers say the real problem is what is legal. They tend to see the large influence of wealth as undue influence—something that is simply a fact of life. The rich always have and always will have more political influence than the rest of us, and no law can change that. What laws can do is reduce the degree of inequality, which is what spending limits in the 1974 FECA would have done.

Whether the problem is political corruption or political inequality, campaign finance is about paying for election campaigns. How much do they cost?

That depends on the kind of election. Presidential elections are the most expensive, and Senate elections generally cost more than nearly all elections for the House of Representatives. Elections for some state offices can cost as much as those for the U.S. Senate and House of Representatives. (State and local elections will not be covered here because the laws regulating them have to be compatible with the same Supreme Court decisions that govern federal campaign finance law.)

The size of the relevant electorate—the number of voters in the country, a state, or a congressional district—is a big factor in determining the cost of elections for these offices. It also matters whether a district is rural, suburban, or urban, or is part of a major media market. Candidates for president have to reach every voter in the country, which is why presidential elections will always be the most expensive.

Senate candidates from most states have to reach many more voters than are in a congressional district, which explains the greater cost of Senate elections. Senate candidates in 2014 spent an average of $7,800,000, while House candidates spent an average of only $1,100,000.[3]

The number of "open seat" elections for any one of these offices will also affect the cost of campaigns. Open-seat elections are ones in which no incumbent is running for reelection, and they are more expensive than ones in which a challenger is trying to unseat an incumbent. Incumbents usually win, so they do not need to raise large campaign funds, and challengers find it hard to raise funds of even moderate size.

The total cost of House elections, on the other hand, is not much affected by the number of open seats. Several members of Congress retire every year, which means the increased cost of electing someone to fill the seats they vacated is a constant feature of House election costs. The much larger number of House candidates—700 to 800 every cycle—and the generally equal size of congressional districts means there is little year-to-year variation in overall spending. The average spending figure of $1,100,000 for 2014 House candidates is close to the average for all House elections since 2000.

There is much more variation in the cost of Senate elections. Only one-third of Senate seats are up for grabs in each election cycle, so the much smaller number of candidates and the widely varying size of state populations can create big differences from one election to the next, even without open seats. The $7,800,000 candidate spending average for 2014 is almost $2 million less than the average for 2012 and $3 million more than the average for 2008.

Do elections cost a lot more now than they used to?

The relative year-to-year stability of House campaign costs makes them a good indicator of the overall trend in the cost of all elections. The average amount that House candidates spend has increased over the years, but it has increased gradually, not in sharp bursts upward.

House candidates in 2014 spent a total of $821,000,000, which is less than the $952,000,000 they spent in 2012. If we looked only at the spending for these two elections we might conclude that the cost of House elections was declining. But the amount of money House candidates spent in 2012 is larger than the $708,000,000 they spent in 2000, and more than twice the $426,000,000 they spent in 1990.[4]

Candidates, however, account for only part of what is spent in campaigns. Party committees and non-party groups, such as political action committees (PACs), super PACs, and formally non-political tax-exempt groups, also make expenditures on behalf of candidates. These are called "independent" expenditures because the groups making them are legally separate from and organized independently of the candidates they support. These expenditures have increased, too, but not always gradually.[5]

All forms of campaign spending have increased, but not all in the same way or for the same reasons. Candidate spending has increased gradually, partly in response to general economic conditions that affect everyone and partly in response to changes specific to campaign finance law and practices. Other spending increases, by party as well as non-party groups, were largely responses to changes in campaign finance law and were episodic.

Is it true that the candidate with the most money always wins?

They usually do. But—and this is an important "but"—that is true because the candidates who get the most money are usually the ones who are most likely to win. They are candidates who have proven themselves by winning other elections, earning the support of party leaders, and achieving name recognition among voters. Candidates who have never won, or even ever run in, an election will not have the full support of party leaders, will be unfamiliar to voters, will not attract much money, and are not likely to win.

But what if these unproven candidates are rich enough to pour tens of millions of dollars into their own campaigns? That usually does not work. It worked for billionaire Michael Bloomberg, who won three terms as mayor of New York City, in 2001, 2005, and 2009, by spending record-shattering sums of his own money to greatly outspend his publicly funded opponents. But it did not work for former eBay CEO Meg Whitman, who broke Bloomberg's record by giving $144,000,000 to her 2010 campaign for California governor, only to lose to the outspent but better-known and more experienced Jerry Brown.[6]

Where money may matter most is when two experienced politicians face one another in an open-seat election. In a contest between two candidates who have both won elections, have the full backing of their parties, and are well known to voters, but who do not both attract the same amount of money, having a bigger campaign fund could be the deciding factor in winning the election.

Money is necessary because campaigns can be expensive, but money alone rarely wins elections. Think of running for an elective office as like playing blackjack in Las Vegas. Having a lot of money is no guarantee that you will win, but without money you cannot even get into the game.

Where do candidates get the money to pay for their campaigns?

All candidates for federal office—president, Senate, and House of Representatives—raise money by soliciting contributions from private citizens. The exception is the public funding program for presidential elections that Congress created in 1974. Beginning in 1976, presidential candidates could draw on a U.S. government fund to pay campaign costs. This program is still available, but in 2012 President Obama and former governor Mitt Romney chose to raise private money instead of using public funds.

Individual contributions made up the great majority of the money President Obama and Governor Romney raised in 2012; PAC contributions made up only a small share of total receipts. Because Obama and Romney depended entirely on private contributions, they had to spend at least as much time asking for money as they did asking for votes.[7]

Congressional candidates also get most of their money from individual contributions, but they get a bigger share of their campaign funds from PACs. Senate candidates may get around 15 percent of their money from PACs and House candidates more than one-third. The great majority of individual contributions they get come from people who live in the same state or congressional district as the candidate they support.[8]

Any citizen can make a campaign contribution, but very few do. In 2012, only 0.4 percent of Americans made contributions large enough—more than $200—to be reported under the FECA; and they accounted for more than 60 percent of all individual contributions. Even fewer citizens made contributions in the 2014 midterm congressional elections. The public pays much less attention to these elections than to those held in presidential election years. Voter turnout drops—from 58 percent in 2012 to 36 percent in 2014—and so does donor turnout. Only 0.23 percent of Americans made contributions of $200 or more in 2014, and they accounted for two-thirds of all individual contributions. Campaign contributions are also closely correlated with family income: the higher a person's income, the more likely he or she is to make a contribution, and to make a large contribution.[9]

What is the role of political parties?

Political parties contribute money to their candidates and make expenditures on their behalf, but party money accounts for only a small share of most candidates' campaign funds. In 2012, party money made up only 1 percent of House candidates' receipts and 3 percent of Senate candidates' receipts. This money was contributed and spent by the two parties' House and Senate campaign committees: the National Republican Congressional Committee, the Democratic Congressional Campaign Committee, the National Republican Senatorial Committee, and the Democratic Senatorial Campaign Committee.[10]

These committees also offer practical advice on how to run a campaign, and help with fundraising, voter registration, and get-out-the-vote drives. These services are especially useful to candidates who are running for the first time or who are in close contests. The Republican National Committee and the Democratic National Committee usually do not get involved in House and Senate races, but they provide similar services to presidential candidates.[11]

How has Congress regulated money in elections?

Congress passed the first regulations early in the twentieth century. The Tillman Act, passed in 1907, prohibited corporations from making campaign contributions; the first disclosure law, passed in 1910, required candidates to publicly report who gave them how much money; and in 1911 Congress imposed a ceiling on congressional campaign expenditures.

These laws were passed in response to a scandal about the funding of the 1904 presidential election. People had long suspected that corporations were making campaign contributions, but no one knew for sure until insurance executives testified under oath in a 1905 investigation. The argument for the Tillman Act was that corporations are not citizens, do not have the political rights of citizens, and should stay out of elections. The purpose of the disclosure law was to tell voters who was paying for election campaigns. And the purpose of limiting congressional campaign expenditures was to make it easier for ordinary citizens to run for office.

In 1940, Congress imposed limits on contributions and set spending limits for presidential campaigns, and in 1947 it extended the ban against corporate contributions to cover labor unions. In 1971, Congress passed the first version of the current law, the FECA. The

1971 FECA strengthened disclosure requirements, but repealed limits on contributions and on most expenditures. It was this law that was in effect during the 1972 presidential election, the one that produced Watergate.[12]

Congress responded to Watergate by passing the 1974 FECA amendments, which revised the FECA so extensively as to be a new start for campaign finance reform. The 1974 reforms began a public financing program for presidential elections, restored and tightened limits on campaign contributions and expenditures, further strengthened disclosure requirements, and created the Federal Election Commission (FEC) to oversee and enforce the new laws.

Majorities of both parties in both houses of Congress voted for the 1974 amendments. But the opponents who lost in Congress took the battle to the courts, where they won a partial victory. In *Buckley v. Valeo*, the Supreme Court upheld most of the amendments, but agreed with the challengers' claim that political spending had the same First Amendment protection as political speech. It was on this ground that the justices struck down limits on all campaign expenditures, whether by candidates or by those spending on their behalf.

What is the state of the Federal Election Campaign Act today?

The FECA today remains much as the Supreme Court and Congress left it in 1976, at least on paper. The presidential public funding system is still on the books, but the last candidate to use it was Senator John McCain (R-AZ), in 2008. The FEC is still in operation, but partisan deadlocks have blocked it from acting on important matters. Candidates, parties, PACs, and groups making political expenditures are still required to disclose their donors, but this law too is less effective. Increasing amounts of money are now spent by officially non-political, tax-exempt groups regulated by the Internal Revenue Service, and they do not have to disclose their donors.

In the 2010 *Citizens United v. FEC* decision, the Supreme Court undermined the oldest reform, the Tillman Act. Citing *Buckley*'s ruling that limiting political expenditures is unconstitutional, the court granted corporations the First Amendment right to make those expenditures. Three months later, in *SpeechNow v. FEC*, the federal circuit court for the District of Columbia struck down the limits on contributions to committees that only made expenditures. These two decisions opened the way for super PACs and for unlimited spending by tax-exempt groups, most of which are nonprofit corporations.

Public funding, contribution limits, and disclosure were intended to free candidates from relying on big donors and to let voters see who was financing election campaigns. The Supreme Court upheld the constitutionality of these provisions in *Buckley*, and they are still law. But big money is back, and it is easy to evade contribution limits and disclosure requirements. In terms of meeting its original goals, the FECA today is in tatters.

2

WATERGATE AND
BUCKLEY V. VALEO

Congress passed the 1974 FECA amendments in response to the Watergate scandal. The amendments were the most comprehensive revision of campaign finance law in history, but they incorporated most of the laws that had been on the books since the Tillman Act in 1907. *Buckley v. Valeo* was the Supreme Court's most comprehensive ruling on the constitutionality of that law.[1]

Buckley was about a challenge to the constitutionality of the entire range of campaign finance law. This was the first time anyone had disputed the very idea of regulating campaign funds, and it was the first time the court had expressed its own doubts about it. By striking down a key part of the 1974 FECA amendments, the court put the constitutionality of regulation at the center of the campaign finance issue for the first time. Debate about the way we should pay for election campaigns became more a matter of constitutional law than of politics, and made the Supreme Court the dominant voice in that debate.

What was Watergate?

Watergate set the standard for a big political scandal. Its impact can still be seen in journalists' tendency to attach the suffix *-gate* to every new scandal. It got its name from a break-in at the Democratic National Committee (DNC) offices in the Watergate, a plush hotel-apartment-office complex in Washington, D.C. It took place in the early hours of June 17, 1972, during that year's presidential campaign. The break-in was discovered when an alert security guard saw that someone had tampered with the locks on the door to the DNC's offices. He called the Metropolitan Police, who arrived quickly and arrested five men inside the DNC offices.[2]

The men did not fit the profile of the ordinary burglar, as they were all wearing business suits or sport coats, and were carrying thousands of dollars in sequentially numbered $100 bills. They also had wiretapping equipment and cameras for photographing documents. Wiretapping is a federal crime, so the police called the FBI. It turned out that the men had broken in to replace wiretaps installed in a previous break-in.

The FBI soon found connections to campaign politics. Documents found on the burglars and in their hotel rooms linked them to President Nixon's campaign committee, the Committee to Reelect the President (CRP), and to current and former members of his White House staff. The CRP was a high-profile operation: Attorney General John Mitchell resigned his office to manage the campaign as CRP director, and Secretary of Commerce Maurice Stans resigned his office to become chief fundraiser as head of the CRP's finance committee.

President Nixon's Democratic opponent, South Dakota Senator George McGovern, was the candidate of the party whose headquarters the burglars has broken into. So it was headline news when the FBI revealed that one of the burglars was CRP's head of security, and that the campaign committee's general counsel and another staff member had overseen the operation from a nearby hotel room.[3]

The FBI soon traced the burglars' $100 bills to a secret CRP slush fund consisting of unreported campaign contributions that had been laundered through a Mexican bank. This fund had been used to pay the Watergate burglars and to finance other espionage and sabotage activities against Democrats and people on the president's "enemies list." Although these discoveries revealed links to the White House, Mitchell took the heat for all of them and resigned as CRP director two weeks after the arrests.[4]

Two months later a federal grand jury indicted the five burglars and the two men who had supervised the break-in. None of these events had much effect on the election, which Nixon won in a landslide. He won 61 percent of the two-party vote, the biggest majority since FDR's slightly bigger victory in 1936.[5]

Things began to go downhill for the president in 1973. The trial of the Watergate burglars began on January 10, ten days before he was sworn in for a second term. Ten days after that, all seven men were convicted (five of them had already pleaded guilty). On February 7 the Senate voted unanimously to assign a special committee to investigate the break-in, political espionage and sabotage, and the financing of the 1972 presidential campaigns. Senators Sam Ervin (D-NC) and Howard Baker (R-TN) were the chair and vice chair, respectively, of the Select Committee on Presidential Campaign Activities, which came to be called the Watergate Committee.

Six weeks after that vote, one of the convicted burglars confessed that they had all lied under oath and had been paid hush money from the secret CRP slush fund. He also said the break-in was not a rogue operation but had been planned by higher-ups. The federal grand jury that had indicted the burglars reconvened to hear more testimony about those higher-ups.

The slow unfolding of events now began to speed up. Grand jury testimony forced the resignations of Nixon's two top aides, H. R. Haldeman and John R. Ehrlichman, and of Attorney General Richard G. Kleindienst. The Watergate Committee began public hearings three weeks later. Then the new attorney general, Elliott Richardson, appointed Harvard Law professor Archibald Cox as special prosecutor to take over the Watergate investigation for the Department of Justice.

The Watergate Committee learned in July that President Nixon had used a White House taping system to record his Oval Office conversations. The committee subpoenaed all of the tapes, but Cox subpoenaed only tapes of specific conversations. Nixon refused to release any of the tapes, and ordered Richardson to fire Cox. Richardson refused and resigned, as did Deputy Attorney General William Ruckelshaus. Nixon then appointed Solicitor General Robert H. Bork as acting attorney general, and Bork did fire Cox.

The resignations and firing took place on October 20, 1973, a Saturday, and came to be known as the Saturday Night Massacre. The immediate result of these events was increased demand for the tapes, from prominent Republicans in and out of Congress, the press, the public, and from the new special prosecutor Nixon was forced to appoint, Texas lawyer Leon Jaworski. In December the president finally did surrender some of the tapes, one of them with the famously unexplained eighteen-and-a-half-minute gap.

The tapes were enough to convince Jaworski, other prosecutors, and the grand jury that the president knew more than he had claimed. The grand jury indicted seven of Nixon's aides, including Mitchell, Haldeman, and Ehrlichman, for conspiracy to cover up crimes. It also listed the president himself as an "unindicted co-conspirator." The Watergate Committee had already uncovered more break-ins, more secret funds, more hush money, and more perjury. Now it had evidence of a White House attempt to cover up its involvement in all those events. The hearings continued into 1974 and kept millions of Americans glued to their TV screens.

Two-thirds of Americans told pollsters the president should be impeached, and the Supreme Court voted 8–0 that President Nixon had to release the subpoenaed tapes. He released them all, including the "smoking gun" tape that showed he was involved in the cover-up less than a week after the Watergate break-in. Soon afterward he resigned to avoid certain impeachment. Never before in U.S. history had a president resigned. As the government helicopter carrying the former president lifted off from the back lawn of the White House, Vice President Gerald R. Ford took the oath of office from Chief Justice Warren Burger. The nation's first unelected vice president became the nation's only unelected president.[6]

What was the campaign finance part of Watergate?

It was the citizens group Common Cause that first made that part of the Watergate scandal public. The newly organized group had been active for months before the break-in, taking maximum advantage of the stronger disclosure requirements in the 1971 FECA. Candidates had to file in their states and in Washington, D.C., and the law required the reports be made available for public inspection. But making reports available for inspection in state and federal government offices did not guarantee that the data in them would get to the public at large.[7]

Getting that data out to the public was what Common Cause wanted to do. It doubted the new law would be enforced any more vigorously than the old one had been, so it decided to take matters into its own hands. Recruiting hundreds of volunteers across the country, the group compiled the data in state and national reports and released it to the press.[8]

But the volunteers soon discovered that CRP had not reported all the required data, and Common Cause had to go to court to get it. The issue in the case was whether the disclosure requirements in the old Federal Corrupt Practices Act (FCPA) still applied in the weeks before the new requirements in the FECA took effect on April 7, 1972.

Both parties had begun fundraising long before the FECA went into effect, which meant they had to comply with both old and new disclosure laws. The FCPA remained in effect through April 6, but the last reporting date under the old law was in February, which put the weeks until April 7 in a gray area. Common Cause asked all campaign committees to report all contributions made in the weeks between the two dates. The CRP refused, and Common Cause sued. The CRP agreed to a partial disclosure in the last days of the campaign, so as to avoid a trial before Election Day. But it resisted a court order to make a full disclosure, and it did not release all of the names until July 1973.[9]

Two of the names grabbed the public's attention: oil and banking heir Richard Mellon Scaife, who gave $1 million, and insurance mogul W. Clement Stone, who gave $2 million. Testimony before the Watergate Committee revealed that the CRP had raised more than $11 million in the weeks before April 7, soliciting large contributions with the promise of anonymity. Some of the contributions the CRP kept secret were later revealed to have been illegal corporate gifts. The biggest of these were $100,000 contributions from the Gulf, Phillips, and Ashland oil companies, whose executives later testified before the Watergate Committee.[10]

As the Watergate Committee learned more about the financing of President Nixon's campaign, the public grew more interested: more than one-fourth of all congressional constituent mail during and after the hearings was about campaign finance, more than on any other issue. After lengthy debates, Congress passed the most comprehensive package of campaign finance reforms ever enacted. Two months after taking the oath of office, President Ford signed the new reforms into law.[11]

How did Congress change campaign finance law after Watergate?

Congress amended the 1971 FECA so extensively as to make it a new beginning for campaign finance reform. The Senate acted first, in 1973. It restored limits on contributions and expenditures, and it created the Federal Election Commission to "oversee and enforce" disclosure requirements and these new provisions. The Senate passed these amendments by an 82–8 majority. The House, however, did not immediately act on the bill.[12]

While waiting for the House to act, Senators Edward M. Kennedy (D-MA) and Hugh Scott (R-PA) tried to add public funding to the amendments the Senate had just passed. Public funding was an old idea, but it had never been tried and was controversial. Public funding for congressional elections was so widely opposed in both parties that Kennedy and Scott quickly dropped it. They did manage to pass a public funding program for presidential elections, but most Republicans opposed it. Republicans voted for the total package, though, and the 1974 FECA amendments passed both houses by large majorities.[13]

Under the new law, an individual could contribute no more than $1,000 per election—the primary and the general each counting as one election—to a candidate; there was no limit on contributions to parties, but there was an aggregate total of $25,000 for all contributions. Parties and other political committees could give up to $5,000 to a single candidate with no aggregate limit. Independent expenditures on behalf of a candidate—expenditures not formally authorized by that candidate—were treated as contributions to that candidate and were subject to the same limits.[14]

The FECA set spending limits for House, Senate, and presidential campaigns, and limits for how much the two parties could spend in those elections. The spending limits for presidential campaigns were part of the public funding program. Congress gave the Federal Election Commission (FEC) the job of administering that program as part of its general responsibility for enforcing the FECA. Congress also strengthened disclosure requirements and gave the six-member FEC—three Republicans and three Democrats—responsibility for enforcing them and for making the data in disclosure reports available to the public.

Who were Buckley and Valeo?

Buckley was Senator James L. Buckley (Cons.-NY), who had led the opposition to the 1974 amendments in the Senate. (He was also the older brother of William F. Buckley, the founder of *National Review* and the leading voice of the conservative movement at the time.) Senator Buckley was joined by: former Senator Eugene McCarthy (D-MN); General Motors heir and major campaign contributor Stewart Mott; the Libertarian Party; the American Conservative Union; the New York Conservative Party; Human Events Inc., publishers of the conservative newspaper of the same name; and the American Civil Liberties Union.[15]

Valeo was Secretary of the Senate Francis R. Valeo. He was not the target of Senator Buckley's suit, but was simply the first of the congressional and executive branch officers who were named as defendants. Those defendants—Valeo, the Clerk of the House, the U.S. attorney general, the U.S. comptroller general, and the Federal Election Commission—were named because the 1974 FECA amendments gave them authority to enforce the new law.[16]

The chief defenders of the law, however, were not the government officeholders named in the suit but, rather, groups of private citizens, chiefly Common Cause and the League of Women Voters, which the court recognized as intervening defendants. An intervening defendant is someone who is not one of the named defendants in a case but has rights and interests that would be at least equally affected by a court's decision. Common Cause and others sought this recognition because they doubted that the Department of Justice would mount an adequate defense of the 1974 law. Their doubts were well founded.

President Ford did not like the 1974 law and signed it reluctantly. He added a signing statement that expressed reservations about the constitutionality of such key provisions as public funding and contribution and spending limits. The Department of Justice shared those reservations.[17]

The Department of Justice (DOJ) is normally responsible for defending the constitutionality of legislation, which is why the attorney general was a named defendant. But no one at the top levels of the department liked the law, either. So great was the department's hostility that top officials seriously considered opposing it or staying out of the case. The chair of the recently formed FEC, however, demanded DOJ representation and got an Oval Office meeting to state his case. At that meeting President Ford approved the highly unusual step of filing two briefs: a perfunctory defense of the law and a longer amicus brief that largely opposed it. The most committed defense of the law came from private citizens.[18]

Why did Senator Buckley and the other challengers think the 1974 reforms were unconstitutional?

Their core argument was that the 1974 law's limits on campaign contributions and expenditures were limits on political speech. Because all political activities require the spending of money, they reasoned that "expenditures for political communication have the same stature as the communication itself." That is, spending on speech is so closely tied to speech itself that the two are constitutionally inseparable and share the same degree of protection under the First Amendment.[19]

They opposed public funding on the ground that there was "no public interest in relieving candidates of the need to raise money to finance their political activities." They did not oppose disclosure in principle, agreeing that it allows voters to make informed choices. But they said the FECA requirements were too broad and that the reporting threshold was set too low. And in addition to finding the FEC to be unconstitutional for violating the separation of powers, they feared that the agency's "intrusive and chilling" enforcement powers would lead to discriminatory enforcement by incumbents against challengers.[20]

The challengers also argued that the stated goals of the law—keeping down the cost of campaigns, reducing political inequality, and curbing the undue influence of rich donors—did not justify the extent of the reforms. They dismissed the rising costs of campaigns by saying that just two of the biggest commercial advertisers had spent more in 1972 than the total spent in all of that year's election campaigns. They also rejected the idea that inequalities of campaign communication between the rich and poor gave political advantage to the rich. And they acknowledged that the Watergate hearings had uncovered some proven and suspected instances of corruption and undue influence, but argued that disclosure requirements were the proper response to that problem.[21]

The U.S. Court of Appeals for the District of Columbia Circuit heard the case first, and upheld nearly the entire law by a 7–1 vote. The challengers then appealed to the Supreme Court, which voted 7–1 to strike down parts of the law.

How did the circuit court decide Buckley v. Valeo?

The appeals court recognized at the start that the 1974 reforms were an attempt to correct "abuses that have spread over the years to infect the nation's federal election campaigns." It noted that Congress passed the reforms after those abuses became the subject of "momentous revelations" in the 1972 presidential campaign. And it agreed that the reforms served important public interests: "No one can doubt the compelling government interest in preserving the integrity of the system of elections through which citizens exercise the core right of a free democracy."[22]

Protecting the integrity of elections meant conducting them under "rules of law," rules set out in what the court acknowledged was the most comprehensive set of election reforms Congress had ever passed. It acknowledged, too, that the reforms were so comprehensive as to affect activities protected by the First Amendment, and so put them under "strict judicial scrutiny." All but one disclosure provision survived that scrutiny. The court upheld the rest of the 1974 reforms 7–1.[23]

The reforms survived because the court held that sufficiently compelling public interests can justify incidental restrictions on First Amendment rights, and because the extent of those restrictions had not yet been clearly defined. They had not been clearly defined because no one knew how the law would work in practice. The court noted several times in its opinion that some of the provisions it found to be constitutional might prove not to be when they were applied. Until then, however, the court said that "these latest efforts on the part of our government to cleanse its democratic processes should at least be given a chance to prove themselves."[24]

And there was another reason why the appeals court upheld the reforms. The court concluded that they enhanced First Amendment values: "By reducing in good measure disparity due to wealth, the Act tends to equalize both the relative ability of all voters to affect electoral outcomes, and the opportunity of all interested citizens to become candidates for elective federal office."[25]

How did the Supreme Court decide Buckley v. Valeo?

The Supreme Court's approach to the case was almost the exact opposite of the circuit court's. The court did not see protecting the integrity of elections as a compelling public interest, so it did not judge the new law by whether it served that interest well enough to justify incidental infringements upon First Amendment rights. Instead, it focused on the First Amendment rights and judged the law by whether it infringed upon them.

The court agreed with the challengers that limits on contributions and expenditures were infringements upon forms of political speech protected by the First Amendment. The challengers were less concerned about limits on contributions than on expenditures, and the court made an even sharper distinction between the two, giving them different degrees of constitutional significance. On the basis of this distinction, the justices upheld limits on contributions but struck down limits on expenditures.

The justices said contributions had less constitutional protection because they were only indirect speech, not the direct speech of the donors. As the majority put it, "the transformation of contributions into political debate involves speech by someone other than the contributor." A limit on the amount of money a person can give to someone else is thus only a "marginal restriction" upon that person's own political speech.[26]

But the justices held that this marginal restriction significantly deters corruption. Because contributions are money given directly to candidates, the justices decided that they had the potential for corrupting candidates. That meant that limits on contributions protect democracy by preventing rich donors from "securing a political *quid pro quo* from current and potential office holders."[27]

Expenditures were another matter. The Supreme Court held them to be the purest form of political speech: "political expression at the core of our electoral process and of the First Amendment freedoms."

It was also direct speech and so, unlike contributions, could not be corrupting. The justices struck down expenditure limits because they were not marginal but "direct and substantial restraints on the quantity of political speech" and because they did not deter corruption.[28]

That was true by definition for expenditures made by candidates themselves, but the court said it was equally true for expenditures made on their behalf by citizens and non-party groups. These are called independent expenditures because they are made without the candidates' authorization. And without that authorization, the justices said, they could not be used to secure political *quid pro quo* from those candidates.

Congress was not so sure, and limited independent expenditures for express advocacy on behalf of candidates to the same $1,000 it had imposed on contributions to those candidates. By 1974, Congress had had more than thirty years of experience with such expenditures and knew that most of them were independent only in a formal, legal sense. Independent expenditures had been used to evade contribution limits since the 1940s, and Congress imposed the $1,000 limit to prevent such evasion in the future.[29]

The Supreme Court, however, chose to believe that independent expenditures really were independent, that candidates who did not authorize them formally also did not do so informally. Such expenditures, the court said, "may well provide little assistance to the candidate's campaign, and indeed may prove counterproductive." If these expenditures could not assist candidates they also could not corrupt them, which meant that limiting them could not prevent corruption. So the court struck down the limit.[30]

The court also made a sharper distinction than Congress did between two kinds of political expenditures: issue advocacy and express advocacy. Congress and both courts generally agreed on how to tell one from the other. Issue advocacy expenditures are advertisements about public policy issues, not candidates. Congress and the circuit and Supreme courts all agreed that this definition held true even if such advertisements mention clearly identified federal candidates.

They also agreed that express advocacy advertisements are those that expressly urge the election or defeat of clearly identified candidates. But it was the Supreme Court that drew a bright line between issue and express advocacy, as advertisements that did and did not use what came to be called "magic words," such as "vote for," "vote against," "elect," and "defeat."[31]

The Supreme Court decided that issue advocacy was not political at all, even if the ads mention candidates in ways that are clearly positive or negative; and because they are not political, they cannot be subject to FECA regulation. The court permitted the government to regulate only ads that expressly urge voters to vote for or against a candidate, because only those ads are political.

The justices made these distinctions on the basis of another one, between two of the three public interests put forward to justify the reforms: promoting equality and preventing corruption. All the justices agreed that preventing corruption was a legitimate public interest, but the majority decided that it was the *only* legitimate interest, the only constitutionally permissible reason to regulate campaign funds.

How did the challengers, the defenders, and the justices deal with the reform goals of curbing campaign costs, preventing corruption, and promoting equality?

They did take the last two interests seriously, but in different ways: preventing corruption was the only public interest that was important enough to justify regulating campaign funds, and promoting political equality was flatly unconstitutional.

The FECA's defenders argued for the need to reduce campaign costs by pointing out that those costs had increased 300 percent between 1952 and 1972, while the consumer price index had increased by only 58 percent. They also emphasized the large amounts of time that candidates must spend raising funds for their campaigns. The appeals court accepted this argument, and agreed that keeping campaign costs down was a legitimate public interest.[32]

The justices, though, agreed with the challengers that the 300 percent increase was of little concern, pointing out that commercial advertising expenditures had increased even more over the same period. They did not see reducing campaign costs as a legitimate public interest: "The First Amendment denies government the power to determine that spending to promote one's political views is wasteful, excessive, or unwise."[33]

But it was the equality interest that really alarmed the Supreme Court. Reform supporters had made an equality argument in favor of expenditure limits. Limits strengthened democracy, they said, by reducing political inequalities that were based on inequalities of wealth: "The political inequality produced by great disparities of wealth, if left unregulated, would upset the premises on which our democracy is based."[34]

Instead of merely dismissing or watering down this interest, the justices attacked it, denouncing it as a constitutionally impermissible goal. It was this attack that produced the most often quoted passage in the *Buckley* opinion: "the concept that government may restrict the speech of some elements of our society in order to enhance the relative voice of others is wholly foreign to the First Amendment." The court equated political equality with the suppression of speech, and suppression of speech not in the abstract but targeted only at "some elements of our society."[35]

Preventing corruption, on the other hand, was a legitimate public interest, one that the justices narrowly defined as preventing *quid pro quo* transactions between donors and candidates. They acknowledged that it was nearly impossible to determine the actual extent of *quid pro quo* corruption. But they added that "deeply disturbing examples surfacing after the 1972 election demonstrate that the problem is not an illusory one." Referring to Watergate, they upheld contribution limits because they believed that even the appearance of such corruption could damage public trust in government.[36]

The majority used its anti-corruption rationale to uphold most of the rest of the 1974 law. They even upheld the public funding program, the most innovative and controversial part of the 1974 law, and the only part that most Republicans in Congress voted against. And they accepted the Federal Election Commission as the enforcer of stronger disclosure requirements; letting voters know who was giving how much to whom, they said, would "deter actual corruption and avoid the appearance of corruption."[37]

Why is Buckley v. Valeo *still important today?*

As the landmark case in campaign finance law, *Buckley* is the reigning precedent that governs every campaign finance case in state or federal courts. For many judges, lawyers, and law professors, this once controversial case has become settled law. But for many others, reform supporters and opponents alike, the case is still contentious.

The Supreme Court's reading of the First Amendment is still the most hotly contested part of the decision. It largely adopted the reform opponents' argument that political money and political speech were so closely linked that they were constitutionally inseparable and shared the same degree of protection under the First Amendment.

Reform supporters counter that this reading of the First Amendment protects money as though it were speech. Which is pretty much what Justice Potter Stewart said when summarizing the opponents' position during oral argument in *Buckley*: "money is speech and speech is money, whether it is buying television or radio time or newspaper advertising." (Stewart wrote the part of the decision that struck down spending limits as a violation of the First Amendment.)[38]

Stewart thought better of including this observation in his part of the decision. But Justice Byron White, who said the majority's decision was based on "the maxim that 'money talks,'" used Stewart's phrase in his dissent to characterize the majority's argument. Reform supporters have used the phrase "money is speech" as a metaphor for the court's argument ever since. The implication is that the court did not so much protect speech as privilege money; the debate over which of these things the court did continues today.[39]

But the biggest and most lasting impact of the *Buckley* decision is the way party and non-party groups have been able to use it to evade the FECA. Torrents of money flowed through the issue-ad loophole, beginning in the mid-1990s in the form of party soft money and continuing through 527 groups and 501(c)(4) social welfare organizations. And it was striking down limits on independent expenditures that made super PACs possible and allowed billionaires to become independent political entrepreneurs.

Reform opponents have their own complaints. They believe the justices did not take the First Amendment argument far enough, that they should have used it to get rid of limits on contributions as well as on expenditures. Here, too, the criticism began with the justices themselves. Chief Justice Warren E. Burger and Justice Harry Blackmun both dissented from this part of the decision, Burger saying that contribution limits were a "severe restriction on First Amendment activity."[40]

Reform supporters say the Supreme Court should have upheld limits on both. Justice Byron White made this argument in his dissent, saying that expenditure limits were necessary to prevent circumvention of contribution limits. White also pointed out something that has received more attention in the years since *Buckley*: that limiting contributions without limiting expenditures would increase candidates' obsession with fundraising, forcing them into "the endless job of raising increasingly large sums of money."[41]

Then there is the anti-corruption argument. Once the court said that preventing corruption was the only constitutionally permissible reason to regulate campaign funds, both sides reshaped their positions to fit into that framework. Most reform supporters believe that the goal of reducing political inequality is even more important today than it was in 1976. Since *Buckley*, though, they have had to refashion their equality argument as an anti-corruption argument.

3

THE RISE AND FALL
OF PUBLIC FUNDING

Public funding for presidential elections was the most controversial and most innovative part of the post-Watergate reforms. It was not controversial with the public, which supported it by large majorities, and every serious presidential contender participated in the program from 1976 through the rest of the century. But as Watergate receded from the headlines and from public attention, so too did support for, and even knowledge of, the public funding program. In 2012, both major party candidates opted out of the program.

While public funding was losing ground at the federal level, though, it was gaining ground at the state and local levels. These programs ranged from ones that offered only tax incentives for small contributions to more ambitious ones that were based on the presidential model. The popularity of publicly funded elections has increased since *Citizens United*, but the immediate future of such programs is at the state and local levels.

How does the Presidential Election Campaign Fund work?

The program is financed by an income tax checkoff. When you pay your U.S. income taxes, you see this question on Form 1040: "Do you want $3 of your federal tax to go to the Presidential Election Campaign Fund?" If you check the "Yes" box under that question, you send $3 into the Fund. Checking that box does not increase your taxes; it simply diverts part of what you have already paid to finance a government program you support. The original checkoff was for $1, but Congress increased the amount to $3 in 1993.[1]

The program uses these checked-off dollars to provide subsidies to qualified candidates: matching funds for small contributions in the primaries and grants for the general election. To qualify for matching funds in the primary elections a candidate must raise at least $5,000 in each of twenty states in contributions of $250 or less. Donors can make contributions up to the FECA limit of $2,700 (as of 2015), but only the first $250 counts toward the $5,000 required for each state. Matchable contributions must be from individual residents of the states, not from PACs or parties. Candidates can still raise money from PACs, but PAC contributions are not eligible for federal matching funds. Candidates with broad support generally raise more money than they get in federal funds.

Congress set the matchable limit at $250 to encourage candidates to solicit small donations. And requiring those donors to be residents of twenty different states ensured that public funds would go only to candidates whose support was not limited to a particular state or region. To be eligible for matching funds candidates also must agree to three spending limits: a limit for each state, which varies by population; an overall limit; and a limit of $50,000 from personal funds.

From 1976 through 2012 the program also provided partial funding for the parties' nominating conventions. Candidates who win their party's nomination get a flat grant for the general election; they must limit their spending to the amount of the grant and cannot raise private funds. Major party candidates began opting out of the program for the primaries in 2000, and in 2012 they opted out entirely, raising private funds for the primary and general elections. As of this writing, none of the candidates for the Republican and Democratic Party nominations have opted into the program for the 2016 primaries, and the eventual candidates will probably raise private funds for the general.

Did Congress come up with the idea of public funding in response to Watergate?

No, public funding is a much older idea. The *Wall Street Journal* proposed public funding as early as 1904, suggesting that it would solve the problem of "the undue and illegitimate use of money in politics." Rep. William Bourke Cockran (D-NY) introduced a public funding bill two years later, saying it might "do away with any excuse for soliciting large subscriptions of money."[2]

Congress did not take the *Wall Street Journal* up on its suggestion, and Rep. Cockran's bill died in committee. But the idea kept popping up. The American Political Science Association suggested in 1950 that public funding would be one "means of checking the irresponsible power of the small minority of large contributors to party funds."[3]

In 1956 Senator Richard L. Neuberger (D-OR) introduced a bill to substitute federal funds "for the present evil of large campaign contributions." Neuberger's bill got no further than Cockran's bill fifty years earlier. But the idea was beginning to get some traction and it briefly became law in 1966.[4]

Senator Russell Long (D-LA) was the first to get a public funding bill passed by Congress and signed into law. It did not stay on the books for very long, though. It soon met with a storm of bipartisan opposition, even from fellow Democrats who supported public funding. The new law had enough support to prevent it from being repealed, but not enough to put it into effect. What happened instead was an agreement to postpone the one part of the law that still survives: the income tax checkoff.

Watergate changed the politics of public funding. The 1974 FECA amendments included a revised version of the 1966 law, and the Supreme Court upheld it in *Buckley v. Valeo*. The new program first went into effect for the 1976 presidential election and public opinion surveys reported strong support for it.

What did reformers hope to accomplish by using public funds to pay for elections?

The main goal has always been to reduce the influence of big donors. This has been cited as the major reason for public funding since the turn of the twentieth century. A related goal is to reduce the amount of time candidates must spend raising campaign funds. The less time they spend on the phone or schmoozing with rich donors at fundraisers, the more time they have to spend talking with voters and doing their jobs as policymakers.

Reformers also hoped that publicly funded elections would be more competitive. Incumbents would always have an advantage, which they earned by getting a majority of the vote in the previous election. But challengers would improve their chances by not having to start their campaigns so far behind in the money chase.

Why was Senator Long's public funding bill so controversial?

There were two cross-cutting lines of disagreement: between the (mostly Democratic) supporters of government subsidies and the (mostly Republican) opponents, and among Democrats who favored some kind of public funding but could not agree on how to design the program. In a Congress controlled by Democrats, it was their intraparty differences over how such a program should work that were the most important.[5]

Where would the money come from? Who would distribute it? Would the money go to parties or candidates? Would it finance primary elections or only general elections? And what was the best way to determine who should get how much money? These are crucial questions for public funding.

They did not get the consideration they needed because Long got around opposition to his bill by pushing it through as one of several riders on a tax bill in the last days of the 89th Congress. So many senators wanted at least one of the riders to pass that no one was willing to vote any one of them down. In the last days of the session, when many members of both houses had already left town, Congress narrowly approved the measure.

That was a very slim base of support for such a far-reaching reform. Too slim, as it turned out. When Congress reconvened in 1967, the law's opponents renewed the attack. The major problem was what to do about the income tax checkoff, which Long had invented as the means for financing his program. An income tax checkoff is a very unusual way to finance a federal government program. Normally, when Congress votes to start a government program, it also appropriates the money to pay for it. In this case, though, Congress voted for a program and decided to pay for it by what amounts to an annual referendum. No other public policy is financed this way, and critics of Long's bill worried that it could set a dangerous precedent.

But the two sides were evenly matched. There were not enough votes either to repeal Long's act or to keep it intact, so both sides agreed to kick the can down the road. They kept the checkoff but postponed indefinitely a decision about what to do with it.

If the income tax checkoff was so controversial in the 1960s, how did it survive the political battles in Congress?

The old battle lines that cut across both parties in 1966 and 1967 became partisan after Vice President Hubert Humphrey's 1968 presidential campaign plunged the Democratic Party $9 million in debt. The party's dire financial straits brought about factional unity behind another public funding bill, which Democrats introduced in the Senate in 1971. Rather than include it in the FECA of 1971, however, they followed Long's tactic of attaching their bill as an amendment to a House-passed tax bill.

The Democrats' proposal had two parts: reviving the checkoff and providing tax incentives for small contributions. The tax incentives provision passed by a large bipartisan majority, and the tax checkoff passed by a slim partisan majority. But the Democrats' unity was not complete: Congress kicked the can down the road again, postponing the effective date of the checkoff until 1973 and barring any payments from the fund until 1976. This was enough to satisfy President Nixon, who signed the tax bill into law.[6]

Then came Watergate, and a rise in support for public funding. Most Republicans still opposed the idea, but the presidential public funding program that Congress passed as part of the 1974 FECA amendments was co-sponsored by Senators Edward M. Kennedy (D-MA) and Hugh Scott (R-PA). The checkoff was now the core of a new way to finance presidential elections. And Congress made the decisions it had put off twice before: it created the Federal Election Commission to administer the Presidential Election Campaign Fund, ensured that the money would go to candidates rather than parties, and decided that the program would cover primary and general elections as well as the parties' nominating conventions.

What happened to the tax incentives for small contributions that Congress passed in 1971?

The 1971 tax bill offered taxpayers a choice between deductions and credits. Donors could claim 50 percent credit for donations up to $25, or deduct the first $50 of donations from their taxable income. Over the next fifteen years, Congress repealed the deduction and doubled the credit twice.

We do not have enough data to gauge the success these incentives had in increasing the number of small donors. Participation was at its highest in the years after the deduction was repealed in 1980, averaging about 5 percent. But we do not know how many of those taxpayers were new donors making small contributions because of the tax credit, and how many were big donors who would have given anyway.[7]

Congress expressed doubts along these lines when it repealed the credit in 1986, as part of President Ronald Reagan's tax reform. Citing IRS data, Congress said that a "significant percentage" of those claiming the credit probably would have made contributions without it, and pointed out that the credit was not an incentive to those who made so little money that they paid no income tax at all.[8]

The same is probably true at the state and local levels, where tax credits for small contributions are still popular. At the federal level, though, the only part of the 1971 public funding law that is still in force is the one that created the Presidential Election Campaign Fund.

Why did the public funding program pay for the party conventions as well as the elections?

Conventions are very expensive events, and corporations had come to play a big role in financing them. Congress provided public funding to make the parties less reliant on corporate money.

Beginning in 2016, corporations will pay for convention costs directly. But when Congress passed the 1974 FECA amendments, corporations were paying for those costs indirectly, by buying advertising space in convention books. The Democrats began this practice in 1936, at the same convention where President Franklin D. Roosevelt delivered his fiery speech against the "economic royalists."[9]

The Republicans also had a convention book in 1936, and they sold ads to many of the same corporations that bought space in the Democrats' book. But the Republicans' book was sponsored by the host committee in Cleveland, not by the party itself. Host committees formed in the city and state where party conventions were held had long been the major source of financing for those events. The Democrats' book, though, was sponsored not by the Philadelphia host committee but by the Democratic National Committee.[10]

The Republicans charged the Democrats with violating the Tillman Act. If the DNC sponsored the convention book, they said, then they were also responsible for soliciting the advertising, which amounted to soliciting campaign contributions. In 1940 the Republican National Committee publicly suggested that both parties scrap their convention books; the Democrats rejected the suggestion. But while the Democrats were selling advertising for their book, Congress passed the Hatch Act, which made such sales illegal by treating them as indirect contributions.[11]

Corporate advertising in convention books did not go away, though, largely because of the Internal Revenue Service. The Hatch Act had prohibited advertising sales to corporations if the proceeds benefited a candidate even indirectly. But the IRS was not especially concerned with how the money was spent. It ruled that the purchase of advertising in convention books was a tax-deductible business expense, no matter how the proceeds were used. The parties even managed to agree on how much to charge for ad space: $5,000 per page.[12]

The Hatch Act and the IRS rule applied to funding for host committees and party committees. Conventions boost local economies, so cities form host committees to compete for them, and those committees have always been financed by local and state businesses and governments. Once a host committee has succeeded in attracting a convention, its primary goal is to welcome the delegates to the city and promote local shops and restaurants. Party funds, which of course cannot come from corporations, are spent on the convention itself, renting the local convention center and buying the services, equipment, and office space the candidates, delegates, and media will need. The goal of the Hatch Act was to keep the two funding streams separate from each other—in short, to prevent a recurrence of anything like the Democrats' 1936 convention book.

Congress tried to do the same thing after Watergate, by providing public funding for conventions and strictly regulating host committee fundraising. The Federal Election Commission required host committees to be nonprofit organizations that could raise contributions only from local businesses. It did not prohibit the sale of ad space in convention books, but it did eliminate the tax deduction the IRS had allowed them to claim for those purchases.[13]

The FEC's bright-line distinction worked for a while, but both parties pressured the agency to relax its restrictions. The parties eventually got their way, and the FEC began allowing host committees to raise money from more sources for more purposes. Convention costs were originally supposed to be covered by public funds, but the result of FEC rulings was that private money raised through host committees began underwriting a larger share of those costs. The share paid for by private sources went up from 14 percent in 1992 to 80 percent in 2008.[14]

In 2014, Congress repealed the part of the public funding program that covered conventions. Beginning in 2016, private money will account for 100 percent of convention costs.

Why did Congress repeal public funding for party conventions?

Congress did not do it in a straight up-or-down vote. The vote was instead on the fourth iteration of a bill originally written to kill the entire program. The first iteration passed the House in 2011 by a party-line vote; the Senate did not vote on it. The bill was reintroduced in the next Congress, but was revised and renamed twice before coming to a vote. The first revision was named the Kids First Research Act, which would have sent all the money in the Presidential Election Campaign Fund to pediatric research. The final iteration—called the Gabriella Miller Kids First Research Act, after a ten-year-old girl who died of a brain tumor—was revised to send only the money that funds conventions to pediatric research. It was this version, promoted as funding for cancer research, that passed. Most House Democrats still voted against it, but the Senate approved it without a recorded vote.[15]

Later that year, Congress passed a massive spending bill that included an eight-fold increase in the amount of money that rich donors can give to parties. Raising the limit from $97,200 to $777,600 per year made it possible for a single donor to give a party more than $1.5 million in a two-year election cycle. Part of the increase— $97,200 in addition to the current $32,400 limit on contributions to the party national committees—was solely to pay for conventions.[16]

How does the public funding program treat minor parties?

How to treat minor parties has been a problem for public-funding supporters since the first bill was introduced in 1904. The solution in the 1974 amendments was essentially the same one suggested seventy years earlier: allocate public funds based on a party's share of the popular vote in the previous election.

Three kinds of parties were eligible for public funds under the 1974 law: major, minor, and new. Major parties are ones whose presidential candidate received 25 percent or more of the popular vote in the preceding election; only the Republican and Democratic parties meet this definition. A minor party is one whose candidate received between 5 and 25 percent of the vote in the previous election. A new party is one that did not run candidates in the previous election but would be eligible for funds if it received at least 5 percent of the vote. Since a new party cannot prove its eligibility until the election is over, it has to finance its campaign with private funds.[17]

The Presidential Election Campaign Fund is essentially for the two major parties. Everyone involved in the creation of the public funding program—the members of Congress who drafted and debated it, the outside reform groups who promoted it, the challengers who tried to kill it, and the circuit court judges and Supreme Court justices who ruled on its constitutionality—knew that there have been no genuine third parties since the demise of the Populist and Socialist parties early in the twentieth century. And they all agreed that some provision had to be made for minor parties and independents. But as a practical matter the program was designed for Republicans and Democrats.

How does the public funding program treat independents?

The law does not even mention independent candidates. That posed a problem for the FEC in 1980, when Representative John

Anderson (R-IL) ran as an independent. He sought post-election reimbursement for his campaign costs, but insisted his campaign committee was not a party and that he did not intend to start one. Commissioners of both parties agreed that independent candidates should not be excluded from the public campaign fund, but the only way they could do that was to treat them as parties. Which is what they did with Anderson, who won more than 5 percent of the vote in the general election and was reimbursed with public funds.[18]

Then there was Ross Perot, the Texas billionaire who bought his way into the public funding system. As one of many third-party candidates who run presidential campaigns they have no hope of winning, Perot could be just another footnote to our political history. But he is important here because he was rich enough to take advantage of a program intended to open presidential elections to donors and politicians who were not rich.

Perot spent more than $68 million of his own money running for president in 1992, making it the most expensive third-party or independent campaign to date. He also got an impressive 18.9 percent of the popular vote, the best showing by any outside presidential candidate since Theodore Roosevelt ran as a Progressive in 1912.[19]

Perot refused to call himself the candidate of a party in 1992, but in 1996 he changed his mind. He spent $8.5 million of his own money to create the Reform Party and ensure he was nominated as its candidate. The FEC agreed to treat the new party as an existing one based on Perot's share of the 1992 vote, and gave him a public funding grant for the 1996 general election. He did not get as many votes this time around, but he got enough to qualify the Reform Party for public funds in 2000.[20]

Most third parties are little more than the campaign committees of their candidates, and they disappear after those candidates are defeated. Like those other third parties, the Reform Party was little more than Perot's campaign committee, and it too effectively fell apart after Perot decided not to run again. The Reform Party might not have been a real party, but thanks to what Perot had been able to buy with his own fortune in 1992 and 1996, it became something just as valuable under the FECA: a name worth millions of taxpayer dollars in 2000.

The shaky state of the Reform Party became clear when its 2000 convention ended with two men claiming to have won the nomination. The FEC eventually recognized Patrick Buchanan, a former adviser to Presidents Nixon, Ford, and Reagan, as the party's candidate. Buchanan, who had tried several times to win the GOP nomination, qualified by being on the ballot in thirteen states. He got less than 1 percent of the popular vote, putting a delayed end to Perot's old campaign committee by making the Reform Party ineligible for federal funds in 2004. Anderson, Perot, and Buchanan are so far the only third-party or independent candidates to receive general-election funds under the public financing program.[21]

Did public funding meet its goal of bringing in new, small donors?

The Presidential Election Campaign Fund did meet that goal. About 80 percent of the tens of millions of people who used the checkoff did not make any other contribution, either individually or through an organization.[22] Checkoff donors also looked more like the general population than the kinds of donors who made contributions to candidates or parties. Most donors who made contributions of $200 or more were well-educated, middle-aged to elderly conservative Republicans who were in the highest income decile. Most checkoff donors were younger, less well educated, moderate-to-liberal Democrats, and only about 10 percent of them had incomes in the highest decile.[23]

Taxpayer participation in the checkoff was at its highest in the years after Watergate. Participation was 27.5 percent in 1976, the year of the first publicly funded presidential election, and went up to just under 29 percent in 1980. Eventually, though, the program began losing the strong public support it had enjoyed at the start. Taxpayer participation fell steadily, dropping below 20 percent by 1989 and below 15 percent by 1993.[24]

Worried that there would not be enough money in the fund to finance the 1996 presidential election, Congress increased the checkoff from $1 to $3 in 1993. That provided the fund with enough money for the 1996 election, but the number of checkoff donors continued to decline. The shrinking size of the fund made candidates give serious consideration to opting out of the program, which they began to do in 2000.[25]

Even now, though, when the program can no longer provide even partial subsidies for presidential campaigns, it is still bringing in small donors. Only 5.4 percent of tax returns used the checkoff in 2015, which was the lowest participation rate in the program's history. But those returns sent $30 million into the fund, which means that several million taxpayers continue to make very small contributions.[26]

Public funding is also supposed to bring in new candidates. Did the presidential program do that?

Yes, the program also achieved that goal. It opened the presidential primaries to politicians who otherwise might not have thrown their hats into the ring. That is especially clear in the early years, as we can see by comparing the candidates who ran in the 1972 and 1976 Democratic primaries. The 1972 primaries are a good place to start for two reasons: with President Richard M. Nixon in the White House, the Democrats had a wide-open primary; and that was the first year the party nominated its candidate by votes in the primaries rather than in the convention.

Seven candidates competed in the primaries, four of whom had the national name recognition and political organization to raise the private funds needed to finance a national campaign: Senator George McGovern of South Dakota, who won the nomination; Senators Hubert Humphrey of Minnesota and Edmund Muskie of Maine, who had been the party's presidential and vice presidential candidates in 1968; and Alabama Governor George Wallace, who had run for president as an independent in 1968 and whose right-wing populism and active opposition to civil rights had made him a perennial protest candidate with substantial popular support.[27]

With the White House still in Republican hands in 1976, the Democrats had another wide-open primary. And this time there were more than twice as many candidates as in 1972, thirteen of whom got federal funds. The eventual nominee—Georgia Governor Jimmy Carter—was almost unknown before the primaries began. Had he run for the nomination in 1968 or 1972, he would have been a dark horse.[28]

Ronald Reagan was another dark horse who got to the top with the help of public funding. When he challenged President Ford for the Republican nomination in 1976, he was a stalwart of the GOP's conservative wing, running against an incumbent president and the party's moderate establishment. The serious campaign he was able to run with government money in 1976 gave him the name recognition and organizational support he needed to win the Republican nomination and the presidential election in 1980.[29]

Reagan's 1984 campaign also shows how public funding achieved the goal of reducing the amount of time candidates have to spend raising private contributions. Harvard law professor Lawrence Lessig says that Reagan attended eight fundraisers for his reelection campaign, and he compares that to the 228 fundraisers Obama attended for his reelection campaign in 2012.[30]

But participation in the tax checkoff had dropped by 2012. Did the same thing happen with public opinion?

Yes, but we cannot be sure how far it dropped. The variety of ways pollsters phrase their questions makes it difficult to gauge the extent of popular backing for the program.

Gallup has been asking a fairly standard question about public funding since the early 1970s, and it is clear from their reports that a majority of respondents approved of the program from the start. In fact, Gallup polls reported majority support for the idea of public funding in 1972 and 1973, before there was a program. Support was highest in the years when the Senate Watergate Committee's hearings were being televised, reaching a high of 71 percent in 1974.[31]

But as memories of Watergate faded, so too did support for public funding. Gallup polls showed continued, but declining, majority support into the mid-1990s. The FEC tried to remedy the situation with an outreach program of public service announcements, brochures, and educational materials for tax preparers. But Congress tended to be stingy when it came to funding FEC projects, and this one did not accomplish its goal of increasing public understanding.[32]

At tax time in 1989, an ABC News–*Washington Post* survey asked taxpayers about the income tax checkoff and found that nearly one-fifth of respondents knew nothing about it. Two 1996 polls showed that the same percentage of people did not even know that presidential elections were publicly funded. What was once a popular reform became just one of many government programs that people knew little or nothing about.[33]

Some polls have shown majority opposition to public funding. Two CBS News polls, in 1999 and 2000, found substantial opposition: 58 percent in the first poll and a big jump to 75 percent in the second. The Gallup report on these polls suggested that the use of the phrase "tax money" in the questions triggered the negative responses. A Campaign Finance Institute report reached the same conclusion about survey questions generally, finding that phrases like "tax money" or "taxpayer dollars" elicit strong opposition.[34]

Gallup got its own negative response to a 2007 survey. Asked whether they thought the presidential candidates should take public funds or raise as much as they could in private funds, 56 percent of respondents said they should opt out of public funding—which candidates had been doing for the primary matching funds since 2000. The most recent Gallup poll, taken in June 2013, asked whether respondents would vote for a "new" system that gave government funds to candidates; half said they would. It is hard to get an accurate reading of public opinion on the subject, however, given how much people's responses depend on the wording of pollsters' questions instead of on independent knowledge.[35]

An interesting development in public opinion is that while support for the federal program declined, existing state programs continued and new ones were created.

What kinds of public funding programs are the states enacting?

Several states use tax incentives much like the federal tax credit that was repealed in 1986. Other states directly subsidize campaigns through programs similar to the one for presidential campaigns. Arkansas, Ohio, and Oregon provide tax credits for the first $50 of an individual taxpayer's political contributions, and Virginia does the same for the first $25. The variety of state programs and the small amount of research on them does not give us much information about participation rates.[36]

An exception is Minnesota's Political Contribution Refund (PCR) program. Minnesota began offering tax credits for small contributions in 1974, but later turned the credits into direct refunds to donors. The state's Department of Revenue administered the program, but kept it separate from the income tax. Individual donors could apply to the department for a refund of the first $50 of their contributions; they usually received their refunds within eight weeks of applying for them.[37]

A Campaign Finance Institute study found the PCR to be very successful. It concluded that the PCR alone, apart from the state's public funding program, was responsible for a higher rate of participation by small donors than in any other state: donations of $100 or less made up 45 percent of contributions from all political donors.[38]

But the PCR, like other kinds of public funding programs in other states, did not always have the strong bipartisan support it needed to survive. In recent years the program's fortunes have depended on which party controls the legislature and who is in the governor's mansion: it was stalled in 2009, revived in 2013, and stalled again in 2015. Even the most successful programs can fail for lack of political support.[39]

Which states subsidize election campaigns?

Maine, Arizona, and Connecticut have programs very similar to the one for presidential elections. All of them provide full funding to candidates for governor, lieutenant governor, and the state legislature. Some cities have also enacted partial public funding programs.[40]

These states went against the national trend by putting their programs into effect at a time when the presidential funding system was losing support from Congress, taxpayers, the general public, and candidates. Maine and Arizona passed their programs by popular vote in the 1990s and put them into effect in 2000. That year also marked the first time a major party's presidential nominee partly opted out of the federal program. The Connecticut legislature passed its law in 2005, one year after both major parties' presidential candidates partially opted out.

These programs also try to bring small donors into the system by requiring candidates to qualify for subsidies by raising a set amount of money in small donations from a set number of contributors. Unlike the federal system, these donations are very small—$5 in Maine and Arizona, $5 to $10 in Connecticut—and are not matched with government funds. Like the federal system, candidates who participate in the system agree to limit their spending to the amount of their public subsidy and to raise no private contributions.

The biggest difference between these state programs and the federal one is that all three states tried to level the playing field between candidates who received public funds and those who did not. Candidates participating in Arizona's program who found themselves outspent by privately funded opponents could even the odds by getting up to three times the amount of their public subsidy. There were similar provisions even in some of the partial funding programs. But in 2011, the Supreme Court struck down the Arizona provision. The justices ruled 5–4 that the Arizona law violated the First Amendment because it "diminishe[d] the effectiveness" of the privately funded candidates' campaigns.[41]

As events in 2015 showed, however, political support for public funding has had its ups and downs even in these three states. A Republican attempt to kill Arizona's program narrowly failed in the state senate. In Connecticut, it was the Democratic majority of the state legislature that proposed suspending that state's program as a budget-cutting measure. But Maine voters easily passed an initiative to increase funding for their state program.[42]

Other states have less extensive programs, ones that cover fewer candidates, provide only partial funding, or both. The Hawaii, Florida, Massachusetts, Minnesota, and Rhode Island programs, for example, cover all state offices, but provide only partial funding of campaigns. Maryland, Michigan, New Mexico, and Vermont provide partial funding only for certain offices. Candidates who participate in all these programs must qualify by raising a certain amount of money in small donations and must agree to spending limits.[43]

One state, Wisconsin, went in the opposite direction from other public funding states. Its 1977 law, which was financed by a $1 income tax checkoff and provided subsidies up to 45 percent of the spending limit for covered offices, made it a reform leader, and the program worked well into the late 1980s. But the state's legislature undermined its usefulness by refusing to index public subsidies to inflation, and repealed it in 2011.[44]

Which cities have public funding programs?

The biggest programs, and the ones that have received the most scholarly attention, are in New York and Los Angeles. But other cities also have public funding programs, some of them older than New York's.

Seattle enacted the first municipal public funding program in 1978. Like more recent partial funding programs, the program provided matching funds for contributions to candidates who agreed to contribution and spending limits. Funding came from a voluntary checkoff on municipal utilities bills. The program ended in 1992 when a state ballot measure banned public funding in state and local elections. A local ballot measure to revive the Seattle program narrowly failed in 2013.[45]

But in 2015, Seattle voters once again made their city a reform pioneer. By a large margin they passed a program that would give $100 vouchers to every registered voter in the city. The vouchers can be used only to make contributions to candidates who accept contribution and spending limits. Seattle's new program, the first public funding voucher system passed at any level of government, will take effect in the 2017 election.[46]

Albuquerque and Santa Fe, New Mexico, provide full funding for mayoral and city council candidates who agree to spending limits. Tucson, Arizona, provides partial funding through matching funds for small contributions. Portland, Oregon's program covered only candidates for mayor and two other executive offices and was intended to be in effect for only two election cycles before being placed on the ballot for voter approval; it failed by a slim margin in 2010.[47]

Los Angeles enacted its program by ballot in 1990, but legal challenges by public-funding opponents delayed it from being put into effect until 1993. As with the presidential fund, candidates have to qualify for the program by raising a certain amount of money in small donations. Once qualified, they got public matching funds for individual contributions up to one-third of an office's expenditure limit for the primary election and one-half of the limit for the general. In 2013, the City Council increased the matches to two-to-one for the primary and four-to-one for the general.[48]

The local program that has attracted the most attention is New York City's. It was enacted in 1988 and is widely regarded as a model for how to do public funding at all levels of government.

How does New York City's public funding program work?

New York City's program began with an old-fashioned political scandal. An investigation into political corruption—not an unusual event in New York—snared some prominent city politicians in 1986. Calls for reform went nowhere in Albany, but in 1988 the New York City Council passed a voluntary public financing law. The original law required candidates to agree to contribution and expenditure limits, but provided a one-to-one match for contributions of up to $1,000.[49]

The 1988 reform was an improvement on the existing law, but over the years the City Council raised the matching ratio and lowered the matchable dollar amount to bring more small donors into the system. Since 2009 there has been a six-to-one match for contributions of up to $175. That means that a $50 contribution, after a $300 match from public funds, turns into $350 for the candidate. The high matching ratio has brought thousands of new, small donors into city elections, and they are a much more diverse group than traditional donors.[50]

Only individual contributions from New York City residents are matched, and not from all of them. Lobbyists and people doing business with the city can write checks, but their contributions are not eligible for public matching funds. PACs, unions, and nonresidents can give, too, but their contributions are also ineligible for matching.

As with the FECA's presidential election law, candidates must meet certain fundraising requirements to qualify for public funding. Candidates for mayor have the toughest requirement: raising $250,000 in $175 contributions. They can get much larger contributions, but only the first $175 counts toward the $250,000 threshold. City Council candidates only have to raise $5,000, but they have to get that money from at least seventy-five residents of their districts, which means they have to get contributions even smaller than $175.

New York City's program is administered by the Campaign Finance Board (CFB). Unlike the FEC, which has six members, with three Republicans and three Democrats, the CFB has five members and is legally required to be nonpartisan. The mayor appoints two members, the Council Speaker appoints two, and they jointly approve the fifth. There is no way to ensure that appointments made by politicians will be nonpartisan, but the CFB has been notably free of the partisan discord that plagues the FEC.

New York City's program provides only partial financing for election campaigns, which means that participating candidates must raise private money to cover most of their campaign costs. In the 2013 Democratic mayoral primary, for example, the four candidates who received public funds got from 60 to 80 percent of their money in private contributions. New York City's program reduces candidates' reliance on private donors, but those donors still provide most of the candidates' campaign funds.[51]

The biggest donor of all was three-term mayor Michael Bloomberg, whom *Forbes* ranks as the fourteenth-richest person in the world. He never participated in the public funding program and was the sole donor to all three of his campaigns. The margins by which Bloomberg won his first and third elections were much smaller than the margins by which he outspent his publicly funded opponents, raising doubts as to whether he could have won without his money. New York City's program allowed his opponents to launch campaigns and recruit demographically diverse groups of small donors, which is a good thing in itself. But it might not have been nearly enough to compete effectively against the kind of big money the program was intended to keep out of elections. The 2013 election was the first since 1997 in which both mayoral candidates were program participants.[52]

How well did the presidential public funding program work?

It worked well for several years. But it was only going to work well for a longer time if Congress made a point of maintaining it, which it did not do. The problem began with the same Congress that voted for the Presidential Election Campaign Fund in 1974. It kept the same $1 checkoff amount that Senator Long had put in his 1966 law, and did not index it for inflation. Congress did increase the $1 check-off to $3 in 1993—but still did not index it to inflation.[53]

Two other dollar figures that Congress did not index for inflation were the $1,000 contribution limit and the $250 limit on contributions to qualify for matching funds. By 1996, twenty years after the first publicly funded presidential election, $1,000 was worth about $300 and $250 was worth less than $80. Had those dollar amounts been indexed for inflation, they would have been raised to $3,000 and $800. In 2002, Congress increased the contribution limit to $2,500, and did index it to inflation.

As one election followed another, the declining value of the dollar meant that the public funding program was less and less able to meet its primary goal of protecting candidates from the need to raise private funds. Opponents of public funding did not need to mount an open attack because the program was gradually hollowed out by congressional inaction. It was an example of policy drift, which political scientists Jacob S. Hacker and Paul Pierson call "the fine political art of producing change by doing nothing."[54]

As public funds shrank, private money ballooned. The independent expenditures the Supreme Court said could not be limited rose quickly in the 1980s, the huge majority of them on behalf of Republicans. Soft money, which was raised outside the FECA, first appeared in 1980 and eventually replaced independent expenditures as the way to raise and spend private money in publicly financed elections. The sharp rise in soft money spending in 1996 and 2000 led campaign-finance experts to conclude that presidential campaigns were conducted as much outside FECA regulations as within them.[55]

It was only a matter of time before a major party candidate would decide not to take public funds. Texas governor George W. Bush was the first to do this, by opting out of the matching-funds program for the primaries in 2000.

Bush was still stuck with the $1,000 limit, but he made the best of that situation by recruiting business executives, venture capitalists, lawyers, and lobbyists into a fundraising network called the Pioneers. Each Pioneer promised to raise at least $100,000 in hard-money contributions from their many connections. The network was a rousing success, raising more than $90 million—almost twice the $49 million Vice President Al Gore was able to raise with matching funds.[56]

As president, Bush did the same thing for his reelection campaign in the 2004 primaries. But this time, so did the eventual Democratic nominee, Senator John Kerry of Massachusetts, who followed Bush's lead by recruiting his own fundraising network. The 2004 election was the first in which both major party nominees had opted out of public funding for the primaries.[57]

By then Congress had passed the McCain-Feingold Act, which raised the contribution limit to $2,500 and indexed it to inflation. But the program was already in such steep decline that even one of the bill's sponsors, Senator John McCain (R-AZ), opted out of it for the 2008 primaries. It was not much of a surprise, then—however disappointing to reformers—when McCain's Democratic opponent, Senator Barack Obama (D-IL), opted out of the program entirely in 2008. In fact, in 2012 all major party nominees opted out of the program entirely. The presidential public funding program is still in effect, but for all practical purposes it ended years ago.[58]

4

DISCLOSURE AND THE FEDERAL ELECTION COMMISSION

The point of disclosure is to let voters see who is financing election campaigns. That was why the Supreme Court upheld the disclosure law in *Buckley v. Valeo* and *Citizens United*, and that was the purpose of the law when Congress passed it in 1910. Getting that first law on the books was not a sure thing, though. Perry Belmont, the former member of Congress (D-NY) who drafted it, explained that disclosure would "turn on the light," which Congress was not eager to do.[1] Belmont failed in his first two attempts to get his bill passed, and it might not have become law but for William Howard Taft.

Taft made two promises when he became the Republican candidate for president in 1908: to voluntarily disclose the funding of his own campaign, and to get a disclosure bill through Congress if elected. When he released his donor list after the election, people saw that he still got some money from the GOP's big Wall Street donors, but that he also had thousands of small donors from well outside New York. Disclosure "never won a greater triumph than this," exclaimed the *Wall Street Journal*.[2]

Taft also made good on his second promise. The law he pushed Congress to pass in 1910 stayed on the books until it was replaced by the one in the 1971 FECA. Congress did not want disclosure to shine a very bright light on its members in 1971, either; and it did not create an agency to enforce the new disclosure requirements. Congress had to change its mind on that point after Watergate, and it created the Federal Election Commission (FEC); but it keeps a tighter leash on the FEC than it does on other regulatory agencies.

What does the FEC do?

The FEC's responsibility for administering and enforcing the FECA covers three main areas: the presidential public funding program, restrictions on the size and sources of campaign contributions, and disclosure. It is still responsible for administering the Presidential Election Campaign Fund, but it has had almost nothing to do with that program since the 2007–08 cycle. None of the 2016 candidates has applied for public funding, and in 2014 Congress repealed public funding for the party nominating conventions.

With the presidential public funding program all but officially dead, the FEC is primarily responsible for disclosure. The task of enforcing the limits on who can give how much to what kinds of political committees can be brought under the broader responsibility for administering disclosure requirements.

Political committees file more than 100,000 disclosure reports with the FEC each election cycle. The FECA requires committees to disclose the name, address, occupation, and employer of every donor who makes a contribution of $200 or more, and every recipient of a committee expenditure of $200 or more. The agency must make this information publicly available within forty-eight hours of receipt.

Many committees have questions about the law, and the FEC answers them in several ways. The agency has publications describing reporting requirements on its website and will fax copies to committees that request hard copies. The FEC staff also hold instructional workshops around the country and answer phone calls to the Washington, D.C., office—about 20,000 calls per election cycle. More complicated questions about how the FECA applies to particular situations are answered by advisory opinions. These opinions are joint efforts by the Office of General Counsel (OGC) and the commissioners.[3]

The result of all this work is the publication of data that tell us how congressional and presidential election campaigns are financed, where the money comes from, and how it is spent. Suppose, for example, that you want to know what kinds of donors gave to which presidential candidates in 2012. One way to answer that question is to find out where most Obama and Romney donors worked:[4]

Top Five Employers of 2012 Contributors

Barack Obama	Mitt Romney
University of California	Goldman Sachs
Microsoft Corp.	Bank of America
Google Inc.	Morgan Stanley
U.S. Government	JP Morgan Chase & Co.
Harvard University	Wells Fargo

Suppose instead that you want to know which states had the most Obama and Romney donors:

Top Five States of 2012 Contributors

Barack Obama	Mitt Romney
California	California
New York	Texas
Illinois	Florida
Massachusetts	New York
Texas	Virginia

Disclosure does today what it was meant to do when the first law was passed in 1910—to "turn on the light" for voters, to tell them who is financing the campaigns of the candidates they vote for. Like any other law, though, disclosure can fulfill its original purpose only when it is enforced, and it has not always been enforced.

Why did Congress create the Federal Election Commission?

It was clear long before Watergate that campaign finance law would not work well without a way to enforce it. The 1910 disclosure law worked fairly well for presidential elections even without a formal enforcement agency because presidential elections always get more attention from the media and the public. And before the FECA, they also got the attention of congressional committees that were appointed to look into their financing. The result was that party, candidate, and other political committees that were active in presidential elections regularly filed reports, and the major newspapers covered the highlights of those reports.

The 1910 law did not work well for congressional campaigns, which get much less media and public attention. That law made the Clerk of the House responsible for enforcing disclosure requirements, but it gave that officer little real authority. William Tyler Page, who was the Clerk in 1924, explained how poorly the law worked without real enforcement: "The filing of these statements has been regarded as more or less perfunctory. . . . In a great many cases no receipts or expenditures are reported at all because the candidate swears that there has been none, and which, of course, must be taken as accurate. . . . Now this law has no teeth in it."[5]

Congress heard plenty of suggestions for how to put some teeth in the law during the next fifty years, and it did strengthen disclosure somewhat in the 1971 FECA. The Clerk of the House and the Secretary of the Senate continued to administer the law for House and Senate elections under the 1971 FECA. But Congress added the comptroller general as a third "supervisory officer" to take responsibility for presidential elections. The comptroller general headed the General Accounting Office (now the Government Accountability Office), and as a presidential appointee with a fixed term of office he was more insulated from political pressure than the House and Senate officers were.[6]

The 1971 disclosure law was an improvement, but it was still weak by today's standards. Political scientist Alexander Heard predicted in 1960 that Congress would not turn enforcement authority over to a genuinely independent agency "unless some startling scandal appears as a catalyst."[7] He was too optimistic. Watergate was the catalyst that persuaded Congress to create the FEC. But Congress made the FEC dependent, not independent. Even after Watergate, Congress wanted to be its own enforcement agency.

How does the FEC work? Is it like other independent agencies?

The FEC is not like any other independent regulatory agency. And when Congress created it in 1974 it was so different as to raise questions about its constitutionality.

The original plan was for the president, the House of Representatives, and the Senate each to nominate two commissioners, one Republican and one Democrat. All six commissioners had to be confirmed by both houses of Congress. To complete congressional supervision of the agency, the Clerk of the House and the Secretary of the Senate would be permanent, nonvoting commissioners. The FEC as originally designed was a separate body but was under the control of Congress.

This was a highly unusual way to appoint agency heads, but here, too, the federal circuit court for the District of Columbia decided to see how the FEC worked in practice before reaching a conclusion about its constitutionality. The court conceded that the FEC's quasi-executive and quasi-judicial powers could be unconstitutional, but decided that was "an abstract question that would be better decided in the context of a particular factual controversy."[8]

The Supreme Court was not inclined to see how the agency worked out in practice. It struck down the method of appointment, ruling that it violated the separation of powers. Focusing on the FEC's enforcement powers, the court found that "it is to the president, and not the Congress, that the constitution entrusts the responsibility to 'take care that the laws be faithfully executed.' "[9] Watergate might have been the catalyst that made Congress create the FEC, but it was the Supreme Court that made the agency independent—or at least more independent than Congress had intended.

Most independent regulatory agencies are, like the FEC, run by presidentially appointed commissioners who serve for fixed, staggered terms, and must be from both parties. The staggered terms are key to an agency's political independence, as it prevents a president from being able to appoint every member. What the president can do is appoint one of the members as the chairperson, to be in charge of the agency. Those other agencies have an odd number of commissioners, usually five or seven. That means that some decisions can be made by party-line votes, but it also means that decisions do get made and that partisan deadlocks are impossible.

That is not true of the FEC, which has six commissioners: three Republicans and three Democrats. Majority decisions are necessarily bipartisan, but the even number means that deadlocks can make decisions impossible. The FEC is like other agencies in that the commissioners serve staggered six-year terms, which overlap so that only two members' terms expire at the same time. Although commissioners are appointed by the president and confirmed by the Senate, the resemblance to other agencies here is superficial.

Independent regulatory agencies are part of the executive branch, which is why appointments to them are made by the president. *Buckley* struck down Congress's original plan for the FEC because it was an extension of the legislative branch, not independent of it. But in fact, presidents make FEC appointments from names submitted by Congress; they confirm congressional choices, not the other way around. This informal practice perpetuates the formal congressional control over the agency that the Supreme Court found unconstitutional in *Buckley*.[10]

The FEC originated in the state to which other agencies sometimes decline: "capture" by the regulated industry. This can happen in other regulatory agencies for several reasons: more agency staff may use the revolving door to take positions in the industry; the agency's need for expertise makes it dependent on industry experts; or insufficient funding leaves the agency unable to attract and retain independent and qualified staff. All agencies are created by Congress, but only the FEC regulates its creators and relies on them for funding.[11]

Congress also made sure the FEC would not be effectively managed. The chairperson is not a presidentially appointed position, but one that rotates among the commissioners, each of whom serves for one year. The chairperson presides over commission meetings and represents the agency before Congress, but otherwise has little more power than any other commissioner. The job title is misleading, as the chairperson leads the FEC only in a ceremonial sense.[12]

How well does the current disclosure law work?

It works very well, but there are still some problems. One problem is the failure to provide required information. Committees are supposed to provide the name, address, occupation, and employer of every donor who gives $200 or more. Not every report filed with the FEC includes this information. Inadequate donor information does not matter much for the majority of the 0.4 percent of Americans who give in the lower ranges of reportable contributions. Part of the debate over disclosure is about whether these donors' names should be disclosed at all. But it does matter for the tinier percentage of donors who make very large contributions.

Imagine a big donor named Jonathan Adam Smith. He can give his name in several different ways: he could spell out his first and middle names in full, use a nickname like John or Jack, use only initials for his middle name, or omit it entirely. (FEC regulations do not allow initials for first and last names.) His wife, Deborah Anne—or Debby—can do the same with her donations.

As a wealthy couple, Jonathan and Deborah probably have more than one house. That means they can list any one of those houses, as well as Jonathan's or Debby's office, as a legal address. They could make large contributions to several committees, giving different addresses and different versions of their names for each contribution, and stay well within the law. But they would also make it very difficult to tell that all those contributions came from the same couple.

This difficulty arises because the FEC does not track contributors; it records contributions. That record shows how many contributions a committee receives, but not all of those contributions are accurately credited to the people who made them. Additional research is needed to turn that raw data from a catalog of contributions into a list of contributors, and additional research is not the FEC's job.[13]

Other problems arise with entries for occupation and employer. The FECA requires this information, but FEC regulations do not. The FEC does ask committees to provide missing information when the blanks for occupation and employer are not filled in. But a committee only has to make one request of the donor to fill in the omissions. If the donor does not respond, the blanks are not filled in and the committee is off the hook for the omissions—that one request counts as a "best effort" to get the information.[14]

Inadequate technology was also a problem in the first ten or fifteen years after the 1974 law went into effect. When it came to getting information out to the public, the FEC in those years was not much better equipped than the Clerk of the House had been in 1910. It met the law's requirement to make the reports public by making microform copies available in public reading rooms. That was an improvement over storing the originals on Capitol Hill, but it still meant that reports were available only to those who went to a government office. How well the law worked still depended on how well the media and political scientists wanted it to work.

The Internet was a huge step forward. Voters now have direct access to disclosure reports, which can be downloaded from the FEC's website. But what a voter sees when she downloads those reports is pretty much what she would have seen had she trudged up to Capitol Hill a century ago: hundreds of pages of raw data. For disclosure to attain its goal of giving voters usable information, someone still has to process that data and make it publicly available in a manageable form. Journalists and political scientists did most of that processing under the 1910 law, but they can no longer do that alone.

The ocean of campaign finance data in FEC databases means that effective disclosure now depends on organizations created for the sole purpose of compiling and analyzing it. Nonprofits such as the Center for Responsive Politics, the Campaign Finance Institute, and the Sunlight Foundation process raw FEC data and provide it to the public in manageable form over the Internet. It is through these intermediaries that the disclosure law attains its goal of turning on the light.

But that light shines only on donors, and individual donors can stay in the dark by contributing through limited liability companies (LLCs). Companies large and small do business as LLCs, and most of them make their officers and operations a matter of public record. But LLCs can also be opaque, which means that contributions they make will be reported to the FEC as coming from the companies, not from the people who created them.

The use of LLCs to hide donor identities first came to light during the 2012 election, when three such companies each made a $1 million contribution to the pro-Romney super PAC, Restore Our Future. The Campaign Legal Center filed a complaint with the FEC, claiming that the practice violated the FECA prohibition against making contributions in someone else's name. When the commissioners got around to voting on the complaint, they deadlocked on whether to investigate it. This does not mean the agency found the practice to be legal, only that it did not find it to be illegal; it is still in a gray area of the law, but it is now a much lighter shade of gray. There were already more LLC contributions in 2016 than there had been four years earlier, and the FEC deadlock may make the practice more widespread.[15]

How does the FEC enforce other parts of the FECA?

Slowly and imperfectly. Congress has never been eager to regulate itself, and it designed a cumbersome enforcement process for the new agency. That process cannot move beyond the preliminary stage until at least four commissioners agree to open an investigation. And four votes are needed to approve each subsequent stage of enforcement.[16]

A case begins when the OGC receives a complaint that a candidate or committee has done something illegal. Based on the response the accused party makes to the allegation—the accused party is called the respondent—the OGC begins the initial investigation by opening a Matter Under Review (MUR). If the OGC finds reason to believe there has been a violation, it recommends that the commissioners approve further investigation.

If the commissioners agree, and the investigation turns up evidence of a violation, the OGC must get majority approval to move on to the next stage, conciliation negotiations with the respondent. If a conciliation agreement is reached, it too needs the commissioners' approval. And if the OGC is unable to reach an agreement with the respondent, another majority vote is required to file a civil suit.

Each of the stages involves OGC communications, called "letters," with respondents. The FECA gives respondents plenty of time to respond to these letters, and requests for extensions are normally granted. Each stage can take weeks, or months, meaning that it can take a year to resolve even routine complaints. More complex or contentious matters take much longer, and most cannot be resolved during the election cycle in which they are filed.

Complex issues also require staff attention, and congressional reluctance to meet the FEC's budget requests has left the agency understaffed. A 1999 audit by PricewaterhouseCoopers found the agency had a "skilled and motivated" staff, but that it was not large enough to handle the volume of enforcement cases. A largely supportive study of the agency done by political scientist Michael

M. Franz in 2009 suggested doubling its budget so it could hire more staff.[17]

The members of Congress who mandated cumbersome enforcement procedures were not entirely self-serving. Fear of overzealous or partisan prosecution was not completely unfounded, so it is not surprising that Congress made the OGC get bipartisan permission from the commissioners to begin each stage of enforcement. And both parties always nominated the "right kinds" of Republicans and Democrats to the commission, people who had close ties to congressional leaders and would not be too independent.

But there were no big ideological battles over nominations until 1999. That is when Senate Republicans nominated Bradley A. Smith, a professor at Capital University School of Law who had recently called for repeal of the FECA in a *Wall Street Journal* op-ed. Supporters of the law immediately opposed Smith, and President Bill Clinton asked the Republicans to name someone else. They not only refused, but also threatened to block consideration of Clinton's judicial nominees unless he agreed to their nominee.[18]

Smith's appointment put Senate Democrats in a bind. They had been no more eager than Republicans to put active reformers on the commission, but they would never have gone so far as to appoint someone who openly advocated repealing the very law he was supposed to enforce. Whatever they thought of the Republicans' choice, though, they too wanted to maintain congressional control over FEC appointments, which is what the Republicans were doing. In the end, Clinton stuck with tradition and appointed Smith, who then won Senate confirmation.[19]

A much bigger ideological battle took place six years later, when Republicans nominated Hans von Spakovsky as Smith's successor. Von Spakovsky also was a staunch opponent of campaign finance reform, but what had made him a more public figure than previous FEC nominees was his record at the Department of Justice: he had supported Georgia's voter ID law and a controversial redistricting plan in Texas. Those activities caused civil rights groups to join FECA supporters in protesting the nomination.[20]

Republicans responded by opposing the appointment of two nominees to fill vacant Democratic seats at the FEC—if von Spakovsky could not be confirmed, neither could anyone else. This time Democrats refused to budge. The result was a standoff that effectively shut down the FEC at the end of 2007 because it did not have enough commissioners to take official action. The standoff ended only when von Spakovsky withdrew his nomination in May 2008.[21]

The FEC was up and running again within a few weeks of von Spakovsky's withdrawal, but only in the sense that it now had a full complement of commissioners. The agency had the quorum it needed to take official action, but more of those actions were being blocked by 3–3 partisan deadlocks.

Why are there so many partisan deadlocks on the FEC?

There is partisan disagreement on that question. A 2015 *New York Times* article about the agency focused on the assessment by Ann Ravel, a Democrat who was then FEC chair. Expressing a view shared by her fellow Democrats, she said she had given up hope of enforcing the law. "People think the FEC is dysfunctional," she said, pointing to the number of 3–3 partisan deadlocks; "It's worse than dysfunctional."[22]

The Republican commissioners disagreed. They said the agency was functioning as intended and that no action at all is better than overly aggressive steps that could chill political speech. In a separate letter to the *Times*, the Republicans acknowledged that "commissioners philosophically disagree on some complex legal questions," but pointed out that 93 percent of their votes were bipartisan.[23]

Which is it? Democrats said Republicans were blocking them from enforcing the law, from checking the arguably illegal ways of raising and spending money that declared and undeclared presidential candidates were using in 2015. Republicans said the low level of enforcement meant that people were obeying the law, and all they were doing was blocking Democratic attempts to suppress political speech.

Partisan clashes were inevitable given the parties' sensitivities about regulation and their differences over the law. And recent scholarship shows that disagreement on how to enforce the law has always split the commissioners along partisan lines. Throughout the twentieth century and into the early years of the twenty-first, however, this mostly meant that the dissenters in 4–2 votes were almost always from the same party.[24]

Partisan deadlocks were rare before 2008. From 1996 to 2004, only about 3 percent of agency votes ended in deadlocks; but that figure rose to 14 percent from 2008 to 2012. Political scientist Michal M. Franz concluded from a study of FEC voting patterns that "[t]he relative consensus that once was an FEC norm has been shattered by an increase in deadlocks."[25]

The media have paid a lot of attention to these deadlocks, but it was not likely that partisan differences in the FEC could have remained at their twentieth-century level as political polarization grew in Congress and the country. Growing polarization may also explain why conservative charges that the FEC is trampling on Americans' First Amendment rights have risen even as the agency's enforcement actions have declined.

An especially prominent charge came not from congressional floor debate or an op-ed, but from the Supreme Court. Justice Anthony Kennedy claimed in *Citizens United* that the FEC regulated political speech and so was in the business of censorship; that when it issued an advisory opinion it was either prohibiting someone from speaking or granting someone "permission to speak."[26] This is a very long way from the *Buckley* court's view of the FEC.

Justice Kennedy differs from other reform opponents in that he couples his accusations against the FEC with support for the idea of disclosure. Disclosure is the business the FEC is actually in, and it is coming under increasing attack from reform opponents outside the court.

Why has disclosure become so controversial?

Privacy is the concern opponents most often raise. The *Buckley* challengers raised that concern, too, but they did not oppose disclosure. They argued that "narrowly drawn disclosure requirements are the proper solution to virtually all the evils Congress sought to remedy."[27] They said the FECA disclosure law was not narrowly drawn, and objected in particular to the $100 threshold for disclosing contributions, saying it was too low.

Congress set the reporting threshold at $100 in 1910. The inflation-adjusted figure in 1971 would have been about $400, so Congress's decision to stick with the original dollar figure is in fact hard to explain. "Even the most corrupt Members of Congress," the challengers said in their *Buckley* brief, "will not be 'bought' for so small an amount."[28] They pointed out that disclosing such small contributions unnecessarily invaded the privacy of people who lacked the means to influence legislators' decisions.

Where should we set the threshold? That became an increasingly important policy question as inflation made small contributions even smaller. And Congress's raising of the threshold to $200 in 1979 did not answer that question. One hundred 1910 dollars would have been worth almost $800 by 1979, and two hundred 1979 dollars would have been worth only about $25 in 1910. Congress did not even index the new $200 threshold for inflation. Had Congress done that, the threshold in 2014 would have been $650. Where to set the threshold is a question that Congress should begin taking seriously.

The privacy argument might have seemed academic in the mid-1970s, when the only way to identify donors was to go to a government office and look through pages of candidate reports. Today, though, the Internet has raised privacy concerns to a new level. You can enter the names of relatives, neighbors, teachers, coworkers, or fellow students in a website, and any reportable contributions they have made will pop up on the screen.

Privacy concerns are also public policy concerns. The *Buckley* challengers cited the associational privacy rights the Supreme Court had protected in several cases involving civil rights workers in the South during the 1950s. They were not afraid of "the kind of focused and insistent harassment" inflicted on NAACP members; what worried them was that excessively low disclosure thresholds would deter people from contributing to parties, candidates, and causes that were unpopular in their social and professional circles.[29]

The purpose of disclosure is to make our democracy work better, not discourage people from participating in it. But some research suggests that this may be happening. Political scientist Raymond La Raja recently did a study to see how the very low disclosure thresholds found in all but a handful of states—half the states set the threshold at from $1 to $50—affect citizens' willingness to contribute. He found that people "who face strong interpersonal cross-pressures from people around them" tend to "cut back on donations or not give at all."[30]

David M. Primo and other political scientists drew a similar conclusion from a brief exercise they conducted in 2012. They asked candidates in every congressional race to post on their websites a notice that the names, addresses, occupations, and employers of donors who gave more than $200 would be made public; all but a few refused, fearing that they would scare away even donors who gave smaller amounts.[31]

These findings are not surprising. What has been surprising is the sharp spike in claims that disclosure causes—is even *intended* to cause—harassment and intimidation of donors, particularly donors to conservative organizations.

What are the intimidation charges raised by opponents of disclosure?

These charges came about largely as a conservative reaction to the liberal reaction to *Citizens United*. That decision allowed corporations to make independent expenditures in candidate campaigns, but nearly all the corporations that took advantage of it were tax-exempt nonprofits regulated only by the IRS. These groups are formally nonpolitical, but can engage in electoral politics as long as that remains secondary to their primary purpose. And as formally nonpolitical groups, they do not have to file disclosure reports with the FEC, which makes them an attractive way to make independent expenditures and keep their donors' identities secret.

Reform supporters call this new form of spending "dark money," and introduced a bill that would have required greater disclosure. Reform opponents call it "anonymous speech," and have said that calls for more disclosure are attempts to intimidate donors to conservative groups. Political science research has revealed reason for apprehension on the part of some small donors, but the recent claims of intimidation have come from sources that are anything but vulnerable.

The U.S. Chamber of Commerce, for example, said in 2012 that the push for disclosure is "all about intimidation. They want to intimidate people from participating."[32] Two years later, the *Wall Street*

Journal said that the purpose of disclosure "is to set up donors as political targets for boycotts and intimidation so the costs of participating in politics will be too steep."[33] Billionaire industrialist Charles Koch agreed: "We get death threats, threats to blow up our facilities, kill our people. . . . So long as we're in a society like that, where the president attacks us and we get threats from people in Congress, and this is pushed out and becomes part of the culture . . . why force people to disclose?"[34]

Claims that disclosure is intended to, and would be able to, cow the *Wall Street Journal*, the Chamber of Commerce, and denizens of the *Forbes* 400 into silence are simply not credible. What is worse is that they distract attention from the legitimate questions about who, what, and how much should be regulated that any regulatory scheme raises. How we answer those questions depends to a large extent on the character of the debate about them. The two sides in *Buckley* made valid arguments about disclosure that were based on factual evidence presented in court cases, and on sworn testimony. Revisiting that old debate, and basing it on recent research, would be a good place to start a reappraisal of disclosure.

5

POLITICAL ACTION COMMITTEES

Non-party organizations form political action committees (PACs) to make the campaign contributions the FECA bans them from making themselves. The FEC defines every PAC as belonging to one of two broad categories: connected and nonconnected. Nearly all connected PACs were formed by corporations, trade associations, labor unions, and membership associations. Nonconnected PACs are a much more diverse group, with super PACs being the newest and most familiar kind.

The 7,500 PACs registered with the FEC at the beginning of the 2015–16 election cycle were the result of two growth spurts: the PAC "explosion" of the late 1970s and the rise of super PACs after 2010, each of which led to different reform priorities. Corporate PACs grew at such an explosive rate in the late 1970s that by 1980 there were almost nine times as many of them as there had been in 1975. Reformers were not alone in concluding that these new PACs greatly increased the amount of business money in elections. Worries about PAC money lasted into the mid-1990s, when soft money (money raised and spent largely outside of FECA regulation) became a greater concern. Thirty years later, the flood of super PAC money released by *Citizens United* and *SpeechNow* made PACs a top reform priority again.

Why do we have PACs? Who created them and why?

Organized labor invented the PAC in 1943, when the Congress of Industrial Organizations (CIO) created the CIO Political Action Committee (CIO-PAC). Its organization and financing was the model on which connected PACs are based today.[1]

The CIO created the PAC in reaction to an attempt by Republicans and Southern Democrats in Congress to squelch labor political activity. Labor unions had occasionally participated in federal elections in earlier decades, but they rarely endorsed a particular party or candidate; they usually spent money on getting their members out to vote rather than by making campaign contributions. That changed in 1936, when a number of industrial unions broke away from the more staid AFL to create the Congress of Industrial Organizations (CIO), which openly worked for President Franklin D. Roosevelt's reelection.

Conservatives were alarmed by organized labor's sudden jump into the political fray in 1936, and in 1943 they saw an opportunity to do something about it. The United Mine Workers went on strike that year, violating the wartime no-strike pledge the AFL and CIO had made after Pearl Harbor. The two labor federations denounced the mine workers for breaking that pledge, but the conservative coalition of Republicans and Southern Democrats responded by passing the Smith-Connally Act, which applied to all unions.

The act was mostly about regulating labor–management relations during wartime, but it also added "labor organizations" to the Tillman Act's ban on campaign contributions by corporations. President Roosevelt vetoed the bill, but Republicans had won enough seats in the 1942 congressional elections to form a veto-proof majority when allied with Southern Democrats to pass it over the president's veto.[2]

The CIO acted quickly, creating the CIO-PAC just two weeks after the veto override. The CIO then spent months conferring with the railroad brotherhoods, AFL affiliates, and farm organizations about how the PAC should work. The CIO formally approved the PAC at its November convention, and member unions donated generously to get it started, giving almost as much money as all unions together had raised in 1936.

The Smith-Connally Act's prohibition against campaign contributions from "labor organizations" meant that no union could use member dues for that purpose, even when authorized by majority vote. The CIO got around that prohibition by creating the PAC as a separate organization with its own treasury, made up of $1 contributions from union members. The PAC was not entirely separate: the CIO used its treasury funds to establish and administer the PAC, and PAC officers were also union officers. But the PAC made contributions only from the voluntary contributions in its own treasury.

The CIO continued this arrangement after a Republican-controlled Congress made the Smith-Connally ban permanent in the 1947 Taft-Hartley Act. This act, too, was intensely partisan, passed by a Republican–Southern Democratic majority that also overrode President Truman's veto. The Taft-Hartley Act infuriated even the AFL, which had not been active in elections since Samuel Gompers's death in 1924. It created its own PAC, Labor's League for Political Education, which followed the CIO-PAC example by making contributions from voluntary contributions made by AFL members.[3]

This established the basic legal form for the connected PAC, now called a separate segregated fund. It was used almost exclusively by labor unions for the next thirty years. That changed after Watergate, when the rush of corporations and trade associations to form their own PACs created the PAC explosion of the late 1970s and early 1980s.

Why did corporations suddenly begin forming PACs in the late 1970s?

Corporations had had political contribution programs for years, most of them informal understandings among top executives rather than formal organizations. They could have gone on using these programs for many more years without turning them into PACs. What made the PAC form suddenly attractive to corporations was Watergate and the 1974 FECA amendments.

We will never know how much business money in politics was illegal. Many corporate programs were not much more than personal solicitations to managers from company presidents or vice presidents for public affairs; others were well organized, but not based on any consistent model. Some of the publicly known ones had filed reports under the old Federal Corrupt Practices Act, but most did not; and some were so secretive that the sponsoring companies would not even acknowledge their existence.[4]

To make sure candidates knew who was contributing to them, these programs used the "double envelope" method: they delivered envelopes containing checks from individual executives inside a larger envelope with the company name on it. Except for the fact that only the individual contributions would be publicly reported, this method served the same purpose as a PAC contribution. But the secretiveness of some of those pre-PAC programs, and the insistence of others that they were not legally required to file reports, gave rise to suspicions that some were breaking the law. And the Internal Revenue Service's successful prosecution of fourteen companies for violating the Tillman Act only added to the whiff of illegality.[5]

Whiffs of illegality are not good for a company's public image or for its bottom line. In the wake of Watergate, corporations moved to legitimize their political contribution programs by reorganizing them as PACs. Almost half the corporations that formed PACs in the late 1970s and early 1980s were simply formalizing preexisting contribution programs.[6]

The $1,000 contribution limit also gave corporations an incentive to form PACs. Under the unenforceable limit that existed before the FECA, and the absence of any limit at all in the 1971 FECA, corporate political programs could make substantial contributions by soliciting only a few top executives. But the $1,000 limit in the 1974 amendments meant that companies would have to do what PACs were designed to do: raise large numbers of small contributions. The Business-Industry PAC's political director explicitly made this point: "The trend away from large single contributions increases the acceptability and importance of PACs."[7]

Acceptability was not the universal reaction to the rapid growth of business PACs, however. Arriving when reform was in the air, they soon became the focus of new concerns about money in elections.

Why did reformers try to curb PACs in the 1980s?

They tried because the PAC explosion looked at first like the return of the very problems reform was trying to solve. The rapid rise of business PACs took everyone by surprise. Labor PACs were an old and familiar feature of electoral politics. They had been making campaign contributions and filing reports under the FCPA since the 1940s. But the rapid adoption of PACs by corporations, trade associations, single-issue groups, and ideological organizations was new and unexpected. By 1986, the number of PACs had increased by 400 percent and the money they contributed to candidates grew by 800 percent.[8]

Corporate executives had been giving money to politicians since the Gilded Age. Between the Tillman Act and the FECA, they gave through corporate contribution programs, most of which were only informally organized and only a few of which filed reports. As long as they were reported only as individual contributions, it was extremely difficult to tell how much business money there was in elections. Labor money in elections had been publicly reported for decades, but the absence of similar reports from corporations made business money almost invisible. That changed when executives began giving through their company PACs: from the late 1970s on, business money became very visible.

Money that suddenly became visible looked like money that had not been there before. Corporate PACs seemed to be pumping lots of new business money into elections. About half of the new corporate PACs were reorganizations of older contribution programs, which means that the other half were formed by companies that had not had such programs. So some of the corporate money was new, making it likely that PACs did bring more business money into elections. But we have no idea how much more. To find out we would have to add up all the corporate executive contributions from pre-FECA elections.

What we do know is that business PACs soon outnumbered labor PACs and were giving more money. When Congress passed the 1974 FECA amendments there were 201 labor PACs and only 89 corporate PACs; ten years later, the numbers were 394 and 1,692, respectively. By 1984, corporate PACs were also giving more money in contributions: $36 million to labor's $27 million. Add the PACs of trade associations and other business organizations, and total contributions by business PACs in 1984 was $67 million—more than twice what labor gave.[9]

PAC money is by definition special-interest money, because PACs are formed only by groups with a particular political interest, either to pass certain kinds of legislation or to elect certain kinds of candidates. So the steep rise in PAC money after Congress passed the 1974 reforms looked like a return of the big money that reform was supposed to stop.

Did politicians begin refusing PAC contributions in the 1980s?

Yes, many of them did, especially Democrats who generally supported reform. The media naturally reported on the rapid rise of PAC contributions in the 1980s, and coverage tended to convey the impression that an unprecedented amount of special-interest money was flowing into elections. Judging by most public opinion surveys, Americans were more likely to think PACs were a bad thing than a good one.[10]

PACs did not get much press coverage in the 1980 election, but they had become a very big issue by 1984. President Ronald Reagan did not turn down PAC funds for his primary campaign, but most Democratic presidential hopefuls publicly announced that they would turn down PAC money. Former vice president Walter Mondale even announced that he would not take contributions from the labor PACs that had been donating to Democrats since the 1940s.[11]

But Mondale's campaign for the Democratic nomination revealed that there might have been less to his pledge than met the eye. He did not in fact take any labor PAC money directly, but his rivals charged that he was being indirectly supported through "independent delegate committees." These ostensibly independent committees, set up to support Mondale delegates to the Democratic convention, were apparently financed by labor PACs. The issue became embarrassing enough for Mondale to call upon the committees to disband.[12]

Publicly refusing to take PAC money came to be something that was expected of Democratic presidential candidates. Arkansas governor Bill Clinton and most of his rivals for the 1992 Democratic nomination made such pledges. And when Senator Barack Obama announced his campaign for the presidency in 2007, he too said he would take no contributions from PACs or lobbyists.[13]

By 1992, however, it was obvious—to the people who paid attention to such things, if not to the general public—that not taking PAC money was not the same thing as not taking money from people in the organizations that sponsored PACs. Refusing contributions from a corporation's PAC, for example, did not mean refusing contributions from that corporation's executives. What appeared to be candidates' principled refusal to take special-interest money through

PACs simply made it harder for voters to know about the special-interest money they took through other means.

Candidates did not reject PAC money because it was special-interest money, but because it was special-interest money on the public record. Given what a bad reputation PACs had with such a broad segment of the public, rejecting their money was understandable as a campaign tactic.

The PAC "scandal" of the 1980s was not at all like the insurance and Watergate scandals. Those exposés revealed once-hidden activities that were either already illegal or were widely regarded as improper and then made illegal. All the PAC did was repackage contributions that had never been regarded as either improper or illegal; it came to be seen as improper only after it had been legalized.

While journalists, reformers, and politicians were trying to figure out what to do about PAC contributions, they also had to deal with the phenomenon of PAC independent expenditures.

Were independent expenditures new?

Independent expenditures were not new. By the 1980s, political committees that claimed to be independent of candidates and parties had been making such expenditures for decades. But the formation of ideological PACs to make such expenditures was new. One of the first such PACs, and the one that got the most attention, was the National Conservative Political Action Committee (NCPAC), which used its funds against moderate Republicans as well as Democrats.

NCPAC's methods raised even more concern than its money. PAC chair Terry Dolan explained how an independent spending group could attack its favorite candidates' opponents while leaving the candidates themselves blameless for running a negative campaign: "A group like ours could lie through its teeth, and the candidate it helps stays clean."[14]

There was nothing reformers could do about such groups. PACs had been legalized under the FECA, which meant they were part of a statute that could be amended. Unlimited independent expenditures, though, were the creation of the Supreme Court, which wrote them into constitutional law, and constitutional law is not easily amended.

NCPAC was also a new kind of PAC, one of a growing number of PACs that did not have sponsors. In 1974 all PACs were what are now called "connected," meaning they were sponsored by an organization, usually a labor union; the corporate and other business PACs that appeared in the late 1970s were also of this type. As early as 1977, though, the Federal Election Commission had to create a new "non-connected" category for the growing number of political committees that had no sponsoring organizations. These two types of committees made up the two categories that are still used to define PACS: connected and nonconnected.

What is a connected PAC?

A connected PAC, or separate segregated fund, has a sponsoring organization, usually a corporation, trade association, or labor union. It is called a separate segregated fund because it must be separate from its sponsoring organization; the fund must be segregated from its sponsor's treasury, and must consist of voluntary contributions. The sponsoring organization can use its funds to create and administer its PAC, and can even use its own officers to manage it. But those officers can solicit contributions only from people who are in some way part of the sponsoring organization, such as union members or corporate managers and shareholders.

This is the way the CIO set up the first PAC in 1943. Over the next twenty-five years, individual unions used this model to form their own PACs. The legality of the PAC form was challenged in 1968, when a federal grand jury in St. Louis indicted the officers of a pipefitters union local, charging that the local's PAC was simply a means to make union contributions that were illegal under the Taft-Hartley Act.

The case ended up in the Supreme Court, which voted 6–2 in favor of the union. It did not matter, the court said, that the union had used its own funds to create the PAC and the people who ran the PAC were the same people who ran the union: "A legitimate political fund must be separate from the sponsoring union only in the sense that there must be a strict segregation of its monies from union dues and assessments."[15] Union officers could also solicit contributions from members, as long as the members understood that the contributions were voluntary and would be used for political purposes.

Once the PAC form was held to be legal, and available to corporations and other organizations in addition to unions, it became more widely adopted. The FEC classifies connected PACs under five categories of sponsors: corporations, labor unions, trade/membership/health organizations, cooperatives, and corporations without stock.

How do the five categories of connected PACs differ from one another?

Corporate and labor committees were the first PACs, and for most of the last forty years they were what came to mind when people thought about PACs. Corporate committees make up more than half of all connected PACs, labor committees only about 10 percent.

Trade, membership, and health committees make up a little less than one-third of connected PACs. The biggest trade PACs include associations of beer wholesalers, cable television companies, real estate developers, construction companies, and banks. The biggest health industry PACs include associations of hospitals, anesthesiologists, dermatologists, and surgeons. Most of these PACs can be included with corporations as representing business interests.

Membership PACs are a more diverse bunch. Some sponsors in this category, such as the National Federation of Independent Business and the National Restaurant Association, are also part of the business community. A few, like PricewaterhouseCoopers and Ernst & Young, two of the world's biggest auditing firms, are themselves active business enterprises. Their PACs are listed under the membership category because they are partnerships, not corporations. The membership category also includes professional associations that are more loosely connected to business interests, such as the National Association of Insurance and Financial Advisors. This category also includes the kind of voluntary associations—such as the National Rifle Association and the League of Conservation Voters—that first come to mind when we think of membership groups. Their PACs are connected because they are incorporated nonprofits and are treated under the law as corporations.

PACs sponsored by cooperatives and corporations without stock make up only about 5 percent of connected PACs. Most of these PACs are small, raising less than $50,000 in an election cycle; the few that raise more than that tend to be mutual insurance companies.

Do business and labor PACs do different things with their money in elections?

They do. With a few exceptions, all put most of their money into contributions rather than independent expenditures. They all give most of their money to incumbents, too, although some are more willing to give to challengers.

Corporate PACs give the huge majority of their contributions to incumbents, and not only to Republicans. The share they give to Republican incumbents can vary from 40 to 60 percent, depending on how control of Congress shifts between the two parties. They very rarely give to challengers and they make almost no independent expenditures. Trade association PACs behave much like corporate PACs, giving more than 80 percent of their contributions to incumbents. But they appear to be even more pragmatic, being slightly more likely to give to Democrats.[16]

Labor PACs also give most of their contributions to incumbents, and 90 percent of their money goes to Democrats. They are much more likely to give to challengers, almost always to Democrats. The big difference from corporate PACs is that a much bigger share of labor PAC money has gone to making independent expenditures, especially in presidential elections. In 2008 labor PACs spent more than $50 million on behalf of Senator Barack Obama, more than twice what they had spent in any previous election.[17]

Corporate and trade PACs give most of their money to incumbents of both parties because the sponsoring corporations want access to powerful decision makers no matter who controls Congress. Giving to challengers is riskier, and corporate PACs, like corporations, tend to be risk-averse. Labor wants access, too, but the GOP has never been particularly friendly, so they give almost exclusively to Democrats. Given the limited access they have in any Congress, labor cannot afford not to take some risks, which is why they give more to challengers and spend so much on behalf of Democrats who share their views.[18]

What are nonconnected PACs?

Nonconnected PACs are not sponsored by organizations. The drawback to having no sponsor is that nonconnected PACs must pay the costs of establishing and administering themselves from the contributions they receive. The benefit is that they are not restricted in whom they can solicit for contributions. Connected PACs must solicit only people who are members, officers, or shareholders of their sponsoring organizations, but nonconnected PACs can solicit anyone.

For decades, nonconnected PACs tended to be formed for ideological or partisan purposes. Of the twenty-five biggest nonconnected PACs active in 2015, twelve were ideological groups—six conservative/Republican, six liberal/Democratic. There were also four other partisan committees—all Republican—called leadership PACs, which are the personal PACs of politicians. Politicians use them to maintain or create support networks by giving money to other politicians, but they cannot use them to finance their own election campaigns.[19]

Super PACs are the newest kind of nonconnected PACs. The FEC's term for them, "Independent Expenditure-Only Political Committees," may be ponderously legalistic, but it also accurately describes what they do. They only make independent expenditures, which they can finance by soliciting contributions of unlimited size from corporations and labor unions, as well as from individuals. Super PACs are the subject of chapter 6.

What do ideological PACs do?

They make contributions and independent expenditures, just as other PACs do. But all the expenses that are covered by the sponsoring organizations of connected PACs—salaries, administrative expenses, even the cost of fundraising—must be paid for out of the money that nonconnected PACs raise.

Look, for example, at how much money the two biggest ideological PACs raised in 2012 and how they spent it. The liberal PAC

MoveOn Political Action raised almost $20 million. It spent $1.2 million on independent expenditures in the presidential election, for Obama and against Romney, and it gave $7 million in contributions to mostly federal candidates; but it also spent $11.5 million for administrative expenses, salaries, and fundraising. The Tea Party Express's Our Country Deserves Better PAC raised $10.2 million. It spent $700,000 on independent expenditures and gave about $300,000 to Mitt Romney and to Republican senatorial candidates; but it spent more than $9 million on fundraising, administration, and salaries.[20]

The only other committees to raise more than $5 million in 2012 were Democracy for America, a liberal PAC, and the Conservative StrikeForce. Democracy for America spent $4.7 million on fundraising, administration, and salaries, but made no independent expenditures and gave only $400,000 in contributions. The Conservative StrikeForce spent $700,000 on independent expenditures and contributions, and $5 million on fundraising, administration, and salaries.[21]

The ideological PACs get a lot of media attention, but many of them may not deserve it. Raising enough money to keep the PAC going and still be able give out meaningful amounts of money is clearly a huge challenge. The total amount of money they raise is not a good guide to how much they give to or spend on behalf of candidates.

What do leadership PACs do?

They do less now than they did before super PACs, but still more than when they were first invented in the 1980s.[22]

Leadership PACs got their name because the first ones were formed by people who were in, or aspired to be in, positions of leadership in Congress. Suppose, for example, that you are in your second term in the House of Representatives and want to start your climb up the ladder of party office by chairing the subcommittee you are on. You can build the kind of support you need to get that spot by forming a personal PAC to make contributions to members of your party's steering committee—they are the ones who make such appointments—and to other subcommittee members.

Your help will be especially welcome to colleagues who are in tight races. You can give them contributions directly and write a check to your party's congressional campaign committee. You can also contribute to your colleagues' state parties and help with polling and fundraising. They will not forget who filled their campaign chests.[23]

There was nothing new about this. Long before there were such things as PACs, leading members of Congress used the networks of friends and donors they had built over the years to send money to the members whose votes they needed.

There were two advantages to doing the same thing with a PAC. Members could "double dip" by soliciting money for their PAC from big donors who had already given the legal maximum to their campaign committee. And they could hand out $5,000 PAC contributions rather than $1,000 (before 2002) individual contributions. Raise and give enough money and you could well get the leadership position you wanted while building a network of friends that would serve you well as you moved up to higher positions.

Members with safe seats could use their PACs to make their incumbent advantage even stronger. They could not legally give the money they raised to their own campaign committees, at least not directly. But they could help themselves indirectly by hiring the political consultants they would need and by handing out money to state and local parties and candidates to shore up support back home.

Leadership PACs also were a way to get around anti-corruption rules that limit what lobbyists can give to legislators. Lobbyists can no longer hand out choice tickets to ball games, or give legislators all-expenses-paid trips to pricey ski resorts or golf courses. But legislators can pay for those things themselves, using money those same lobbyists contribute to their personal PACs.[24]

Some reform-minded members tried to ban leadership PACs. But when even backbenchers began forming such committees, members found them too useful to support a ban. It was not long before people realized how useful the PACs could be to politicians seeking the nation's highest office.[25]

In 1995, Senator Bob Dole (R-KS) was able to use his personal PAC, Campaign America, to start his unofficial campaign for the presidency without having to announce that he was a candidate.

During what political scientists call the invisible primary, in the odd-numbered year before the official primaries, Dole gave contributions to state and local candidates and party committees in the early-voting states of Iowa and New Hampshire. He had been doing the same thing since 1988, but in 1996 it paid off by helping him get the Republican nomination.[26]

Senators Barack Obama and Hillary Clinton did the same thing in 2007 with their personal PACs, Hope Fund and HillPAC, respectively, and Governor Mitt Romney followed suit in 2011. Times change, though, and by 2011 the leadership PAC was already old news. It still had its uses, but the big new thing was the super PAC.[27]

6

SUPER PACs

Super PACs are independent expenditure committees that can take contributions of any size from any American individual, corporation, or labor union, and spend without limit. They made a huge splash when they were first formed in 2010, turning candidates' attention away from the merely rich and toward the fabulously wealthy. These are the fruits of *Citizens United*, and they go a long way toward explaining why that decision is still so widely opposed years after it was handed down. What all the attention paid to that decision misses, however, is that the roots of super PACs go much deeper. Like the other ways used to raise and spend money outside of FECA regulation, super PACs can be traced directly back to *Buckley v. Valeo*.

Where did the super PAC come from?

It came partly from *Citizens United*, which gave corporations the First Amendment right to make independent expenditures. And it came partly from *SpeechNow v. FEC*, a lower-court decision that struck down FECA's $5,000 limit on contributions to PACs that made only independent expenditures. Both decisions were based on the distinction *Buckley* made between contributions and expenditures.[1]

The $5,000 limit was on contributions to all PACs, something that Congress added to the 1976 FECA amendments. No one challenged it right away because it was so similar to the limit on individual donations upheld in *Buckley*. Those limits help prevent corruption, the court said, because a contribution is a direct gift to a candidate, a *quid* that can be exchanged for a corrupting *quo*. Not so for independent expenditures, which the court chose to believe really were independent. They were the pure speech of the spenders, not a way to corrupt candidates, and so fell squarely under the First Amendment's protection.

But if independent expenditures could not corrupt candidates, could the contributions made to finance them be corrupting? SpeechNow said they could not, and that the $5,000 limit on them did not serve the constitutional purpose of preventing corruption. The federal circuit court for the District of Columbia agreed, and struck down the limit on contributions to PACs that did only independent spending.[2]

The FEC acted a few months later to comply with the circuit court decision. Citing *Citizens United* and *SpeechNow*, the agency announced that what it called independent-expenditure-only PACs could now solicit unlimited contributions from individuals, corporations, and unions. Thus was born the super PAC.[3]

Many super PACs were formed in the months before the 2010 midterm elections, but by 2012 there were fifteen times as many and they had become the mega-fundraisers of the PAC world, raising more than all corporate and labor committees combined.[4]

What makes super PACs super?

Getting rid of the $5,000 limit was essential, as the great majority of super PAC funds come from individuals. The *Citizens United* grant of corporate First Amendment rights to make independent expenditures was not enough by itself to create super PACs. For-profit business corporations neither made their own independent expenditures nor, as far as we know, contributed much to PACs that did. But 501(c)(4) social welfare groups, which are nonprofit corporations, did both.

Super PACs are just super-sized versions of the kinds of political committees that had been regulated under the FECA since 1971, so they still had to report their donors to the FEC. That is not true of 501(c)(4)s; they can hide their donors, which made them ideal companions for super PACs.

Republican political strategist Karl Rove was one of the first to see the advantage of pairing a super PAC with a 501(c)(4). His American Crossroads was the first big super PAC, formed just three weeks after *SpeechNow*. He had spent months pitching the idea for American Crossroads to the GOP's biggest donors, and they had pledged to contribute $30 million. But in the first month after launching the PAC it had received only $200. Donors still wanted to honor their pledges, but they were reluctant to go public. Rove solved that problem by creating a sister organization, a 501(c)(4) called Crossroads Grassroots Policy Strategies. That did the trick. The American Crossroads/Crossroads GPS combination raised $325 million in 2010, which at the time was a record for a non-party group.[5]

It was not long before someone tried to super-size a traditional PAC by creating a hybrid PAC.

What is a hybrid PAC?

A hybrid PAC is the grafting of a super PAC onto a standard non-connected PAC. The FEC's official name for it is "political committee with non-contribution accounts." Like the super PAC, the hybrid PAC was born out of a suit against the FEC.

Rear Admiral (ret.) James J. Carey, founder and treasurer of the National Defense PAC, brought the suit against the FEC. The NDPAC is a nonconnected committee that contributes to (mostly Republican) candidates who share its hawkish foreign policy views.[6] After *Citizens United* and *SpeechNow*, Carey thought his PAC should be able to raise and spend unlimited sums of money for independent expenditures while also maintaining the account it used to make contributions. Citing those cases, Carey asked the FEC for an advisory opinion in 2010.

The FEC's general counsel presented the commissioners with two draft opinions. One would have permitted the NDPAC to add an independent expenditures-only account to its existing contributions account; the other would not have permitted it. The FEC deadlocked on each draft. Carey then filed suit against the agency, and the federal district court for the District of Columbia ruled in his favor, permitting him to turn the NDPAC into a hybrid PAC.[7]

Before *Carey*, connected and nonconnected PACs could make contributions and independent expenditures from one account, but that account could not accept contributions from corporations and unions, or from individuals in amounts greater than $5,000. Now a nonconnected PAC can have both a "traditional" contribution account and a second "super PAC" account. So far there has been no serious attempt to do the same with connected PACs.[8]

Hybrid PACs were not the only super PAC problem the FEC had to face. The biggest one was the old issue of coordination with candidates.

Why is coordination between candidates and super PACs a problem?

Super PACs make only independent expenditures, which *Buckley* defined as being made without coordinating or consulting with the candidates they support. This was the first legal definition of independent expenditures, but they and the coordination problems they created were already decades old by the time the *Buckley* decision was handed down.

Independent expenditures date back to 1940, when the Hatch Act imposed contribution and expenditure limits on party and candidate committees. To evade those limits, both parties created ostensibly independent committees; big donors could donate to them after they had given the maximum contributions to party and candidate committees.

The rapid proliferation of these groups greatly complicated the job of congressional committees appointed to investigate campaign funds. To deal with the hundreds of supposedly independent, nonparty actors in the 1944 election, that year's Senate investigating committee had to decide how to distinguish a genuinely independent committee from a candidate committee. The senators decided that a genuinely independent committee was one that engaged in activities intended to affect the outcome of an election, but was neither sponsored nor financed by a candidate or a political party.[9]

That distinction was clear in theory but proved to be nearly impossible to make in practice. In its post-election report, the 1944 Senate committee said its investigations were "hampered by the fact that it is not unusual for a regular party organization to set up 'dummy' committees, which may have a suite of offices separate from the regular organization, have distinctive letterheads, publish advertising and literature, or sponsor radio broadcasts, and yet be wholly controlled and financed by the regular party organization."[10]

Some degree of coordination was assumed, even if it could not be proved. But from the 1940s to the 1970s, the only thing Congress did about the problem was to prohibit labor unions from making independent expenditures. Congress did no more than that partly because few members were inclined to prohibit a tactic they themselves found so useful.

Senator Al Gore Sr. (D-TN) described how he used the independent spending dodge in his own campaigns: "I have had barbers for Gore, farmers for Gore, teachers for Gore, businessmen for Gore, and as we approached a limit ... why, we just established another committee. This is clearly within the law, which means we really have no law."[11]

What did Congress do about independent expenditures after Watergate?

Congress had known for more than thirty years that most independent expenditures were made to evade contribution limits. So when it enacted a $1,000 limit on contributions to candidates in the 1974 FECA amendments, it imposed the same limit on independent expenditures made to benefit those candidates. Evasion, which is to say coordination, was no easier to prove in the 1970s than it had been in the 1940s, which meant that laws prohibiting it were bound to be ineffective. But if Congress could not prohibit evasion, it could limit it by imposing a ceiling on independent expenditures.

Buckley struck down that solution. The Supreme Court came up with a definition of independent expenditures that was essentially the same as the one devised by the 1944 Senate committee. But instead of using it as a standard for measuring the independence of expenditures, the justices saw it as a statement of how independent they actually were. In their view, independent expenditures were not a way to evade limits on direct contributions by making indirect ones but, rather, "pure speech" that could not be limited.

Congress knew more about independent expenditures than the court did, but there was not much it could do under the circumstances. The best it could do was to include in the 1976 FECA amendments the requirement that any PAC or person making independent expenditures in support of a candidate had to certify "under penalty of perjury" that they are not made "in cooperation, consultation, or concert with" that candidate. The phrase "under penalty of perjury" was not in the 1974 law, but it appeared three times in the 1976 FECA amendments.[12]

Congress's repeated warnings about perjury suggest that it did not buy the *Buckley* court's blithe assurance that merely calling a committee independent was enough to make it so. But that assurance now had the force of constitutional law, which meant that Congress's definition of independence, even with its strong statements about legal penalties, had no more practical effect than the definition drawn up by that Senate committee in 1944.

Then came *Citizens United* and *SpeechNow*. The super PAC made the weakness of the law's bar against coordination even more glaring.

How did Citizens United *and* SpeechNow *make coordination between candidates and super PACs such a big problem?*

They did that by changing the law about who could give how much to whom. Before the Bipartisan Campaign Reform Act (BCRA) there were two campaign finance systems: the one under FECA regulation and the parallel soft money system that was effectively unregulated. The FECA prohibited corporate and union contributions and imposed limits on contributions from individuals; soft money was mostly raised under state laws that did not have these restrictions.

But BCRA went a long way toward ending soft money by drawing a bright line between the two systems. Congress could do nothing about state laws, but it could prohibit federal candidates from raising nonfederal funds. So BCRA barred federal candidates from soliciting "any funds that are not subject to the limitations, prohibitions, and reporting requirements" of the FECA.[13]

Citizens United blurred that bright line by permitting independent expenditures to be financed by corporate and union money. And when *SpeechNow* struck down the $5,000 limit on individual contributions to PACs that made those expenditures, it blurred the *Buckley* distinction between contributions and expenditures. By ruling that contributions to independent spending PACs could not be limited, *SpeechNow* effectively redefined those contributions as being themselves a form of expenditures. There were now gray areas where there had once been clear distinctions.

The FECA still prohibited corporate and union money and imposed limits on individual contributions, but now there were exceptions. The old restrictions applied to candidates, parties, and traditional PACs, but not to the new super PACs. Super PACs had to meet the same FECA registration and reporting requirements as other political committees, but they were funded in the same way as the old non-FECA soft money committees. Funds that were not subject to the limitations and prohibitions of the FECA were nonetheless now in the FECA. And if those funds were now in the FECA, did that mean that federal candidates could now solicit them?

The FEC soon had to answer that question. In May 2011, conservative lawyer James Bopp Jr. formed the Republican Super PAC, which he said would raise funds in coordination with the candidates it supported. He said this would not violate the FECA ban against coordination because that ban applied only to a super PAC's expenditures, not to its fundraising. He was so sure his plan was legal that he did not even bother to request an advisory opinion from the FEC.[14]

Democrats were not so sure, and they did ask the agency for an advisory opinion. Majority PAC and House Majority PAC, super PACs formed to help Democrats win seats in Congress, asked the FEC whether the candidates they supported could solicit unlimited contributions to them and attend PAC fundraisers.

The FEC's answer essentially supported Bopp's position. It did say that candidates were still bound by pre–*Citizens United* laws about raising campaign funds. But it also said that candidates could attend super PAC fundraisers at which unlimited sums would be solicited from corporations and unions, as well as individuals; they could stay within the law as long as they personally solicited only individual contributions of $5,000 or less.[15]

What the FEC said in effect was that candidates could hit up rich donors and corporate executives for five- and six-figure contributions under the legal cover of soliciting only the first $5,000. Some reformers tried to portray the $5,000 limit as a victory, but Bopp knew better. He said the FEC "approved our goal," and called the $5,000 limit "a fairly meaningless and technical restriction."[16]

What are the rules against candidates coordinating with super PACs?

The FEC has a "three-prong test" to determine whether an expenditure for a campaign ad was coordinated with a candidate, but essentially it comes down to whether the candidate does any one of five things:

- Requested, suggested, or assented to the ad
- Was materially involved in the ad's creation, production, or distribution
- Had substantial discussion with the PAC before the ad was created, produced, or distributed
- Employed the same vendor the PAC employed to create, produce, or distribute the ad
- Employed a person who created, produced, or distributed the ad for the PAC

The FEC test lays down clear lines between legal and illegal conduct, which is what regulations are supposed to do.[17] The problem is that candidates and PACs can work together without doing any of those things. That means coordination cannot be prevented and that it is next to impossible to enforce the rules against it.

This dilemma appeared soon after *Buckley*, in response to the burst of independent expenditures by conservative groups in 1980. After that year's election, reformers asked the FEC to narrow its definition of independence. As members of that 1944 Senate committee could have told them, though, "independent" was an elastic term.

Political scientist Larry J. Sabato explained in his 1984 book on PACs that direct consultation was not necessary to coordinate expenditures with candidate campaigns: "The network of friends and associates among campaigns and PACs is so large and so informed that anyone seriously desiring to know a candidate's campaign needs or plans has very little trouble doing so."[18]

By 2001, the Supreme Court itself acknowledged that supposedly independent expenditures were made with a "wink or nod" from the candidate they supported.[19] But it took the rise of the single-candidate super PAC in 2012 to show how close coordination with candidates could get and still not count as coordination under the law.

How close did candidates and super PACs get in 2012?

The presidential super PACs are a good example. "We don't control outside groups," President Obama's press secretary told the press soon after the pro-Obama Priorities USA Action super PAC was formed; "These are not people working for the administration."[20] That was true: the people in question had left their White House jobs several weeks before founding the PAC. And the co-founders of the pro-Romney Restore Our Future super PAC had not worked for Romney since his 2008 primary campaign.[21]

The distinction between coordination and independence "essentially collapsed" in 2012, said legal scholar Richard Briffault; reform lawyer Paul S. Ryan saw things the same way, saying "many super PACs are joined at the hip with candidates."[22] Not everyone saw something to worry about. Legal scholar Bradley A. Smith thought that super PACs' impact on elections had been overblown; what worried him was that arguments like Briffault's and Ryan's "can create a cynicism among the general public."[23]

Smith realized that in the "commonsense" definition of the term, candidates were coordinating with single-candidate super PACs formed by their associates and former aides. But it is the legal definition that matters, he said, and it requires something more: "the opportunity for *quid pro quo* bargaining. Absent actual coordination—that is, actual discussions and dealings between the parties—that crucial link is missing."[24] Smith saw no need either for new rules or stronger enforcement of existing ones.

Calls for new rules continued after 2012. Briffault proposed a rule change that would treat single-candidate PACs run by the candidates' former aides, and for which the candidates themselves solicit contributions, as coordinated with those candidates' official campaign committees. Rep. David Price (D-NC) introduced a bill that would reclassify single-candidate super PACs as part of the candidate's campaign.[25]

The pattern begun in 2012 shows no sign of ending. There were about twice as many single-candidate super PACs in 2014 as in the 2012 congressional elections, and there will likely be even more in 2016. In the presidential race, Priorities USA Action shifted to supporting Hillary Clinton in 2016, a change made clear when Guy Cecil, the political director for her 2008 presidential campaign, became the

PAC's co-chair. There is no chance that Congress or the FEC will do much to strengthen enforcement of the rules against coordination.[26]

How did the super PAC change the way presidential candidates run their campaigns?

The same laws that were in effect for the 2008 and 2012 presidential elections are still in effect for the 2016 election. But the super PAC gets around those laws, and candidates are using them to do more of the tasks that used to be done by exploratory committees and candidate committees.

Forming exploratory committees used to signal the start of the invisible primary, when presidential hopefuls compete to win the support of party leaders and voters in the year before the actual primaries begin. What makes this period so important is that, with very few exceptions, over the last nine presidential elections the major-party candidates who had the most party endorsements and were ahead in the polls and in fundraising by the time of the Iowa caucuses went on to win the nomination.[27]

An exploratory committee is not a candidate committee, but a way for a politician to explore the possibility of becoming a candidate, to "test the waters." Such a committee is advantageous for a politician who genuinely does not know whether it is feasible to become a candidate. The committee must raise funds in compliance with FECA limits and prohibitions, but it does not have to file disclosure reports; and if the politician decides not to run, there will be no public record of the committee's activities.

The advantage for politicians who are simply being coy about announcing themselves as candidates is that the exploratory committee allows them to raise and spend money on such activities as travel and polls without triggering the FECA requirement to form a candidate committee. Spending more than $5,000 on such activities through their leadership PACs would trigger that requirement.[28]

The 2008 presidential election started off the same way as elections going back to 1980. By mid-January 2007, the most prominent presidential hopefuls in each party—Senators Barack Obama, Hillary Clinton, and John McCain, and Governor Mitt Romney—had all formed exploratory committees. Within three weeks all had announced their candidacies. The pattern continued in 2011, as Romney and other Republican contenders formed their own exploratory committees.[29]

The 2016 election did not start off this way, though. Some candidates quickly realized that super PACs could take the place of exploratory committees. Super PACs are legally independent committees, not formed by or coordinated with candidates, so they can spend unlimited sums of money without triggering the $5,000 limit. Candidates can test the waters without forming the exploratory committee that would allow them to raise money legally, because legally they are not raising any money at all. And as long as candidates are not officially candidates, they can work with and raise funds for the super PAC that supports them without breaking any laws. Initial 2016 front-runners Hillary Clinton and Jeb Bush, for example, both had super PACs, but neither one formed an exploratory committee and both put off announcing their candidacies.[30]

Super PACs became campaign necessities. Despite being legally independent of the candidates they support, some candidates used them to pay for the kinds of jobs that candidate committees used to do—jobs such as phone banks, get-out-the-vote drives, data collection, and opposition research. PACs that became super because they were formally independent of candidates' and parties' campaigns grew even more super as subcontractors for those campaigns.[31]

Stephen Colbert formed a super PAC on his Comedy Central TV show, The Colbert Report. What was that about?

It was about making fun of the unenforceable rules about disclosure and coordination. It did not start out that way, though. Apparently Colbert did not have a very good idea what to do with his idea for the Americans for a Better Tomorrow, Tomorrow super PAC. Trevor Potter, who was the PAC's lawyer, said that decisions to make fun of flimsy rules "evolved in wonderful spontaneity."[32]

Colbert told his audience that he had a "simple dream: to use the Supreme Court's *Citizens United* ruling to fashion a massive money cannon that would make all those who seek the White House quake with fear and beg our allegiance . . . in strict accordance with federal election law."[33]

Colbert thought his super PAC would get tons of corporate money and was disappointed when he got none. Potter told him that super PACs have to disclose their donors, and explained that corporations were not eager to make their contributions public because they might upset shareholders and customers. But he added that they might be willing to give to tax-exempt 501(c) groups that did not disclose their donors.

So Colbert formed a 501(c)(4), initially called Anonymous Shell Corporation, but later renamed Colbert Super PAC SHH. Potter reminded him that the group's major purpose had to be social and educational, and Colbert assured him that it would educate Americans by telling them that gay people cause earthquakes.

Colbert was pleased to hear that he could keep contributions to his super PAC secret by routing them through his 501(c)(4), but he needed assurance that this was legal:

COLBERT   You mean I can take secret donations from my 501(c)(4) and give them to my supposedly transparent super PAC?

POTTER   And it will say "Given by your (c)(4)."

COLBERT   What is the difference between that and money laundering?

POTTER   It's hard to say.[34]

One week later, Colbert sent an email to supporters of Americans for a Better Tomorrow, Tomorrow, telling them how to make secret contributions to the super PAC: "Already we have gotten a massive donation from [name withheld], a kind and [adjective withheld] person who only wants to [objective withheld]."[35]

Colbert then decided that he wanted to be a candidate himself. Told that he could not run his super PAC while running for office, he turned the PAC over to Jon Stewart, who was then host of Comedy Central's *Daily Show*. He then announced he was forming an exploratory committee to lay the groundwork for his possible candidacy for "President of the United States of South Carolina."

Stewart wanted to use the super PAC to run ads supporting Colbert's campaign. But to emphasize his compliance with the laws that required him to operate completely independently from Colbert, he renamed the Colbert PAC the Definitely Not Coordinating With Stephen Colbert Super PAC.[36]

Potter cautioned Stewart that he and Colbert could not discuss what the ads would say, or when and where they would air, because that would meet the legal definition of coordination. What Colbert could do was to speak on television, simply as a citizen, to say what he wished Stewart's super PAC would do—and "take the risk" that Stewart might be watching and use that information.[37]

Colbert announced his candidacy too late to get on the ballot for South Carolina's Republican primary, so he and Stewart's super PAC urged Republicans to vote for former Godfather's Pizza CEO Herman Cain as a proxy. The Tea Party favorite was actually not a candidate anymore, having suspended his own presidential campaign after allegations of sexual misconduct. But he was still on the ballot and Colbert was not. Colbert and Cain held a joint campaign rally the day before the vote to whip up interest, but received only 1 percent of the vote.[38]

Jeb Bush's super PAC did not help him at all. And Hillary Clinton's super PAC did not help her fend off Bernie Sanders. So how big a deal are super PACs, really?

One of the biggest surprises of 2015 was the yawning gap between the large sum of money in Jeb Bush's super PAC and his low ranking in the polls. No one predicted such a thing. Nor could anyone have predicted that Hillary Clinton, whose super PAC far outstripped those of her few Democratic rivals, would see her fifty-six-point lead in the polls over Senator Bernie Sanders (I-VT) shrink to just eight points by April 2016. And Sanders shot up in the polls despite having no super PAC.[39]

The biggest shock was the startling rise of billionaire real estate mogul and reality TV star Donald Trump to the top of the polls in the Republican primary. Trump came in from outside the party, with no experience in politics and government, and no ties to the GOP establishment. He also had no super PAC, but he did not need one. His name recognition as host of "The Apprentice" and the prodigious talent for populist demagoguery he demonstrated on the stump earned him tens of millions of dollars' worth of free media.

We have seen other right-wing demagogues use their candidacies to stir up grassroots nativism, but they remained on the political fringes; Trump became a front-runner, which has never happened before.[40]

Only slightly less shocking was the rise of Texas senator Ted Cruz. Unlike Trump, Cruz was an insider, a Republican politician with several years of experience in federal and state government. And he had the second-biggest Republican super PAC. But this Tea Party favorite was also a true-believing conservative ideologue who challenged the GOP establishment from his first days in the Senate, putting himself on the outside of his own party, and making himself one of the most detested men in politics. That did not stop him from rising to second place in the polls, despite spending only a bit more than Trump on ads.[41]

Bush, on the other hand, spent tens of millions of dollars on ads without raising his poll numbers above 15 percent or winning a single primary. Yet the Right to Rise super PAC might have been a bigger help to his campaign than these figures suggest. It paid for 95 percent of his ad buys because there was three times more money in the super PAC than there was in his campaign committee. Bush might have needed his super PAC simply to stay in the race.[42]

Maybe we are having difficulty gauging the impact of super PACs because the impact they have had is not what we expected. Most people expected that a flood of super PAC money would quickly eliminate candidates who did not get the biggest contributions. What happened instead was that candidates who could not get the biggest contributions were still able to get enough backing from big donors to keep their campaigns alive. Rather than speed things up by giving one candidate an unbeatable lead early in the race, super PACs may instead slow things down by scattering rich donors' money among several candidates.

As of this writing, in the first months of 2016, it is too early to say that super PACs do not matter. We know they mattered by changing traditional patterns of raising and spending campaign funds. But we have no way of knowing what further effect they might have had without the populist wave that hit both parties in the primaries. And we have yet to see how they will be used in the general election.

7

BILLIONAIRES

The rise of the super PAC was also the rise of the politically active billionaire. Dropping the old restrictions on who could give how much to whom did more than turn the attentions of fundraisers from millionaires to billionaires. It also freed billionaires to be more than mere donors. They could now become political entrepreneurs in their own right.

There seem to be a lot of billionaire donors these days. Is this new?

Not entirely. The tiny slice of the population made up of the very rich has always provided a hugely disproportionate share of campaign funds. There is nothing new about that. What has changed in recent decades is that their share has been increasing. In 1980 the richest .01 percent of Americans accounted for about 15 percent of all campaign contributions, a share that rose to about 30 percent over the next thirty years. Then came *Citizens United* and *SpeechNow*. In just the next two years the .01 percent's share of contributions shot up to more than 40 percent.[1]

The upward trend continued into 2015. Two analyses of midyear reports submitted to the FEC in June 2015 by presidential candidates and the super PACs that support them made the pattern clear. The *New York Times*'s analysis reported that just 358 families, those who gave $100,000 or more, provided "well over half" of all the money contributed to the Republican and Democratic presidential campaigns in the first six months of the year.[2]

A more detailed study, by the Campaign Finance Institute (CFI), reported a similar finding: the 376 donors who gave $100,000 or more provided 54 percent of the money contributed to the candidate committees and super PACs of both parties. The CFI analysis also shows the striking difference between the two parties. The Democrats had only thirty-five $100,000-plus donors, and they accounted for only 21 percent of all Democratic contributions. The 441 Republican donors who gave that much accounted for 64 percent of all Republican contributions. A February 2016 *Politico* study made another comparison, finding that the 100 biggest donors gave as much as the 2 million small donors combined.[3]

The role of parties has also changed. From the nineteenth century through the end of the twentieth, there was a clear division of labor in both parties: the rich provided the money, and the parties provided the candidates and ran the campaigns. Rich donors who wanted to be politically active were active in the party.

Today is different. Big donors today give much of their money to super PACs and other non-party groups. Most of the parties' biggest donors still do not want to take on the tasks of picking candidates and running campaigns themselves, but some do. The old division of labor is no longer a good description of the way campaigns are funded.

What is different about megadonors today?

Billionaires have used super PACs to become independent political players alongside the parties, playing the kind of large and public political role that is new in American politics. This trend began in the 2012 presidential primaries.

Former Massachusetts governor Mitt Romney came out of the 2011 invisible primary as the front-runner. A string of victories made him the most likely winner even before Super Tuesday gave him enough delegates to clinch the nomination. At this point in previous primaries, rival candidates would have dropped out, unable to raise enough money to keep their campaigns going.

But two of Romney's rivals, Newt Gingrich and Rick Santorum, did not drop out, even though strings of primary defeats had left their campaign committees drained of cash. They did not drop out because in 2012 they did not have to rely solely on their campaign committees to stay in the race. They kept running because a few conservative billionaires poured millions of dollars into the single-candidate super PACs that supported them. Those billionaires were not under the illusion that Gingrich or Santorum could win; they just wanted to make sure that their conservative voices remained a part of the campaign for a while longer.

Las Vegas casino mogul Sheldon Adelson and Texas corporate raider Harold Simmons accounted for more than 90 percent of the $24 million in the pro-Gingrich Winning Our Future PAC. Wyoming investor Foster Friess, Louisiana oil and gas mogul William J. Doré, Sr., and Harold Simmons's wife Annette contributed about 70 percent of the $7.5 million in the pro-Santorum Red, White, and Blue Fund.[4]

Money has always been one of the ways to gauge a candidate's strength. The invisible primary has often been called the money primary, but money was entwined with party, tending to go to those who had the most party endorsements. And candidates with the most endorsements and the most money also tended to have the highest poll ratings. A few billionaires disrupted that pattern in 2012. By using their wealth to buck the party rather than fund it, they forced Romney to raise and spend additional money to defend a victory he had already won. The RNC stated in its postmortem of the 2012 campaign that super PACs were "a wild card that weakens our eventual nominee."[5]

Today's billionaires are breaking the traditional division of labor between fat cats and politicos. They are using super PACs to turn private wealth into a political force in its own right. The bigger role big money is playing showed up in the way presidential hopefuls raised money for the 2015 invisible primary.

How did fundraising by presidential candidates in 2015 differ from that of previous elections?

The difference was greatest for the Republicans, who reversed the fundraising practices of 2011. Super PACs were still new in 2011, and candidates tended to use them as add-ons to traditional campaigns. Four years later it was the campaign committees that were treated as add-ons. Having a billionaire-backed super PAC was almost a requirement for being taken seriously as a candidate at the start of 2015.

Jeb Bush raised the most money. The $103 million the pro-Bush super PAC, Right to Rise USA, had raised by the June 30 reporting date was four times as much as all super PACs combined had raised by the same point in 2011. But he had raised only one-tenth as much, $11 million, in hard-money contributions for his campaign committee. Campaign committees were still a legal necessity for declared candidates, but Bush and other candidates saw fundraising for them as something that could be postponed. By June 30, Republican candidates had raised much less money for their campaign committees than their predecessors had by the same point in 2007, the last open-seat presidential election.[6]

In the years before *Citizens United* and *SpeechNow*, candidates used their campaign committees to pay for all campaign costs—polls, voter data, staff salaries, phone banks, websites, travel, ad buys, and so on. To raise the millions of FECA-regulated dollars needed to finance a presidential campaign, candidates had to get checks from thousands of donors. To do that they relied on people called "bundlers."

Bundlers tended to have fortunes that fell well short of *Forbes* 400 entry requirements, but their ability to raise the necessary funds from their extensive business, professional, and social connections made them indispensable. Then came *Citizens United*, *SpeechNow*, super PACs, and bigger spending by 501(c)(4) nonprofits. Now a rich donor can write one check for an amount that bundlers would have needed weeks to raise. Which is why the bundlers' phones were not ringing as the invisible primary began in 2015.[7]

By trading bundlers for billionaires, candidates narrowed their financial constituencies and brought about a new division of labor in campaign spending. Before *Citizens United*, candidates had to pay for the air war and the ground war—television and radio ads and get-out-the-vote drives—with the hard money they raised for their campaign committees. Since *Citizens United*, candidates have turned the air war, and even some parts of the ground war, over to super PACs. Republican candidates' campaign committees paid for 99 percent of ads in 2007, about one-third in 2011, and less than 20 percent in 2015. On the Democratic side, Clinton paid for nearly everything through her campaign committee.[8]

Jeb Bush was the establishment candidate who raised the most
money from billionaires, but his campaign never got off the ground.
So were the billionaires really all that important?

Billionaire support did not determine candidate strength in 2015, and that was a continuing surprise. Another surprise was that the Republican establishment was also unable to determine candidate strength; and when Bush dropped out, it could not manage to unite behind anyone else. So it is true that money did not determine candidate strength, but it is also true that we do not know for sure what did.

Bush was the very definition of the establishment candidate. As the son and brother of two presidents, and the former governor of a state that is important for money and votes, he was the presumed front-runner even before he got into the race. Confident of corralling the GOP's biggest donors, he planned to "shock and awe" his rivals by raising so much money so quickly that other Republicans would abandon their campaigns.[9]

And it looked at first like he might do it. He personally solicited contributions for his super PAC, most spectacularly at a jaw-dropping $100,000 per plate fundraising dinner on Park Avenue. And the money did come rolling in. The fundraisers brought in so many fat checks from so many rich backers that Bush's advisers worried about how it would look to voters. To avoid the impression that he was running a billionaires-only campaign, he asked donors to keep their contributions down to a modest $1 million.[10]

Bush was the only candidate who had the party and donor connections to pull that off. And he was probably the one who was most shocked by how little good it did. At midyear he had the broadest support from the party's traditional big donors and many times more endorsements from party leaders than his rivals. In past elections, party endorsements helped fundraising, growing campaign funds attracted endorsements, and success in both showed up in public opinion polls. But in the second half of 2015 Bush's poll numbers dropped, his fundraising stalled, party support began to wane, and massive media spending could not stem the reverses.[11]

Donald Trump and Ted Cruz were the only ones who did well in the Republican primaries. The billionaire real estate magnate had no support from other billionaires but shot up to the top of the polls almost at once. The right-wing Texas senator had a lot of billionaire money behind him, albeit from a narrow base of finance and fracking, but he did not need to spend much of that money to shoot up to second place in the polls.[12]

Money did not cause the rise of these far-right outsiders, but neither could money stop it. Thanks to the rise of super PACs, billionaires were more important in 2015 than in any other invisible primary. But most of them put their money behind candidates who lagged behind in the polls and later lagged behind in the primaries. The Republican party was very publicly at odds with itself, which goes a long way toward explaining why the big donors backed losers rather than winners.[13]

And once the candidates they backed had lost, the billionaires were left with only two unattractive choices of where to put their money. The Koch brothers' network ended up spending very little money in the primaries because its members could not agree on which candidates to back against Trump. Other billionaires decided to oppose Trump not by backing a rival candidate but putting their money into anti-Trump ads. Given the untraditional role big money has played in the primaries, it is anyone's guess what role it will play in the general election.[14]

Were billionaires any more important in the Democrats' race?

Billionaires might have been even less important for the Democrats. They, too, had an unusual invisible primary, but it played out mostly by the old rules, with the party's big donors backing the establishment front-runner.

Hillary Clinton entered the race as the front-runner, and she maintained that status through the end of 2015. She did not need a quick infusion of big money to cement her lead, so she postponed hitting up rich liberals and focused first on raising hard money for her campaign committee. Clinton went for bundlers first and billionaires second, and the difference from Republican candidates showed up in the numbers: the $77 million in her campaign committee by the June 30 reporting date was more than four times the $16 million she had in her super PAC. Almost three-fourths of her super PAC money came in million-dollar contributions from the Democratic Party's traditional big donors.[15]

Clinton's chief rival was Senator Bernie Sanders of Vermont, who appealed to the party's progressive base. He rejected the very idea of a super PAC, not that he would have gotten much billionaire backing anyway. The big surprise about Sanders was not that he rose quickly in the polls during the invisible primary—previous progressive challengers had done that—but that he remained a strong challenger by winning votes and delegates in the primaries. He did not win more delegates than Clinton, but by early 2016 he was raising more in hard money.[16]

The Democrats were also at odds with themselves during the primaries, if not quite as spectacularly as the Republicans were. Which explains why Clinton could not fend off Sanders despite backing from liberal billionaires, most noticeably a late $8 million contribution from financier George Soros. There was never much chance that Sanders would get more than a handful of party endorsements, and he did not. But the lack of establishment and billionaire support was the point of Sanders's campaign.[17]

Citizens United and *SpeechNow* did bring out the billionaires, though. And even if their money did not have much effect on the 2015 invisible primaries, many of them used what the Supreme Court had given them to set themselves up as political entrepreneurs. The Republicans were the most active, and the Koch brothers' network is the biggest of the big-donor groups. The Democrats eventually followed suit by forming their own big-donor group, called the Democracy Alliance.

What is the Koch brothers' network?

It is a coalition of tax-exempt groups put together by Charles and David Koch. They are the owners of the giant conglomerate Koch Industries, and are tied for sixth place on *Forbes*'s list of the richest people in the world. The groups in the network are funded by about 400 mostly unidentified donors who attend the Kochs' twice-yearly political conferences. The Kochs raised and spent $400 million through their network in the 2012 election, and they plan to spend about $750 million in 2016.[18]

The Koch brothers are not newcomers to conservative politics: their father Fred, who founded Koch Industries, was one of the original members of the John Birch Society, and David ran as the Libertarian Party candidate for vice president in 1980. The Kochs also founded and still finance many of the organizations in the conservative political infrastructure. In the 1970s they founded two of the biggest conservative think tanks—the libertarian Cato Institute and the Mercatus Center at George Mason University—and they are major funders of the Federalist Society, the Heritage Foundation, and the American Legislative Exchange Council.[19]

The brothers began holding their twice-yearly conferences in 2003, reportedly after becoming dissatisfied with the George W. Bush administration. The conference agendas are kept secret, as are the identities of the wealthy donors who attend them, and reporters are not welcome. The meetings also serve as fundraisers for conservative groups the donors fund, and the Kochs invite selected Republican politicians to make their pitch for campaign contributions.[20]

Barack Obama's 2008 election spurred the Kochs to get more directly involved in elections. One of the 501(c)(4) groups in their network, Americans for Prosperity (AFP), became a key provider of seed money for Tea Party groups in 2009, and helped organize their demonstrations at House Democrats' town hall meetings in the summer of 2010. AFP has since become part of the "set of organizations" that make up the Tea Party.[21]

When Obama ran for reelection in 2012, AFP took full advantage of *Citizens United*. It was already "the most muscular arm" in the Kochs' network, but the Supreme Court's decision gave it even more muscle, allowing it and other tax-exempt corporations in the network to spend $400 million on express advocacy.[22]

The $400 million figure is a conservative estimate, because the network's spending must be calculated by adding up the amounts spent by each member organization, and many of those organizations gave money to each other. Most of those organizations are registered with the IRS as social welfare groups, and swapping funds back and forth is a way to preserve their tax-exempt status by claiming they are spending money on the social welfare activities that are their official purpose. The network's complicated structure was designed to hide its finances from public view, so we do not know for sure how much it spends, where the money comes from, or where it goes.[23]

What did the Koch network do in the 2012 and 2014 elections?

It got deeply involved in the ground war, registering voters and getting them to the polls on Election Day. Americans for Prosperity paid for a small army of people to knock on voters' doors, and armed them with detailed information about those voters from a massive database built by i360 LLC, another part of the network.[24]

Recruiting and mobilizing voters is a party's core function. It has traditionally been a labor-intensive operation, the job of ward and precinct party operatives who knew the voters and jotted down "data points" about them on 3x5 cards. Knocking on doors is still a labor-intensive function, but now there is also plenty of capital behind it. In the era of "big data," even the newest volunteer door-knocker has detailed information on voters and nonvoters, drawn from consumer data; vehicle registrations; newspaper, magazine, and cable TV subscriptions; even hunting and fishing licenses.[25]

Thanks to i360, the Kochs proved to be better at the ground war than the GOP. The party knew it needed expertise in data analytics, and the RNC entered into a data-sharing arrangement with the Koch network for the 2014 midterms. The Kochs and the RNC had access to each other's data, and any new data provided by GOP or network activists would be available to both. Measured by the number of Republicans elected to Congress that year, the data-sharing arrangement was a big success.[26]

But that arrangement expired after the 2014 midterms, and the Kochs still had the GOP's voter file. By the summer of 2015 a fight over ownership of the file broke out into open warfare. The real problem for the GOP is that there seemed to be general agreement, even within the RNC, that the Kochs' interface with the voter file was better than anything the RNC had.[27]

Voter data is a party's lifeblood. But accumulating, maintaining, increasing, and analyzing the information in those massive databases is expensive. Big data costs big money, and the GOP was slow to invest in a dashboard that gave its candidates easy access to that data. Which meant that many Republican candidates had reason to think it made sense to get what they needed from the Kochs.

The RNC said the party's voter data should be controlled by those who are accountable to voters, not by a private group. Koch aides said that giving candidates easier access to that data made the network better able to achieve the common goal of electing conservatives. The conflict became so heated that the RNC accused the Kochs of wanting to control not just the data but the party itself.[28]

How are other conservative billionaires becoming active in elections?

Mostly by using their money to promote their own policy agendas. Several of the party's biggest donors have done this by forming their own super PACs and political groups.

One reason for this move is lingering anger at Karl Rove's assurances that Mitt Romney would win in 2012. Some of the donors who gave generously to Rove's American Crossroads super PAC decided they could do better by making their own political decisions. Others struck out on their own simply because *Citizens United* gave them the opportunity to push their preferred issues and candidates directly. Some took advantage of this opportunity even before the disappointments of 2012.[29]

TD Ameritrade founder J. Joe Ricketts and his wife Marlene founded their Ending Spending Action Fund super PAC in 2010. As the name suggests, they use their PAC to support candidates who want to reduce the size of government. Ricketts and other family members provided the huge majority of the PAC's funds for the first two election cycles. But this PAC, too, appears to have benefited from the 2012 disappointments, as most of the larger fund it has raised since 2014 has come from donors outside the family circle. In 2016 the Ricketts family started the Our Principles super PAC solely to run ads against Trump; the $12.5 million it spent in just the first two months was almost as much the ESA Fund had spent in all of 2012.[30]

The biggest of the donors to both Ricketts family PACs was hedge fund billionaire Paul Singer. Singer, who has a gay son, formed American Unity PAC in 2012 to back Republicans who supported gay rights. He is one of the Koch network donors, but late in 2013, he formed his own big-donor group, called the American Opportunity Alliance. Singer, too, holds twice-yearly seminars for the forty members who pay annual dues of $50,000. Toward the end of 2015 Singer rallied his Alliance donors in a failed attempt to build up Florida senator Marco Rubio as the GOP establishment's counter to Trump.[31]

Another hedge fund billionaire, Robert Mercer, has been a big donor to the Koch brothers' network and to the Ricketts and Singer super PACs. In 2015 he topped all his previous contributions by putting $11 million behind Ted Cruz's quest for the GOP nomination. But he also became a political operator in his own right by buying into Cambridge Analytical, a data analytics firm that specializes in psychological profiles of likely voters. Cambridge Analytica provided voter data to Cruz's campaign, and to other Republican candidates and organizations.[32]

Something the Kochs, the Ricketts family, Singer, Mercer, and others have in common is that they were big Republican donors before 2010, and they continue to give to party committees. David Koch, Paul Singer, and Robert Mercer, for example, gave $1.8 million to the GOP in 2015. This is far less money than they gave to their own and other personal political organizations, but it shows that they still value their ties to the formal party organization.[33]

That is not as true of corporate raider Carl Icahn. He has made few contributions to the party over the years, and he has not been a fundraiser or otherwise been very active politically. Then, in October 2015, he announced that he, too, would become a political entrepreneur, committing $150 million for a single-issue super PAC to advocate for lower corporate taxes. It remains to be seen whether this wide-open era of campaign finance will draw in even less politically active members of the *Forbes* 400.[34]

Are liberal billionaires doing anything similar to what the Koch brothers are doing?

Yes. Democrats are not as well supplied with liberal billionaires as Republicans are with conservative ones, but they are making an effort to catch up with what the Kochs and other conservative billionaires have been doing for decades.[35]

The Democrats' version of the Koch brothers' network is the Democracy Alliance. It, too, holds twice-yearly get-togethers in posh resorts, keeps its membership secret, and bars reporters from its meetings. And its members also contribute to an approved list of political organizations. Another similarity between the two groups is the way their founders have reacted to election losses.[36]

The conservative political infrastructure the Kochs helped build had been in place for a generation or more by the turn of the new century, but it was the Republicans' defeat in 2008 that spurred the brothers to get directly involved in elections. And it was the Democrats' narrow defeats of 2000 and 2004 that persuaded rich liberals to form the Democracy Alliance.

The 2004 election was especially frustrating, as many of those same rich donors had poured millions of dollars into pro-Democratic groups to do voter registration and get-out-the-vote drives. The Democracy Alliance was created in 2005 to direct their money away from elections and toward investing in a progressive political infrastructure to counter what conservative money had been building since the 1970s.

Unlike the Kochs' network, the Democracy Alliance was not created by, and is not run by, one or two big donors. Currency trader George Soros and insurance magnate Peter Lewis provided seed money for the new group, but it was not their idea. The idea came from Democratic Party activist Rob Stein, who explained it in presentations to groups of unhappy Democrats. Stein urged rich liberals to stop putting their money into meeting the short-term needs of election cycles and start making long-term investments in reinvigorating the political left.

Alliance partners, as members are called, pay annual dues of $30,000 to underwrite the twice-yearly conferences, and they commit to contributing at least $1 million over five years to approved progressive groups. A group that wants to get on the Alliance's approved list must submit an application that includes financial information and a business plan. Among the approved groups are the think tank Center for American Progress, media watchdog Media Matters for America, progressive legal association American Constitution Society, and data analytics firm Catalist LLC. The massive voter database built by Catalist was a big factor in the success of the Obama campaign's ground war in 2008 and 2012.

One big difference from the Kochs' network is that many members of the DA, as the Democracy Alliance is called by insiders, are labor unions, such as the Communications Workers of America and the Service Employees International Union. Called institutional investors, they too commit to making at least $1 million in contributions but pay more in annual dues. In 2014, the DA's board of directors elected a union executive, the National Education Association's Tom Stocks, as chair.

As the Kochs formed their network to the right of the RNC, the DA was seen as being to the left of the DNC. The Alliance withheld approval for centrist groups like the Democratic Leadership Council, for example. Factional divisions within the Alliance led to a falling-out in the lead-up to the 2008 presidential primaries, when many of Hillary Clinton's supporters—some of them among the Alliance's founders—left the group in protest, charging other members with putting a thumb on the scale for Obama. The DA was still lukewarm toward Clinton eight years later, finding her to be too hawkish on foreign policy, not progressive enough on domestic issues, and too close to Wall Street.[37]

The Alliance's liberal tilt worried many in the DNC, as the Koch network's libertarian tilt worried the RNC. The Democrats did not go as far as Republicans by accusing the DA of trying to take over the party. But both parties do seem to be uneasy about the rapidly growing importance of non-party groups and of the increasing amount of money spent outside of the formal party organizations.

Are individual liberal billionaires building personal political operations, as rich conservatives are doing?

Not nearly to the same extent. The best-known liberal organization is NextGen Climate Action, the super PAC formed by hedge fund billionaire Tom Steyer. He formed his PAC in 2014 to help elect candidates who backed policies to combat climate change, and he provided more than 85 percent of the $78 million the PAC took in that year. It was a Republican year, though, and all but two of his candidates were among the Democrats who lost. The money he poured into his super PAC made him the biggest donor of the 2014 election cycle and second only to Sheldon and Miriam Adelson as the biggest donors to either party since 2010. He and his super PAC are gearing up for another attempt to elect green Democrats in 2016, and he is also joining the Latino Victory Fund's effort to elect more Hispanics to higher office.[38]

The only other personal super PAC that largely supports Democrats is Michael Bloomberg's Independence USA. Bloomberg himself has not been a Democrat since 2001. He switched to the Republican Party to run for mayor of New York City, and in the middle of his second term he switched again, this time to become an independent. In 2012, toward the end of his third term, he formed Independence USA to back candidates who supported stronger gun control. He has always been the PAC's sole donor.[39]

8

OUTSIDE MONEY

By 2015, "outside money" had come to mean spending by super PACs and politically active tax-exempt groups. Super PACs are registered political committees under the FECA and must disclose their donors; their spending is labeled "outside" only because it is done outside the formal structure of candidate and party committees. Politically active tax-exempt groups are not registered political committees that disclose their donors; they are registered with the IRS as nonpolitical groups and do not have to disclose their donors. Their spending is labeled "outside" because it is done not only outside the formal party structure but also largely outside the FECA; because it is not disclosed, their spending is called "dark money."

Raising and spending money for federal elections, but largely outside federal election law, is a practice that is almost as old as the FECA. The parties themselves began the practice in the 1980 election by inventing what came to be called "soft money," which was raised mostly under state laws. It was only after Congress severely curbed party soft money by passing the McCain-Feingold Act in 2002 that outside money began to flow through tax-exempt groups that were regulated only by the IRS. And it was after *Citizens United* that the money flowing through tax-exempt groups and super PACs turned into a flood.

What was soft money?

Soft money began in the 1980 election cycle as a way to get private money into the presidential public funding program. Ronald Reagan accepted public funds for his campaign, which means he also agreed not to raise private funds. He and the Republican Party were ideologically opposed to the program, though, and soon found a way to circumvent it. More accurately, they realized the FEC and Congress had recently provided the means for circumventing it.

That Congress would make adjustments to the FECA after the 1976 election was a given. The 1974 FECA was the most comprehensive campaign finance law ever enacted, and no one could know exactly how it worked in practice until after the first election. And no one could know for sure how the new federal law would mesh with fifty different state laws, few of which regulated the size and sources of contributions as strictly as the FECA.

Both parties in Congress agreed that the FECA had unintentionally restricted party-building activities in the 1976 election by treating grass-roots activities such as registering voters, getting voters to the polls, and distributing bumper stickers, yard signs, and sample ballots as in-kind contributions to federal candidates. Treating them as contributions, which the FECA restricted, put a damper on what had always been a standard part of election campaigns. The 1979 FECA amendments allowed parties to raise and spend unlimited sums of money for such party-building activities—as long as it was hard, FECA-regulated money.[1]

The FEC, however, had already created an opening for non-FECA money in federal elections. Elections for federal office in most states coincide with elections to state and local offices, and most state laws were more permissive than the FECA. The laws covering contributions were clear: state law regulated gifts to state candidates and the FECA regulated gifts to federal candidates. What was not clear was how much of which kind of money they could use to pay for the generic grass-roots activities that affected both state and federal candidates.

The FEC said they could use both state-regulated and FECA-regulated money. In response to a 1978 request from the Kansas Republican Party, the FEC ruled that parties could use state-regulated money in proportion to the number of state and federal races in an election. As there were almost always more state and local than federal candidates, this ruling meant that state-regulated money could be used to finance most generic grass-roots activities. The FEC went further in 1979, ruling that the national parties could raise state-regulated money as long as they used it to assist state parties.

Congress acted to remove barriers to grass-roots participation in the 1980 elections while keeping the FECA in place. By themselves

the 1979 amendments would have attained that goal. But the new
FEC rules weakened FECA rules, which made 1980 the first federal
election that was financed in part by nonfederal, or soft, money.
How big a part is not clear, as the FEC did not require the parties to
disclose the sources of their soft money until 1992.

Many state laws permitted corporations and unions to make contributions, so money from these sources, banned under the FECA,
nonetheless found their way into federal elections. Again, there is
no way to know how much of such money the parties raised before
1992. From 1992 through 2000, FEC figures show that the majority
of soft money came from corporations and their executives; only a
small minority came from labor unions.[2]

Did both parties raise soft money?

Yes, they did. The Republicans were the first to see the possibilities
in the FEC rulings, but the Democrats soon caught up to them.

To get private funds for Ronald Reagan's publicly funded campaign, the Republican Party set up a soft-money operation to raise,
distribute, and spend state-regulated money. They could raise and
spend money from corporations in states that permitted corporate
funds in elections; but they could also raise corporate money in
states that did not permit it if it was spent in states that did. Rich
donors who lived in states with no contribution limits could start
writing checks to state parties after giving the maximum allowed
under the FECA.[3]

This sort of thing has to be well organized, and the GOP set up a
national "nonfederal" account in Washington, D.C., to manage it. It
was in effect a parallel campaign finance system that was regulated
neither by the FECA nor by the laws of any particular state. The
FECA was a national system authorized by federal legislation, but
the soft-money system had no authorizing law. It was a nationally
centralized legal arrangement for taking advantage of the differences among state laws.

The Democrats eventually caught on to what the Republicans
were doing, but it was late in the game by then and their feeble
attempts to catch up in 1980 did not amount to much. They were
a bit better organized in 1984, although still no match for the GOP.

But they launched a much more aggressive fundraising campaign in 1988, which raised three times more soft money than in 1984, and matched the Republicans' soft-money operation dollar for dollar.

It was also in 1988 that both parties decided to voluntarily disclose at least some of their soft-money donors. The public learned that 267 people had made $100,000 contributions to the GOP, and that 130 donors had given the same amount to the Democrats. That was more $100,000 donors than in the 1972 election, and some of them were corporations. The "fat cats" of pre-Watergate days were back in force.[4]

Reformers had seen soft money as a problem since 1980. The FEC did not share their concern, though, and did not meet their persistent requests to require the parties to disclose their soft-money accounts until 1992. It is only for the years 1992 to 2000 that we know how soft money was being raised and spent.

Soft money was supposed to pay for state-level party-building activities such as voter registration and turnout drives, administrative costs, and building funds. And when the parties began filing soft-money disclosure reports in 1992, it turned out that they did spend the great majority of that money on activities that could fall into a stretched definition of party building. The parties spent far more money than was necessary to achieve the goal Congress had set out in the 1979 FECA amendments. But for twelve years and four presidential elections, there was surface plausibility to the parties' claim that they were doing no more than paying for generic campaign activities.[5]

The nature of soft money changed after 1992, though. That is when the parties began to raise much more money and spend it for purposes that had nothing to do with party building.

How did the nature of soft money change after 1992?

The change began in the 1995–96 election cycle, when the parties began taking advantage of *Buckley*'s issue-advocacy loophole. Recall what the Supreme Court said about issue and express advocacy. "Express advocacy" meant political ads that expressly urged the election or defeat of clearly identified federal candidates. Issue ads, on the other hand, even those that portrayed clearly identified candidates in a positive or negative light, were not political under the court's definition and could not be regulated by the FECA. Money for issue ads could be raised in unlimited amounts from corporations, labor unions, and individuals, and it did not have to be reported to the FEC.

The court knew that no one "would have much difficulty devising expenditures that skirted the restriction on express advocacy ... but nevertheless benefited the candidate's campaign"; they knew, that is, that one did not have to be unusually clever to devise ads that were effectively express advocacy yet escaped regulation as issue advocacy. The Democrats took advantage of this loophole to initiate the second phase of soft money.[6]

That second phase began in 1995, when the Democrats raised soft money to pay for issue ads to support President Clinton's reelection campaign. This went well beyond party building. What was being stretched now was the definition of "nonpolitical." Issue ads were supposed to be nonpolitical simply by virtue of not expressly advocating the election or defeat of a candidate. But saying that such ads were still not political even when they were financed by a political party required a very elastic reading of *Buckley*. Which turned out not to be a problem for either party. Although FEC auditors thought the ads should be regulated as hard money, the commissioners did not challenge their legality. Both parties tacitly agreed that even issue ads directly financed by a political party were nonpolitical.[7]

The parties aired a torrent of sham issue ads in 1996, and they raised nearly four times as much soft money as in 1992 to pay for them. In 2000, they ran even more ads and raised twice as much money as in 1996. Political scientists who studied those two elections concluded that the FECA regulatory structure had effectively collapsed.[8]

That the FECA should show signs of collapse only twenty years after it went into effect caused alarm inside and outside Congress. After the 1996 election, the Citizens' Research Foundation, the Brookings Institution, and the Committee for Economic Development, all mainstream organizations, convened groups of campaign-finance experts to study the problem of soft money; all called on Congress to ban it.[9]

Congress also had its say about 1996 fundraising. Senators John McCain and Russ Feingold changed the focus of their reform bill from PACs and independent spending to soft money, but this latest version, too, fell before a Republican filibuster. A congressional investigation of President Clinton's reelection campaign was almost inevitable, given press attention to such questionable practices as White House coffees, Lincoln bedroom sleepovers for big donors, and rumors of foreign money. The Senate committee chaired by Senator Fred Thompson (R-TN) got the most media attention, as Thompson was a cosponsor of the McCain-Feingold bill.[10]

The Senate investigation began and ended in partisan rancor, but both parties agreed, in the words of the Thompson Committee's final report, that soft money had "eviscerated" the FECA, which was "in serious need of an overhaul."[11] Which is what happened when Congress eventually passed the McCain-Feingold bill in 2002.

What was the McCain-Feingold Act?

Formally called the Bipartisan Campaign Reform Act (BCRA), it prohibited the national parties and federal candidates and office-holders from raising and spending soft money—money that did not comply with FECA contribution limits and prohibitions. The law also expanded the FECA to cover elections that include candidates for both state and federal office. In those elections, the kind of grass-roots and party-building activities that were once partly financed with state-regulated money now must be financed only with hard, FECA-regulated money.

To cover some sham issue ads, BCRA created a new category of federally regulated expenditures called "electioneering communications." These communications are defined as television or radio ads that mention a clearly identified federal candidate and are aired within thirty days of a primary and sixty days of a general election. BCRA required that these ads be financed with hard money even if they did not use any of the "magic words." The Supreme Court upheld the law by a 5–4 vote in *McConnell v. FEC* (2003).[12]

The parties and non-party groups now had to find new ways to get outside money into federal elections. The first way was through a new, and less regulated, variant of a familiar and fully regulated political committee: the 527.

What is a 527?

Congress added section 527 to the Internal Revenue Code in 1975, to clarify the tax status of political committees. Their tax status was unclear because there had never been anything in the tax code to tell the Internal Revenue Service (IRS) how to treat them. In practice, the IRS already treated political committees as tax-exempt organizations by not requiring them to pay income taxes on the contributions they received. The people who made those contributions had to pay taxes, though, because the IRS treated political contributions as gifts, which were covered in the tax code.[13]

Section 527 applied only to political committees and ensured that contributions to them would not count as taxable income if they were solicited for the "exempt function" of electioneering, defined as influencing the election of candidates to public office. The section also provided that contributions to 527 political committees would no longer be treated as taxable gifts (but neither would they be treated as tax-deductible gifts).[14]

Candidate committees, party committees, and PACs registered with the IRS as 527s and with the FEC as political committees. Section 527 was passed just months after the 1974 FECA amendments, and in those pre-*Buckley* days Congress assumed that 527s would always be subject to those amendments, raising and spending hard money and filing disclosure reports with the FEC.

Congress was overly optimistic. Less than a year after section 527 was added to the tax code, the Supreme Court's *Buckley* decision significantly restricted the scope of FECA regulations. The 1974 FECA counted issue advocacy as an activity under the exempt function of electioneering, meaning that organizations doing issue ads had to register with the FEC as 527 political committees and file disclosure reports. Then the *Buckley* court said issue advocacy was not political, that only express advocacy counted as political spending.[15]

But if issue advocacy could not be regulated by the FECA because it was not political, did it still count as an exempt function of electioneering under the tax code? That question remained unanswered for another twenty years.

The answer came in the late 1990s, after the Sierra Club and other tax-exempt groups went to the IRS with another definition of issue advocacy. They argued that, whatever the Supreme Court had said in *Buckley*, their issue ads were electioneering because they were intended to influence the outcome of elections. The IRS agreed and retained issue advocacy as an exempt function under the tax code.[16]

The IRS ruling opened a regulatory gap between the FECA and the tax code. New 527s formed to make issue-advocacy expenditures enjoy the same tax-exempt status as older ones. But these new "stealth PACs" were not counted as political committees under the FECA, so they did not have to register or file disclosure reports with the FEC and could raise money outside FECA restrictions on the size and sources of contributions.

In 2000, Congress made it harder for 527s to evade disclosure by requiring them to report their donors to the IRS. That fell far short of the FECA requirement, though, as the IRS had no way to make those reports public. Congress took a bigger step in 2002 by passing BCRA, which expanded the FECA's regulation of campaign spending. BCRA's new "electioneering communications" category included the express advocacy the FECA had always covered, and added sham issue ads that aired within thirty days of a primary election and within sixty days of a general election. All groups making electioneering communications, even those that were not registered as political committees, had to finance their ads with hard money and had to file disclosure reports with the FEC.[17]

The tightened regulations aside, 527s were still the best way to take the place of party soft money in 2004. Sham issue ads did have to be financed with reportable hard money when aired within BCRA's thirty- and sixty-day reporting windows, but nonreportable soft money could still pay for them outside those windows. And some 527s made very large expenditures just before the reporting windows in the 2004 presidential primaries.[18]

Did 527s just replace party soft money?

Not entirely. Section 527 groups were the best alternative to party soft money after BCRA, and the $440 million they spent in 2004 was almost 90 percent of the $500 million in soft money spent in 2000. But while 527s raised impressive sums of money, it was not the same kind of money as the parties could raise before BCRA.[19]

Section 527 groups were formed by non-party groups, not by parties. To be sure, many of the bigger groups were formed and managed by former party and government officers, who worked with interest groups that were very close to the parties. But giving to 527s was not the same thing as giving directly to parties, so those who did give had different motives from party soft-money donors. "It's not access money," Grover Norquist said of 527s, "it's movement money. They are not writing checks to sit down with congressmen."[20]

Another difference from party soft money is that 527s were not more or less equally divided between the two parties—the great majority of 527s were pro-Democratic groups. Only fifteen of the fifty biggest 527s were Republican, and the two biggest Democratic groups, America Coming Together and the Media Fund, spent more than all fifteen of the Republican groups combined. Soft money had become more important to the Democrats over the past two decades, and 527s were a way to keep the new kind of outside money flowing.[21]

The mix of funding sources changed, too. Corporations and trade associations contributed much less to the new 527s in 2004 than they had to party soft-money committees in 2000, while labor gave almost three times as much. Individual contributions also tended to be much larger, especially from Democratic donors: investor George Soros, Progressive Corporation CEO Peter Lewis, and Shangri-La Entertainment CEO Stephen Bing together gave more than $60 million; Soros and Lewis each gave more than the four biggest Republican donors combined.[22]

Reformers said the new 527s were so active in federal elections that they should have registered with the FEC as political committees and been subject to FECA limitations on fundraising. The FEC eventually agreed, at least in retrospect and regarding only a few groups. In 2006 and 2007, long after it would have had any deterrent effect, the agency levied heavy fines on the biggest 527s, including the Democratic groups Americans Coming Together and MoveOn.org Voter Fund, and the Republican groups Club for Growth and Swiftboat Veterans for Truth.[23]

Spending by 527s continued at a lower level in the 2006 midterms but dropped sharply in the 2008 presidential election. The biggest Democratic 527s in 2004 were mere shadows of themselves in 2008, if they still existed at all. The FEC's ruling that the most active 527s were PACs under the FECA was partly responsible for the drop, as it had led some 527s to disband. The presidential candidates also played a role: Barack Obama discouraged 527s and John McCain had led the opposition to them since 2000. For all the publicity they got at the time, 527s were just a blip compared to the twenty-two-year run of party soft money.[24]

But the decline of 527s did not mean a decline in outside money, which flowed almost as freely in 2008 as in 2004. FEC penalties might have had some effect here, too, by causing some of the groups that had formed 527s to switch to other kinds of tax-exempt groups, such as 501(c)s, which were the conduits of choice for outside money in 2008.[25]

What are 501(c) tax-exempt groups?

Where 527s had electioneering as the function that exempted them from having to pay taxes on their income, 501(c)s are exempt because their principal purpose is, in some nonpolitical way, to improve conditions for their members. That applies to both 501(c)(5) labor unions and 501(c)(6) business associations, and it also applies to 501(c)(4) social welfare organizations, which can serve very vaguely defined constituencies. These groups are not excluded from all political activity, as they may lobby Congress to advocate for the kinds of legislation that will promote their principal purposes.[26]

These groups may also participate in elections as long as that participation is not their primary activity. To be sure, labor unions, corporations, and trade associations have long participated in elections indirectly through their PACs. So did some of the larger 501(c)(4)s, such as Planned Parenthood and the National Rifle Association; but they registered their PACs with the FEC, which treated them the same way as other connected PACs. Direct participation in elections was permissible only if it was a secondary activity. It is that supposedly nonprimary political activity that has drawn so much attention to 501(c)s.[27]

That political activity began to increase in 2004, when BCRA drove some soft money to the kind of "stealth" 527s that many of those groups had already formed. It continued in 2008, after the Supreme Court's decision in *FEC v. Wisconsin Right to Life* (2007) made them a more attractive channel for outside money by allowing them to get around BCRA.

What was Wisconsin Right to Life v. FEC*?*

The case began when Wisconsin Right to Life (WRTL), an incorporated 501(c)(4), sought an exemption from BCRA's electioneering communications provision.[28]

The Supreme Court that heard the case in 2007 was not the same one that had upheld BCRA in 2003. President George W. Bush had not been able to appoint any new justices in his first term, but in the first year of his second term he made two appointments—Chief Justice John G. Roberts and Associate Justice Samuel A. Alito— that made an abrupt change in the constitutionality of campaign finance law.

The court heard WRTL's appeal not long after the two new justices took their seats. The issue was about three campaign ads the group had aired in 2004. The ads mentioned Senator Russ Feingold (D-WI), who was a candidate in the Wisconsin Democratic Party primaries, and were aired during the thirty-day window before those primaries. They fell squarely under BCRA's definition of electioneering communications, which required that they be financed with hard money. But WRTL had paid for them out of its treasury funds, which included contributions from business corporations, and corporate funding for electioneering communications was illegal. The FEC took WRTL to court for violating the law.

WRTL sought an "as-applied" exemption from the electioneering communications provision. That is, it did not challenge the BCRA provision itself, but claimed only that its three ads should be exempted because they were not political, but were genuine issue ads, even if they did mention Feingold and were aired within the thirty-day pre-primary window. The Supreme Court granted the exemption in a 5–4 vote, holding that the ads were merely about issues and were not "the functional equivalent of express advocacy."[29]

The court gutted BCRA's electioneering communications provision without having to strike it down. It was still on the books, but it no longer applied to all ads that mention clearly identified federal candidates because the court had held that some such ads were subject to BCRA's funding restrictions and some were not. It was now up to the FEC to decide on a case-by-case basis which was which. A decision that formally did no more than grant an exception to three ads actually reopened a hole that BCRA had closed, allowing soft money to flow freely again, this time through 501(c)s.

Was there still a lot of outside money in the 2008 election?

Yes, almost as much as in 2004. The difference is that the money came through different channels in the two elections. There was about $400 million of outside money in the 2008 election, which was not a great deal less than the $490 million in 2004. The difference is that the 527s that spent almost 90 percent of the outside money in 2004 accounted for less than half of the money in 2008. The big spenders in 2008 were 501(c)s, which spent at least three times as much as in 2004 and 2006.[30]

And unlike the 527s in 2004, the great majority of the 2008 501(c) money was Republican. There were almost as many Democratic groups as Republican ones among the forty-three biggest 501(c)s, but Republican groups spent almost two and a half times what Democratic groups spent. In an almost exact reversal of 527 spending in 2004, the two biggest Republican groups, the U.S. Chamber of Commerce and the Sheldon Adelson–funded Freedom's Watch, spent more than all twenty-one Democratic groups combined.

Part of the reason for that ratio might have been the return of corporate money. We do not know that for sure, though, because the FEC weakened disclosure rules by allowing the 501(c)s to keep many of their donors secret.

How did the FEC weaken disclosure rules for tax-exempt groups?

When the FEC wrote new regulations to comply with *Wisconsin Right to Life v. FEC*, it narrowed the scope of its disclosure rules. Under the rules it had issued after BCRA, a group spending $10,000 or more on electioneering communications had to disclose all of its $1,000-plus donors. Under the 2007 rules they now had to disclose only those donors who gave "for the purpose of furthering electioneering communications."[31]

The FEC had a superficially plausible explanation for this ruling. Officially, tax-exempt groups are not primarily engaged in politics, so requiring them to disclose all their donors would violate
the privacy of people who gave to support the groups' nonpolitical purposes. Privacy is an important public interest, one the FEC
is obliged to protect; but neither BCRA nor *Wisconsin Right to Life*
required the disclosure of donations to nonpolitical groups. What
they did require was the disclosure of donations to pay for those
groups' electioneering communications. The FEC could have protected both privacy and disclosure, even for groups that really were
primarily nonpolitical, by requiring them to make separate solicitations for their political and nonpolitical expenditures. What it did
instead was use its obligation to protect privacy as a cover for not
protecting the public's interest in disclosure.[32]

The ruling set off a round of challenges to the new regulation in
the federal courts. In 2011, Representative Chris Van Hollen (D-MD)
filed suit to reverse the FEC regulation, claiming the agency had read
BCRA and *WRTL* too narrowly. As of this writing, the most recent
event in the back- and forth- between the federal district and circuit
courts in Washington, D.C., was the circuit court's January 2016 rejec-
tion of Van Hollen's challenge. By then, *Citizens United* had made
501(c)s, and particularly 501(c)(4)s, immensely more valuable as conduits for political money.[33]

What are 501(c)(4)s?

Section 501(c)(4) social welfare groups get their exemption for being
"primarily engaged in promoting in some way the common good
and general welfare of the people of the community."[34] This is a very
broad definition, and it covers a wide variety of organizations: the
American Civil Liberties Union and the American Association of
Retired People are both 501(c)(4)s, as is the National Rifle Association.
In addition to the few nationally known organizations there are tens
of thousands of smaller ones, such as Rotary Clubs, volunteer fire
departments, and neighborhood associations.

Like other 501(c)s, social welfare groups are supposed to devote
most of their time, money, and other resources to their primary
activities—the ones that got them a tax exemption. Thanks to the

IRS's vague definition of "social welfare," 501(c)(4)s are easier to form than other politically active 501(c)s: 501(c)(5) labor unions and 501(c)(6) business associations serve well-defined communities of beneficiaries, but a 501(c)(4) can claim to be providing some kind of social benefit to the entire country. Just how easy it was to form 501(c)(4)s became clear when *Citizens United* made them even bigger conduits for outside money than they had been in 2008.

How did Citizens United *change the role of 501(c)s in elections?*

Like Wisconsin Right to Life, Citizens United was a 501(c)(4) nonprofit corporation that sought an as-applied exemption for a campaign ad it had financed with funds from its treasury. The ad was a feature-length film, *Hillary: The Movie*, that attacked Senator Hillary Clinton (D-NY) when she was a candidate in the 2008 presidential primaries.

The Supreme Court got the case in 2009, but did not decide it then. In a highly unusual move, the conservative majority of justices asked Citizens United to submit supplemental briefs on whether the court should overturn previous decisions upholding long-standing restrictions on corporate money in elections. The conservative justices' request amounted to asking Citizens United to change its as-applied challenge to BCRA into a constitutional challenge to the court precedents they wanted to overturn. In January 2010, they did just that. In another 5–4 decision, they held that corporations and unions should never have been prohibited from making express advocacy expenditures.[35]

Most 501(c)(4)s are, like WRTL, nonprofit corporations, and the FECA treated them the same way as for-profit business corporations. They could use their treasury funds to pay for issue ads, as they did in 2004 and 2008. But they could not use those funds to make express advocacy expenditures, and could not contribute to PACs that did. *Citizens United* allowed them to do both.[36]

Social welfare groups could now engage in an even wider range of political activities, all the while retaining their tax-exempt status as nonpolitical groups that could keep their donors secret. Just how valuable these groups became can be measured by the sudden increase of interest in forming new ones. The number of applications for new 501(c)(4)s submitted to the IRS barely changed from 2009 to 2010, but they doubled in the two years after *Citizens United*. The result was more than $1 billion in independent spending in 2012, almost seven times as much as in 2008; 501(c)(4)s spent more than all 501(c)s combined had spent in 2008.[37]

The sources for most of this money were not fully disclosed, which was a big change from previous elections. More than 95 percent of outside spending was fully reported in 2004, and almost two-thirds was fully disclosed even in 2008. But only 40 percent of outside spending was fully disclosed in 2012, and 30 percent was not disclosed at all.[38]

Alarmed at the sharp increase of undisclosed money in independent expenditures, reform supporters coined the term "dark money" to dramatize the problem. Dramatizing the problem, however, does not solve it, and the use of dark money continued to evolve. The most recent development is the single-candidate dark-money group, which makes its own political expenditures.

The best example of single-candidate dark-money groups in 2015 was in the Republican presidential primary: the Conservative Solutions Project, a 501(c)(4) that was paired with the Conservative Solutions super PAC backing Senator Marco Rubio (R-FL). Other candidates in both parties were buying ads directly with their campaign committee funds or indirectly through the super PACs supporting them, which meant that the money was fully disclosed. Most of Rubio's ads, though—$8.5 million worth of them—were bought by his dark-money group.[39]

When *Citizens United* greatly expanded the kinds of political activity that could be regulated more loosely under the tax code than under the FECA, a rush of applications to form new 501(c)(4) social welfare groups was inevitable. That the IRS would scrutinize these new applications was a given. That this scrutiny would create a controversy that brought the agency itself under scrutiny was probably unavoidable.

What was the controversy over the IRS's scrutiny of applications to form social welfare groups?

The sudden interest in promoting social welfare after *Citizens United* raised suspicions that many of the new 501(c)(4)s would merely be fronts for taxpayer-subsidized politicking.

The IRS is responsible for ensuring that this sort of thing does not happen, but its vague definition of "social welfare" gives it almost no guidance for determining whether a 501(c)(4) deserves its tax exemption or is a political committee in disguise. To determine what kinds of groups were filing the new applications, the IRS sent detailed questionnaires to many of them. Conservatives cried foul, charging that the agency was targeting Tea Party groups, and House Republicans held hearings to grill IRS officials.[40]

The Treasury Inspector General for Tax Administration (TIGTA), an independent office that oversees the IRS, conducted its own investigation of the Republican complaints. It concluded that IRS staff had used inappropriate criteria for selecting groups to examine and had asked unnecessarily intrusive questions. The report concluded with the seemingly sensible recommendation that the IRS and Treasury provide "guidance on how to measure the 'primary activity' of . . . 501(c)(4) social welfare organizations."[41]

That recommendation did not even come close to the core of the problem, which is whether IRS staff should be regulating political activity at all. And it was the Treasury Department itself that allowed political activity to slip in under the tax code. In the statute that added the 501(c)(4) exemption to the tax code, Congress defined qualifying groups as those that are "operated *exclusively* for the promotion of social welfare." But the regulation the IRS wrote to administer that statute relaxed Congress's definition by opening the exemption to groups that are only *primarily* engaged in promoting social welfare.[42]

It seems clear that Congress wanted to keep political activity out of the tax code; it was the IRS that opened the way for 501(c)s to participate in elections. Had the agency stayed with the statutory definition, there probably would have been no dark money and it would not now be mired in controversy. The American Bar Association had seen the potential for a political problem nine years earlier, when soft money began migrating to 501(c)(4)s. It issued a report in 2004 that also called for a better way to define the "primary" activities of tax-exempt groups.

What did the American Bar Association recommend the IRS do about political activity by nonpolitical groups?

The American Bar Association (ABA) was concerned about the "vague and uncertain" standards for regulating 501(c)(4) political activity, and recommended that Treasury and the IRS adopt "bright line" definitions of primary and secondary activities. But not much had changed when the Congressional Research Service (CRS) issued its own report in 2009. The CRS found that the tax code and IRS regulations were still unable to "address how to determine whether a 501(c)(4)'s campaign activity . . . is its primary activity."[43]

If the bright-line standards the ABA called for still do not exist, it is not for lack of trying. Congress thought it had set such a standard when it added section 527 to the tax code in 1975. Congress believed nonpolitical 501(c)s would use the new section to form their own PACs if they wanted to participate in elections. The Senate Finance Committee was optimistic about this:

> a section 501(c) organization that is permitted to engage in political activities would establish a separate organization that would operate primarily as a political organization. . . . In this way, the campaign-type activities would be taken entirely out of the 501(c) organization to the benefit both of the organization and the administration of the tax laws.[44]

This must have seemed reasonable at the time, but in retrospect it looks like wishful thinking. Rather than taking their electioneering out of the tax code and under the FECA, the 501(c)s themselves became prominent political actors, using IRS regulations to shield their donors.

Using the tax code to regulate politics poses two problems: how to define campaign activity, and how to determine whether a tax-exempt group's campaign activity is its primary purpose. The ABA addressed these issues in its 2004 report.

The ABA suggested that the IRS's "facts and circumstances" test for defining campaign activity was unconstitutionally vague, and called for a clearer definition. To determine whether a group's participation in election campaigns was in fact less than primary, it recommended setting a percentage of a group's expenditures as a bright-line test. It suggested 40 percent as the less-than-primary standard, but acknowledged that the IRS had in practice accepted the groups' own standard of 49 percent. There is still no formal standard.[45]

In 2013, the Congressional Research Service issued another report, which said that IRS regulations still did not provide a clear definition of campaign activity. The agency did try to clarify its definition by issuing new draft regulations in 2014; but it quickly retracted them when they were met with a storm of criticism from liberal and conservative groups, which found them too restrictive.[46]

The problem with a clear definition may be that it would restrict the range of activity the vague definition makes possible. The IRS said it would try again, but Congress put a stop to that, at least for the 2016 fiscal year. The omnibus spending bill passed at the end of 2015 contained a rider that prohibits the agency from writing a clearer definition. President Obama did not protest the rider and signed the bill into law.[47]

Using the tax code to regulate campaign activity was what Congress hoped to avoid when it added section 527. That savvy politicians in 1975 thought it would be so easy to keep taxes and politics separate shows how different their political world was from ours. In the post–*Citizens United* world, the ability to make unlimited expenditures from undisclosed sources through supposedly nonpolitical organizations makes the political benefits of tax exemption too big a prize for either party to give up.

9

CORPORATIONS, UNIONS, AND *CITIZENS UNITED*

Citizens United undermined more than 100 years of campaign finance law when it gave corporations the First Amendment right to spend money in elections. Congress had said in 1907 that corporations did not have that right; that First Amendment rights were the rights of citizens, and corporations were not citizens.

Citizens United is one of the Supreme Court's most controversial decisions. Polls taken just weeks after the decision was handed down showed that large majorities of Republicans and Democrats opposed it. A poll taken five years later showed even greater opposition: 80 percent of Republicans and 83 percent of Democrats said the decision should be overturned. At a time when Americans are deeply divided along party lines on most major public policy issues, this bipartisan hostility is striking. Concern about corporate money in elections got the first reform movement going at the turn of the twentieth century, and it appears to be reviving that movement in the first decades of the twenty-first.[1]

What can corporations do in elections now that they could not do before Citizens United?

Citizens United made only one change in the law by permitting corporations to make independent expenditures to support or oppose candidates. All the other laws regulating corporate (and union) participation in elections, such as being able to make campaign contributions through their PACs, remain the same. As a practical matter, it is tax-exempt nonprofit corporations, not for-profit businesses, that have taken full advantage of *Citizens United*.

Defenders and opponents of the decision differ over its significance. Defenders focus on its practical effect and point to the comparative trickle of business corporation money that has found its way into elections to argue that the decision was not as important as its critics claim. Opponents say that the real significance of the decision lies not in its immediate practical effect but in the political theory behind it. By declaring corporations to be members of our democratic community, with much the same political rights as citizens, the court took it upon itself to redefine our democracy by fiat. Very few of us are political philosophers, but the overwhelming popular opposition to *Citizens United* suggests that most of us knew at once that the court had acted against widely and deeply held opinions about what it means to be a democracy and how our democracy should work.

Did Citizens United *overturn the Tillman Act's ban on political contributions?*

No, it did not. The 1907 ban on corporate contributions is still on the books, but *Citizens United* undermined its constitutionality. When Congress passed that law it made no distinction between contributions and expenditures, because at the time there was no such thing as independent expenditures. The only way to get money into elections was by contributing to parties or candidates, so Congress prohibited corporations from making contributions. And in 1947, when independent expenditures became another way to get money into elections, Congress added a ban on independent expenditures.

The *Buckley* court did not change that ban, and the challengers did not ask it to do so. But that court did strike down limits on independent expenditures by political committees, ruling that such expenditures could not corrupt candidates. The *Bellotti* court used that ruling to overturn state laws prohibiting corporations from making such expenditures in ballot-measure elections. And in *Citizens United* the court expanded *Bellotti* to strike down the federal ban on corporations making independent expenditures in candidate elections.

Having made that big constitutional leap, it would take only a relatively small step to strike down the Tillman Act. Corporations would presumably be subject to the same restrictions as flesh-and-blood citizens, who cannot give candidates more than $2,700 per election—a limit the Supreme Court has upheld as an anticorruption measure. If corporations have the First Amendment right to make independent expenditures because they cannot corrupt, then there does not seem to be much reason not to grant them the right to make contributions, which also cannot corrupt.

The Tillman Act is still good law. The question is for how long.

Did the Tillman Act work? Or did corporations keep making campaign contributions after it banned them?

Some corporations almost certainly did keep making contributions, but there is no way to know for sure. We should be clear about something: the Tillman Act was, is, and always will be unenforceable. You cannot enforce a law if you cannot tell when it has been violated, and the only evidence that a corporation has made an illegal contribution is in private company records. And there may not be any evidence even in those records.

Illegal corporate contributions are most easily concealed by routing treasury funds through the private bank accounts of corporate executives. When the executives write personal checks to candidates, the candidates report them as individual contributions. No one but the executives themselves know that the funds came from the company treasury. Corporate contributions usually come to light by accident, when revealed by a whistle-blower, or through secondhand accounts.

An early secondhand account was a 1912 *Washington Post* article that said corporations were violating the Tillman Act. A later one came in 1956, when a *Fortune* editor reported that many company presidents simply dipped into the till to give money to politicians. And of course there were the company presidents who told the Senate Watergate Committee that they had made illegal contributions.[2]

Much of the suspicion about the legality of corporate contributions before the mid-1970s came about because company executives made them through informally organized programs that did not file disclosure reports. The individual contributions were reported, but the existence of the corporate programs often was not. That suspicion largely vanished when corporations began making contributions through PACs.[3]

When did corporations and unions begin using their money to influence elections?

Corporations began putting money into elections in the nineteenth century, many decades before labor did, or could. The political influence of corporations first became the subject of campaign debate during the 1904 presidential election. After the 1905 scandal about insurance company contributions in that election, Congress passed the Tillman Act to keep corporate money out of elections.

The American Federation of Labor (AFL) under Samuel Gompers began participating in elections in the 1906 midterm elections. It did not make campaign contributions, but it did send political messages to members—what today would be called internal communications—to let them know which candidates it supported. Even that limited election activity ended with Gompers's death in 1924.[4]

Union participation in elections revived in 1936, when President Franklin D. Roosevelt ran for reelection. The AFL stayed out of the 1928 and 1932 presidential elections, and was planning to do the same in 1936. But many industrial unions broke away from the AFL to form the Congress of Industrial Organizations (CIO), which backed FDR's reelection. The differences between the two groups were more about labor strategy than politics, but the CIO jumped into the election with both feet. The CIO and more than fifty independent, railroad, and AFL unions made direct contributions to candidates, parties, and other political groups, spending twice what labor had spent in all previous elections.

Labor participation is a familiar part of elections today, but the amount of money and on-the-ground activity the CIO put into the 1936 elections marked a dramatic change in American politics. Political scientist Alexander Heard said that it "provoked a fierce howl that clearly marked 1936 as a watershed year in the political alignment of social and economic interests."[5]

The 1936 election was an ideological battle, with big business and Republicans trying to defeat the New Deal, and labor and Democrats trying to keep it going. The Democrats' victory temporarily settled the ideological dispute, which did not break out again in 1940. Labor supported Roosevelt again, although with less than one-fourth of what it had spent in 1936. Unions were also active in the 1940 and 1942 congressional races, and labor participation in federal elections was on its way to becoming a permanent feature of political life. Conservatives were not happy about that and began a long campaign to curb labor political activity.

How did conservatives try to limit labor participation in elections?

United Mine Workers president John L. Lewis gave them their first opportunity when he led a strike in 1943. A labor strike during the war was hugely unpopular, which is why the CIO and the AFL had made a wartime no-strike pledge after Pearl Harbor. The coal strike broke that pledge and the CIO and AFL denounced the UMW for its action. Republicans and Southern Democrats in Congress—an alliance known as the conservative coalition—responded with the Smith-Connally Act, which regulated labor–management relations but also included a wartime prohibition against union political contributions. Congress passed the act over President Roosevelt's veto.[6]

The CIO got around Smith-Connally by inventing the political action committee (PAC). In 1947 the conservative coalition made the wartime contribution ban permanent. The Taft-Hartley Act, passed over President Harry Truman's veto, brought unions under the Tillman Act and added a ban against independent expenditures by corporations and unions. The CIO had already invented the PAC to get around Smith-Connally's temporary ban, and that invention became permanent with Taft-Hartley's permanent ban. Organized labor has participated in elections through union PACs ever since.

But union PACs, too, eventually came under attack. At first, they were only secondary targets of attacks on the union shop. There were many private suits against unions in the 1950s and 1960s, some of which reached the Supreme Court. The plaintiffs in the first one, *International Association of Machinists v. Street* (1961), did not get the injunction against the union shop they wanted, but they did begin a change in union practices by getting a partial refund of membership dues.

Under union shop contracts, unions negotiate wages, benefits, working conditions, and so on for all employees, even those who are not union members. To prevent nonmembers from being free riders, who share the benefits of membership but not the costs, all employees covered by a contract are required to pay dues. The court did not give the *Machinists* plaintiffs the complete refund they sought, but it did order the union to refund that portion of dues that financed political activities the dissenters opposed. The court handed down similar decisions in later cases, and dissenter rebates became a well-established practice.[7]

But the practice worked because PACs themselves were well established. No one had ever challenged the legality of the PAC form, but that changed when just such a challenge reached the Supreme Court in *Pipefitters v. United States* (1971).

Why did the Department of Justice challenge the legality of labor PACs in Pipefitters v. United States?

The case began in St. Louis, where federal prosecutors had for years been trying to make charges stick to the mobbed-up head of a pipe-fitters union local. The union president had served time for extortion, but his mob ties got him excellent legal representation, and he was also close to the city's Democratic machine. Understandably frustrated with seeing him repeatedly slip through their fingers, the prosecutors turned their fire on the local's PAC.[8]

No one had challenged the legality of the PAC the CIO formed in 1943. Nor had anyone challenged the legality of the PACs that individual unions later formed on the CIO-PAC model. Republicans often claimed that those PACs were no more than a ruse for making illegal union contributions, but they did not put their claims to the test by bringing formal charges. It was the Democratic prosecutors in St. Louis who did that, by charging that the pipefitters' PAC was merely a subterfuge for making contributions that were prohibited by the Taft-Hartley Act.

The charge of illegality alarmed all unions, because their PACs were organized the same way as the indicted one in St. Louis. They were even more alarmed when the St. Louis local lost in the district court, lost again in the Eighth Circuit Court, and saw the Nixon administration bring a similar suit against the Seafarers International Union. The Chamber of Commerce and the National Association of Manufacturers had already announced that they would work with the administration to restrict labor PACs, and the AFL-CIO saw the Seafarers indictment as evidence of a plan "to silence the trade union movement."[9]

To protect its PACs, labor had to fight in Congress as well as in the courts. The Department of Justice indictments and court rulings came down while the 1971 FECA was under debate in Congress, and conservative Republicans in the House tried to add amendments that would have made PACs illegal. The AFL-CIO was part of the bipartisan coalition behind the FECA, but it could not have backed a law with such provisions. The labor group worked with moderate Republicans to introduce an amendment that formally legalized PACs. Two-thirds of Republicans and most Southern Democrats voted against the amendment, but it passed and became part of the FECA of 1971.

The Supreme Court did not decide the *Pipefitters* case until after the FECA became law, and ruled 6–2 in favor of the union. The court acknowledged that Congress might have legalized something that had been illegal, but concluded that the Taft-Hartley Act did not clearly either permit or prohibit the PAC form. The justices ruled that a PAC was legal as long as the fund from which it made campaign contributions consisted only of voluntary donations made for political purposes and was kept separate from the union treasury. By upholding the legality of the PAC form, the court also blunted some of the attempts to further restrict the role of labor political money.

Seven years later the court expanded the role of corporate political money. One of the *Pipefitters* dissenters, Justice Lewis Powell, wrote the decision for a split court in *First National Bank of Boston v. Bellotti* (1978).

What was the issue in First National Bank of Boston v. Bellotti?

The case was about a Massachusetts law that prohibited corporate expenditures in ballot-measure elections. After Congress passed the Tillman Act in 1907, Massachusetts joined most other states in passing its own version of the federal law. Like many of those other states, Massachusetts later added a ban against corporate expenditures in initiatives and referendums. *Bellotti* was a challenge to the constitutionality of this ban.

The *Bellotti* plaintiffs, the First National Bank of Boston, Gillette, Digital Equipment, and other companies, wanted to defeat a referendum that would have authorized a personal income tax in Massachusetts. The companies raised a First Amendment challenge to the state law because they wanted to buy ads against the tax using corporate treasury money, which had been illegal under state law for more than half a century. They lost in the Massachusetts Supreme Judicial Court, which unanimously upheld the law, ruling that "a corporation does not have the same First Amendment rights of free speech as a natural person."[10]

They fared better in the Supreme Court, which voted 5–4 to reverse the state court's decision. The court did not say outright that corporations had the same First Amendment speech rights as people, however. That was not even the issue in the case, according to Justice Powell. He did grant political speech rights to those corporations, but did so in a roundabout way by recasting the issue as the voters' "right to hear." He said the First Amendment furthers this right by protecting all speech, whatever its "source." By not extending that protection to corporate spending in ballot measure elections, Powell said, Massachusetts had discriminated against the bank and other plaintiffs because of their "corporate identity."[11]

The *Bellotti* decision relied heavily on *Buckley*—specifically its ruling that preventing *quid pro quo* corruption was the only constitutionally permissible reason to regulate campaign funds. And if expenditures had almost no corruptive potential in candidate elections, the court reasoned that there was no corruptive potential at all in elections that had no candidates.[12]

Bellotti's grant of limited First Amendment rights to corporations created a stir at the time, but that soon died down. Ballot-measure elections are held only at the state and local levels, so few people thought the decision would have any effect on the FECA's regulation of federal elections. *Bellotti* was seen as something of an outlier for decades. Then it came back as the core precedent for *Citizens United*.

Why did the Supreme Court give First Amendment rights of political speech to corporations in Citizens United?

Strictly speaking, it did not do that. Rather than make the argument that corporations had those rights, it begged the question by claiming they had always had them.[13]

That was not a widely held opinion before *Citizens United*. No one had challenged the constitutionality of the Tillman and Taft-Hartley Acts for keeping corporate money out of elections, and both the *Buckley* challengers and the *Buckley* court simply accepted them as established law. For most of the twentieth century we did not regard corporations as members of the democratic community, or as having the same rights as the flesh-and-blood citizens who were members.

Citizens United turned this long-standing assumption on its head. According to the court, it had recognized corporate First Amendment rights decades ago, long before *Bellotti* and even before the Taft-Hartley Act. Writing for the majority, Justice Anthony Kennedy cited a long string of cases, going back to the 1930s, in which the court had ruled in favor of corporate litigants to uphold First Amendment rights.

The great majority of these cases involved charges of obscenity or libel against newspapers, magazines, theaters, and cable television companies. The few political-speech cases were about newspapers and the NAACP, an incorporated membership association. Because the court ruled in favor of some kind of corporation in each case, Justice Kennedy concluded that it had recognized the First Amendment rights of *all* corporations.[14]

Justice John Paul Stevens, writing for himself and the other three dissenters, devoted most of his opinion to attacking Kennedy's conclusion, arguing that the majority's opinion was not based on decades of precedent but instead "marks a dramatic break from our past." With tongue in cheek, he supposed it may be "a First Amendment problem that corporations are not permitted to vote, given that voting is, among other things, a form of speech."[15]

Another way the court dodged the issue of corporate citizenship was to redefine it as one of equality between corporations and people. The justices did not have to be so bold as to say that corporations *are* people because *Bellotti* had already treated people and corporations as equally important "speakers." And *Buckley* had said that reforms aimed at reducing political inequality between what came to be called "speakers" were unconstitutional, so it was easy to portray the spending ban as being out of line with precedent.

How big a change did Citizens United *make to the way campaigns are financed?*

It brought about some very big changes, the rise of super PACs and dark money being the biggest. Not everyone saw it that way at the time, though. The decision's supporters claimed that it did not make much difference. Pointing out that corporations had been financing sham issue ads since the 1990s, they said there is very little difference between an ad that tells people to call Senator Jones and tell him to stop mistreating puppies and one that tells people to vote against him.

The difference is that while sham issue ads do serve the same function as express advocacy, corporate financing of sham issue ads was done outside the FECA, under more permissive state laws. It was soft, outside money, not hard, inside money. Emphasizing the similarity of the ads distracts attention from the fact that *Citizens United* brought outside money inside.[16]

That the decision would result in super PACs and dark money was not immediately evident. But the corporations the court freed to make independent expenditures included officially nonpolitical nonprofits that are regulated by the IRS and do not disclose their donors to the FEC. *Citizens United* led to a steep rise in applications to form such nonpolitical nonprofits, and to the resulting rise of dark money.

What about corporate personhood? Did Citizens United *say corporations are people?*

No, the Supreme Court has never said that corporations are people. Corporations have been *legal persons* since the nineteenth century.

They gained this status so the state would recognize and protect their rights to do such things as make contracts and own property. Individuals, or what the law calls "natural persons," had always had these rights, and when the corporation became a common way of organizing a business, they were extended to corporations.[17]

Courts eventually recognized corporations as having additional constitutional rights, such as due process of law and protection against unreasonable search and seizure. But corporations did not get other rights, such as the Fifth Amendment's protection against self-incrimination. They cannot claim that right because, as incorporeal entities, they cannot testify at all.

The court might never have said that corporations are people, but it can be argued that they have treated them as though they are people. And in a sense the court *is* claiming that corporations are people. For the first time in a majority opinion, the *Citizens United* court defined even for-profit business corporations as voluntary associations of citizens. Justice Antonin Scalia had been promoting this definition for twenty years in his dissenting opinions, and Justice Anthony Kennedy made it part of the *Citizens United* decision.[18]

Did Citizens United *release a flood of corporate money for independent expenditures?*

It almost certainly did not do that. It is impossible to know for sure because the explosion of independent expenditures after *Citizens United* included a large amount of untraceable dark money.

It is very unlikely, though, that there was anywhere near enough money to be called a flood. The alarm expressed after a decision as controversial as *Citizens United*—most notably by President Obama in his 2010 State of the Union speech—may be understandable, but political scientists were not surprised when the flood of corporate independent expenditures did not appear.[19]

Corporations did finance most of the sham issue ads of the 1990s and early 2000s, which were express advocacy in all but name. But that was money given directly to the parties, which was another way of buying access to members of Congress; and both parties got most of their soft money from business, so it was also bipartisan.

It is true that corporate officers are largely Republican and conservative in their individual contributions. But the contributions they make through their corporate PACs are predictably pragmatic, suggesting that corporations will not soon spend much money on partisan independent expenditures.[20]

But the absence of a flood of corporate money does not mean there was none at all, which seems to be what some supporters of *Citizens United* believe. In an attempt to counter reformers' claims about the radical nature of the decision, they point to disclosure reports filed with the FEC, which show that few corporations report making independent expenditures or contributing to groups that do. But in the long history of corporate money in elections, corporations have never been eager to report their contributions and expenditures.

As a Business Roundtable vice president explained in 2013, "90-something percent of corporate CEOs" would not make openly partisan expenditures for fear of offending customers.[21] Target Corporation is a case in point. In 2010, Target gave $150,000 to an independent spending PAC that backed a Republican candidate who opposed gay marriage. While that was not a major point in his campaign, it was enough for marriage equality advocates to launch very public demonstrations against and boycotts of Target stores.[22]

Citizens United *also permitted unlimited spending by labor unions. Has that happened?*

Organized labor does a lot of political spending. But *Citizens United* was not greeted with warnings that it would release a flood of union money because organized labor is so much weaker than it once was.

Union membership was still rising, if only fitfully, in the 1970s, but it has steadily declined since 1980. From 1980 to 2010, the number of people in the labor force increased by more than 40 percent while the number of union members decreased by more than 25 percent. Union funds are made up of member dues, so shrinking membership means fewer dollars available for the kinds of expenditures the Supreme Court legalized.[23]

Another big difference between unions and corporations, whether business for-profits or tax-exempt nonprofits, is that unions have to spend a lot of their money just to protect their existence. The

Republican Party has always been hostile to organized labor, and that hostility appears to have grown stronger as labor grows weaker. The Republican assault on public-sector unions in Wisconsin, for example, is almost without precedent. It was conducted not only by the national and state GOP, but also by an array of non-party organizations such as the Koch-backed Americans for Prosperity, Tea Party groups, and Glenn Beck's 9-12 Project.[24]

Organized labor is still the biggest and best-organized part of the Democratic coalition. Unions have been the most loyal member of the party's constantly shifting financial constituency, and they provide a reliable source of manpower and votes during election campaigns. But the Democrats have done very little to reverse the steady decline of this valuable ally. They can take labor for granted because they know it has no place else to go, that it has no choice but to keep supporting Democratic candidates and policies. Unions will continue to be a vital part of the Democratic coalition even as they get weaker, but *Citizens United* did nothing to make them stronger.[25]

Critics of Citizens United *also said it would let foreign money into U.S. elections. Has that happened?*

The alarm about foreign money was first raised when *Citizens United* used the "identity of the speaker" holding to allow corporations to spend money in federal elections. "If taken seriously," Justice John Paul Stevens said in his dissent, "our colleagues' assumption that the identity of a speaker has *no* relevance to the Government's ability to regulate political speech would ... appear to afford the same protection to multinational corporations controlled by foreigners as to individual Americans."[26]

The FEC ruled at least as early as 1989 that the American subsidiary of a foreign corporation could not form a PAC because it would be financed by the foreign corporation and foreign nationals would participate in making PAC decisions. Whether the bar against foreign participation in American elections still held after *Citizens United* was soon tested in a case that made its way to the Supreme Court.[27]

In 2010, two Canadian citizens who were living in the United States cited *Citizens United* to challenge the constitutionality of the law prohibiting them from making contributions to candidates for the U.S. Congress. A three-judge panel of the federal district court for the District of Columbia unanimously dismissed the suit, and the Supreme Court summarily affirmed the court's decision on appeal. Foreign nationals still cannot give or spend money in our elections.[28]

What foreign corporations and foreign nationals can do is put their money into American elections through dark-money groups. They can contribute to the officially nonpolitical tax-exempt groups—501(c)(4) social welfare organizations and 501(c)(6) business associations—that make independent expenditures on behalf of candidates. There is no reason to think there is a lot of foreign money in our elections, but under current FEC and IRS regulations there is no way to know for sure. And as long as there is no way to know for sure, there will always be doubts.[29]

Holes in the law also raise doubts. It is not clear, for example, that the ban against foreign participation in candidate elections holds true for ballot-measure elections. This hole was exposed when two European companies spent $327,000 to defeat a Los Angeles County ballot measure in 2012. The measure's supporters complained to the FEC, and three years later the notoriously slow-moving agency voted to investigate.[30]

Although the FEC counsel believed foreign nationals had made the decision to spend foreign money in that election, he advised against pursuing the matter. While the FECA clearly bans foreign money from candidate elections, he explained, it does not clearly do so for ballot-measure elections. The Democratic commissioners still voted to investigate the matter, but the Republican commissioners voted against it. What this means for the future of foreign money in state referendums and initiatives is anyone's guess.

Is the Republican Party financed by business and the Democratic Party by labor?

Business definitely favors Republicans and labor is even more solidly Democratic. But a few unions have supported Republicans and the Democrats have always raised most of their money from business. Even most of the Democrats' soft money came from business: from 1992 to 2000, business provided five times as much soft money as labor did. Corporate, trade association, and other business PACs are generally pragmatic and bipartisan in their contributions, so it is not surprising that in 2012 they gave Democrats more than twice what labor PACs gave. Organized labor has always been the Democrats' most reliable financial backer, but it has never had nearly enough money to be the party's financial mainstay.[31]

What about corporate lobbying? Isn't that at least as big a problem as campaign finance?

Lobbying and campaign finance are a joint problem, not separate ones. Given FECA contribution limits, corporations naturally spend much more on lobbying members of Congress than on giving them PAC contributions—about thirteen times as much, according to political scientist Lee Drutman. But lobbyists also see campaign contributions as a necessary part of their job: "It's all about having prior relationships, which is why fundraisers are important. It's a lot easier working on an agenda with someone you helped get into office."[32]

Lobbying and campaign finance sustain one another. Until the 1980s, though, lobbying and making campaign contributions were still different operations, however much they overlapped. That is, campaign contributions opened congressional office doors for lobbyists, but the lobbyists themselves largely stuck to lobbying. That was a division of labor that made sense when most lobbyists were employees of the company whose interests they represented in Washington.[33]

That division of labor became less clear-cut with the rise of lobbying firms, which allowed corporations to outsource their Washington representation. Once lobbying became a Washington-based business in its own right, it attracted the kind of Washington insiders who used to be the ones being lobbied—insiders such as former members of Congress. Thus was created the now-notorious revolving door, through which former government employees leave office to make much more money as lobbyists, often working on behalf of the same industries that had once lobbied them.

As more members of Congress and congressional staff have become lobbyists, Congress has strengthened its lobbying regulations.

Congress had long restricted the kinds of gifts that members and staff could receive from lobbyists, but it did not begin to regulate the growing campaign finance part of lobbying until the Jack Abramoff scandal. Super lobbyist Abramoff pleaded guilty to corruption charges in 2006, accepting a plea deal that committed him to cooperate with a federal corruption investigation.[34]

The following year Congress passed the Honest Leadership and Open Government Act of 2007, which required lobbyists to disclose how much they contributed to and bundled for candidates. The Lobbying Disclosure Act of 1995 had focused on requiring lobbyists to register and to report how much they spent on lobbying. At the time, few lobbyists made direct campaign contributions. By the time Abramoff pleaded guilty, however, more lobbyists were making their own contributions and bundling the contributions of others. The 2007 law was the first to recognize that raising campaign funds had become a part of lobbying.[35]

Super PACs have made raising campaign funds an even more important part of lobbying. In addition to making and bundling contributions and hosting fundraisers at D.C. restaurants, lobbyists showed up as creators, managers of, and advisers to some of the biggest super PACs in 2012. A lobbyist co-founded the first of the big super PACs, American Crossroads, and other lobbyists were advisers to and directors of House Majority PAC and Majority PAC, the Democrats' House and Senate super PACs. A more recent trend is to host "destination fundraisers" at pricey resorts, where the informal setting allows lobbyists to build closer relationships with members. Lobbying and campaign finance have always sustained one another, but in the last decade they have merged to become a single operation.[36]

10

CONCLUSION

Even a week can be a long time in politics, so predictions about longer periods should be made, and read, with caution. That said, it does not feel like much of a risk to say that the future looks bright for opponents of reform.

Why does the future look bright for reform opponents?

It is certainly not because people are satisfied with things as they are. Eighty percent of Republicans and 83 percent of Democrats told a Bloomberg Politics poll in September 2015 that *Citizens United* should be overturned. Three months earlier, 80 percent of Republicans and 90 percent of Democrats told a CBS News/*New York Times* poll that money has too much influence in elections and that our campaign finance system must be fundamentally rebuilt. That is a lot of discontent.[1]

By the end of 2015, 152 organizations—including old and new reform groups, single-issue organizations, labor unions, and civil rights and religious groups—had signed on to a statement of principles to check the "undue influence of money in politics."[2] *Citizens United*, super PACs, billionaires, social welfare groups, and dark money have caused the recently disillusioned to join longtime reformers in calling for big changes in campaign finance law.[3]

No one expects those changes to come about in the near future, though. Reform bills introduced in Congress over the years have died in committee, and a deadlocked FEC is not even enforcing existing law. Actual changes are taking place only at the state and local levels, where citizens, legislatures, and city councils have been experimenting with public funding. It is various kinds of public funding programs that have been the focus of reform efforts at all levels.

Is there is any chance for reviving public funding for presidential elections?

The presidential program may not be legally dead, but it is flat on its back. Congress has shown no interest in restoring it to good health, but reformers keep coming up with good ideas.

In 2003, Senators John McCain and Russ Feingold introduced a bill to strengthen the presidential system. They proposed modest adjustments such as raising the checkoff amount again, making a bigger grant to candidates, and setting higher limits for party spending on behalf of candidates. They also called for a four-to-one match for contributions in the primaries.

The bill went nowhere in 2003, but revised versions of it have been introduced in every succeeding Congress, and along the way it has become a bolder vision of reform. The current version, called the Empowering Citizens Act, would completely rewrite the presidential funding system. It treats funding for the primary and general elections the same way, by eliminating spending limits and providing a six-to-one match for the first $250 of contributions up to a maximum of $100 million for the primaries and $200 million for the general. Every version of this bill has died in committee.

Public funding for Senate elections is the goal of another bill, the Fair Elections Now Act, which Senator Richard Durbin (D-IL) has been introducing in every Congress since 2007. His bill would impose a tax on payments made to corporations with government contracts and offer donors a refundable tax credit of up to $50. Every version of this bill has died in committee. The prospects for reviving presidential public funding in the near future are the same as they have been for at least a decade: approximately zero.

What about public funding for state and city elections? Is that likely to continue?

Yes. These programs continue to have their ups and downs, but several states and cities have either strengthened existing forms of public funding or introduced new ones.

The most ambitious proposal is public funding vouchers. Rather than giving subsidies directly to candidates, a voucher program would distribute a fixed sum of money to registered voters. It would answer the question of how to distribute public funds by turning that decision over to voters, allowing them to give their allotted sums to the candidates or parties of their choice. The only voucher program in the country is the one Seattle voters passed in 2015; it will take effect in 2017.

There are few genuinely new reform ideas, and vouchers are no exception. Senator Lee Metcalf (D-MT) was probably the first to come up with the idea, during the 1967 debate over Senator Long's presidential public funding act. Vouchers got little attention after Congress passed the current presidential public funding program, but they began to look attractive again with the rise of soft money. Several law professors revived the idea in the 1990s, and they and others have fleshed it out in recent years.[4]

All public funding programs have been at least partly designed to recruit small donors, and the voucher idea takes both goals to their logical conclusions. Small-donor programs are intended to increase political participation by finding ways to convince otherwise uninvolved citizens to part with some of their money. Citizens with vouchers would not have to pay to participate. A voucher program would immediately give voting-age citizens something candidates and parties want, and that could increase citizen participation in elections by giving a big boost to grass-roots political organizing.

The boost that vouchers would give to grass-roots organizing may be the most valuable thing about them. Winning an election has always required organization, but as getting out the vote became a more capital- than labor-intensive operation, block-by-block party organization was no longer necessary. Once every registered voter on every block gets a $100 voucher, though, each one of those voters becomes someone candidates and parties will very much want to talk with.

That is all speculation, of course. Voucher programs hold great promise and are very much worth trying. But we have no practical experience with them, and will have to see how they work in practice. That is not so with small-donor programs, which have been in effect at the national, state, and local levels for years.

Will small-donor programs be able to counter the surge of rich donors and democratize campaign finance?

Probably not. Reducing the influence of big donors has always been the goal of small-donor programs. But very few campaigns—very few winning campaigns, anyway—have ever been funded mostly by small contributions. Which raises the question: if so many people think small money is such a good thing, why have we not seen more of it? It is not for lack of trying. Small-donor programs go back to 1908.

Burned by scandals that revealed their dependence on big contributions from Wall Street, both parties in the 1908 presidential election launched serious attempts to attract small donors. This was not a one-time event, either, something they abandoned when the scandal faded from popular memory. Instead, the parties made the programs a regular part of their campaign fundraising.[5]

Big donors kept giving, too, of course, and kept providing a disproportionate share of campaign funds, as they had done for decades. But their share did not rise to alarming levels until 1972, when rich donors wrote fatter checks than they had done since the Gilded Age. Those fat checks became part of Watergate, and they were what revived the call to curb big donors by encouraging small ones. Congress responded by amending the FECA to impose strict contribution limits and require presidential candidates to get small donations to qualify for public funds. And that seemed to work for a while: "The role and power of the 'fat cats' in the process has been diminished," said RNC chair Richard Richards in 1981.[6]

The fat cats' role did not stay diminished, though. It expanded again in the era of soft money, which Congress banned by passing the Bipartisan Campaign Reform Act (BCRA) in 2002. The BCRA was hailed as another democratizing breakthrough when the parties responded by raising unexpectedly large sums of hard money from small donors. And now that the fat cats are back yet again, so too are calls for reducing their role by increasing the number of small donors.[7]

The parties probably knew as early as the 1920s that small donors were important mainly for public relations. By reporting large numbers of small donors, the parties showed that they were not dependent on a small number of big ones. But small donors were never going to provide enough money to put them at the center of campaign fundraising.

What has changed since 2010 is the idea that they *can* matter to the bottom line and should be put at the center of campaign fundraising. Implicit in this idea is the belief that a large enough number of small donors can reduce the political influence of big donors.

Small donors, though, need much more encouragement than big donors, and federal, state, and local programs have had varying degrees of success in recruiting them. New York City's six-to-one matching program has been among the most successful, bringing tens of thousands of new, small donors into electoral politics. The new donors are also more diverse, by race, ethnicity, education, and income, than traditional donors.

The New York program's success showed up in the numbers: more than half of the donors in the 2013 election were giving for the first time, and two-thirds of them made small contributions. But a highly skewed distribution of big and small donors showed up even here. The two-thirds of donors who made small contributions provided only a little more than 10 percent of the total amount contributed. That means 90 percent of the total came from just one-third of the donors. And that was with a low contribution limit of $4,950.[8]

An important measure of success for small-donor programs is, or should be, whether donors give more than once. Big donors give in election after election because they are politically involved or have business or social connections to those who are. If small donors are going to give as regularly as big ones, they too will have to become politically involved. That is something that tax credits and matching funds by themselves cannot do.

Politics requires organization. Small-donor programs are organized to increase the number of small donors, but not to organize the donors themselves. Large numbers of unorganized donors are a statistic, not a political force with the kind of voice in Washington that would justify the term "democratization." People have been chasing the dream of a small-donor democracy for more than 100 years, and it still eludes us.

Well-financed non-party groups seem to be more active than the parties in recent elections. Are the parties getting weaker?

Changes to campaign finance law necessarily change the way the parties operate, and *Citizens United* and *SpeechNow* made substantial changes. Super PACs and politically active tax-exempt groups brought big money back into elections in a big way, and the big donors even formed their own organizations. These groups created many more points at which campaign funding decisions are made. This decentralization may not be weakening the parties, but neither is it making them stronger. Money that flows through non-party groups may end up in the coffers of major party candidates, but it still means less money flowing through the formal party organizations.

These new groups will probably be around for a while. Successful candidates use super PACs to buy ads without having to dig too deeply into the hard money they raise for their campaign committees. Less successful candidates also use them to buy ads, which keep their campaigns alive on the air after their hard-money fundraising has stalled. So they may survive as more or less autonomous adjuncts of parties and party factions. Tax-exempt groups may eventually be more widely used for similar purposes, as they have the added benefit of keeping donor identities secret.

The rich donor groups are another matter. Super PACs and 501(c)s are immediately valuable to candidates and can be formed by people close to them; when a candidate's campaign is over, they can be disbanded. That is not so with the rich donor groups. The donors formed them to serve their own long-term political purposes, to promote favored policies or to push the country in a particular political direction. The Koch brothers' network in particular has begun to operate on the scale of a political party.

It is not clear, though, that the donor groups have what it takes to last in the long run. For one thing, they lack a crucial feature that the parties have: a succession plan. This could be a problem for the Koch network. Eighty-year-old Charles Koch is the "lead investor," and the network will probably flourish as long as he remains in good health. But network staff is understandably worried that many donors will stop giving once he is gone.[9]

Parties do not have that problem. They have split and come back together several times over the last 150 years or so, while usually managing to elect new leaders at regular intervals. Political parties are what make democracy work, so it is hard to imagine our democracy existing without them. And voters identify with parties, not with super PACs, tax-exempt organizations, or groups of billionaires who meet in expensive resorts. The parties have a legitimacy those groups do not have and cannot have.

Which is not to say that a party establishment cannot lose legitimacy in the eyes of the party rank-and-file. That seems to be what was happening during the 2015–16 primaries, when people inside and outside the GOP thought the party was cracking up. The most destabilizing forces for both parties tend to be internal, not external.

Can the FEC be made to work?

People keep coming up with ideas to make it work, mostly by making the FEC more like other agencies. The Federal Election Administration Act, introduced by Senate Tom Udall (D-NM) on March 1, 2016, would replace the FEC with a five-member Federal Election Administration. The president would appoint all five members with the advice and consent of the Senate, as is done at present. Four of the five members—only two of whom could be from the same political party—would have staggered six-year terms. Rather than have the office of chairperson rotate among the commissioners, it would be a separate, presidentially appointed position, as it is in other agencies. The chairperson would be the FEC's chief officer, with broad management and administrative powers, including the power to prepare the agency's budget. This bill is a revised version of one that Senators John McCain (R-Ariz.) and Russ Feingold (D-Wisc.) first introduced in 2003. That it has been introduced and reintroduced so many times over the years without ever getting out of committee suggests that the current version will not fare any better.[10]

Will disclosure survive?

The survival of disclosure is no longer as sure a thing as it used to be. The *Citizens United* court reaffirmed the *Buckley* court's support for disclosure as serving the public interest of telling voters where political money is coming from. But it was also *Citizens United* that released the flood of big money that changed opposition to disclosure from occasional grumbling to a full-on ideological assault.

The decision's immediate result was the rise of dark money, money raised and spent by tax-exempt nonprofit corporations that do not have to disclose their donors. That led reformers to call for stronger disclosure requirements, which in turn led reform opponents to attack the very idea of disclosure. The opponents' argument, that disclosing the names of conservative donors subjected them to liberal and government intimidation, is one the Supreme Court bluntly rejected in *Citizens United*.

Disclosure seemed to be safe, given decades of support by an increasingly conservative court. But a hint that the opponents may be onto something came in January 2016, when a three-judge panel of the federal circuit court for the District of Columbia handed down a decision on disclosure that criticized the Roberts court from the right.

The circuit court's decision was the latest in a long-running case about an FEC regulation that allows tax-exempt groups to hide the names of donors who finance their independent expenditures. The judges praised *Citizens United*, which they called "the most expansive, speech-protective campaign finance decision in American history." Yet they also said the Supreme Court's support for disclosure requirements was a "startling intrusion" on the right of "anonymous speech." The judges' point is that speech is a constitutional right, while disclosure is only "an extra-constitutional value," and the court was wrong—apparently has been wrong since *Buckley*—to treat them as equivalents.[11]

That federal court judges should criticize the Roberts court for being insufficiently hostile to campaign finance reform is surprising. But it is alarming that the judges should have turned on what has for more than a century been the one reform that even reform opponents supported. Those observers who think that a long-term goal of the Roberts court is the near-total deregulation of campaign finance have also assumed that disclosure would be the one law left standing. Maybe not.

There seems to be a lot of support for a constitutional amendment to overturn Citizens United. *Is that likely to happen?*

It is hard to take this idea seriously. Even if amending the Constitution were a good idea, an amendment would have to get the votes of two-thirds of both houses of Congress and be ratified by the legislatures of three-fourths of the states. There is no chance that either of these things could happen in the near future.

And what if the amendment were ratified? It would free Congress and state legislatures to ban corporate political spending and set limits on independent expenditures. But that does not mean they would do those things. And if they did, the constitutionality of the new reforms would be determined by the same Supreme Court the reforms were meant to get around.

Some things do need to be done by amending the Constitution, such as giving women and eighteen-year-olds the vote, limiting the president to two terms, and giving electoral votes to the District of Columbia. But other things have been accomplished through changing interpretations of an unchanging text: labor unions used to be illegal combinations in restraint of trade, racial segregation used to be constitutional, the minimum wage used to be a violation of the freedom of contract, and Congress used to have no authority to prohibit child labor.

These social and economic changes happened as the Supreme Court itself changed. The same is true of campaign finance. The problem is the court, not the Constitution, and the court is a product of our current politics. Changing the Constitution without changing the Supreme Court would be a legal solution to a political problem, which means it would not be a solution at all. But to get a better court we will need better politics.

Why are the prospects for reform so poor?

It mostly comes down to the Supreme Court and political polarization. Neither was an important factor for more than half a century after the first campaign finance reforms were passed in 1907 and 1910. During that half-century, the court played only a small role in campaign finance law, and partisan polarization in Congress was declining from a high point in the 1890s. Today the Supreme Court dominates the issue and congressional polarization has gone back to nineteenth-century levels.

Campaign finance has become thoroughly judicialized, a term used to describe a situation in which key decisions on fundamentally political issues are made by judges rather than legislators.

Judicialization began with *Buckley*, which was handed down in 1976, when polarization was beginning to increase. The court had become more conservative under the Nixon administration, and it made an even sharper turn to the right under George W. Bush. The Roberts court is the most conservative one we have seen since the 1930s, and three of its eight (as of this writing) justices—Roberts, Alito, and Thomas—are among the five most conservative justices to sit on the court in that time. (The late Justice Scalia was also one of the five most conservative justices.)[12]

By the time President George W. Bush appointed John G. Roberts and Samuel Alito to the court, partisan polarization in Congress was greater than at any other time in modern history. Congressional polarization has been asymmetrical, increasing not because each party was moving away from the ideological center, but because Republicans made a sharp turn to the right. Part of the GOP's increasing conservatism was a committed opposition to campaign finance reform.[13]

This is why reformers have put so much energy into passing reforms at the state and local levels. The hope is that the success of those reforms will cause them to spread across the country. But even the successful reforms passed in blue or purple states and cities may never spread to red ones. The states already have different kinds of voting laws—blue ones to make it easier to register and vote, red ones to make it harder—and the same could happen with campaign finance laws.[14]

It does not matter that *Citizens United* may be the most hated Supreme Court opinion in recent memory. Nor does it matter that 80 percent or more of Republicans and Democrats think the decision should be overturned and that Congress should curb super PACs by imposing limits on independent expenditures. And it does not matter that bipartisan agreement on these points is especially striking at a time when the public may be as polarized as the politicians.[15]

None of these things matter, because our political system is not very responsive to public opinion. This was the conclusion two political scientists reached after a detailed study of 1,779 policy issues: "even overwhelmingly large pro-change majorities, with 80 percent of the public favoring a policy change, got that change only about 43 percent of the time."[16]

They also do not matter because what that 80 percent of Americans dislike so much is rooted in *Buckley*. There would have been no *Citizens United*, no super PACs, and no opening for billionaires to spend unlimited sums of money in elections without *Buckley*'s rulings that preventing corruption is the only permissible justification for regulating campaign funds, and that independent expenditures cannot be limited because they are pure speech. Curbing the role of big money in elections would mean overturning the landmark case in modern campaign finance law, and the chances of that happening are a lot less than 43 percent.

The chances of curbing big money in elections would be a lot better if the 5–4 split on the Supreme Court went the other way. How likely is that?

The death of Justice Antonin Scalia has already shown us just how far we are from getting the better politics we need to get a better Supreme Court.

CHRONOLOGY

1907

An Act To prohibit corporations from making money contributions in connection with political elections (Public Law 59-36, Tillman Act)
   http://legisworks.org/congress/59/session-2/publaw-36.pdf
Chap. 420
   This was the first federal campaign finance law. The original bill was drafted and introduced by Senator William E. Chandler (R-NH) in 1901, but it never got to the floor for a vote. Chandler had it reintroduced by Senator Benjamin Tillman (D-SC), which is why it is called the Tillman Act.

1910

An Act Providing for publicity of contributions... (Public Law 61-274)
   http://legisworks.org/congress/61/publaw-274.pdf
   The first federal disclosure law. Required national political committees to disclose campaign receipts and expenditures. It covered only general elections and required reports to be submitted after Election Day.

1911

An Act To amend an act entitled "An Act Providing for publicity of contributions... (Public Law 62-32)
   http://legisworks.org/congress/62/publaw-32.pdf Chap. 33

Strengthened the 1910 disclosure law by extending it to cover primary elections and requiring political committees to file disclosure reports before Election Day; and imposed a limit on congressional campaign expenditures.

1918

An Act To prevent corrupt practices in the election of Senators, Representatives, or Delegates in Congress. (Public Law 65-222)
http://legisworks.org/congress/65/publaw-222.pdf Chap. 187
Prohibited the bribery of voters.

1921

U.S. v. Newberry, 256 U.S. 232
https://supreme.justia.com/cases/federal/us/256/232/
Senator Truman H. Newberry (R-MI) appealed his conviction for exceeding the spending limit in his 1918 campaign. The court overturned Newberry's conviction, but did so without coming to a clear decision about the scope of the 1911 law.

1925

Federal Corrupt Practices Act, 1925 (Public Law 68-506)
http://legisworks.org/congress/68/publaw-506.pdf Chap. 368,
Title III (rider on postal salaries bill)
Recodified and revised existing campaign finance regulations. Congress strengthened disclosure by requiring reports to be filed in nonelection years; but it also read *Newberry* to mean that it had no authority to regulate primary elections, and revised the disclosure and spending limit laws to apply only to general elections.

1934

Burroughs v. U.S., 290 U.S. 534
https://supreme.justia.com/cases/federal/us/290/534/
A Virginia political group charged with violating the 1910 disclosure law challenged its constitutionality. The court upheld the law on the odd ground that it was intended to prevent the bribery and intimidation of voters.

1939

An Act To prevent pernicious political activities (Public Law 76-252, Hatch Act)

http://legisworks.org/congress/76/publaw-252.pdf Chap. 410

Extended civil service protections to all federal government employees, prohibiting them from taking an active part in election campaigns whether on or off duty. It originated with the conservative coalition, which wanted to curb actual abuses of the large numbers of relief workers in the Works Progress Administration, but also wanted to prevent President Roosevelt from using those same workers in his 1940 reelection campaign.

1940

An Act To extend to certain officers in the several States and the District of Columbia the provisions of the Act entitled "An Act to prevent pernicious political activities" (Public Law 76-753, Hatch Act II)

http://legisworks.org/congress/76/publaw-753.pdf Chap. 640

The second Hatch Act (Hatch Act II), which also originated with the conservative coalition, extended the prohibition against political activity to state government employees who were at least partly paid from federal government funds. Pro–New Deal Democrats added a $5,000 contribution limit and a $3 million campaign spending limit as what they hoped would be poison-pill amendments that would cause Republicans and Southern Democrats to kill the bill. Their tactic did not work, and the limits became part of the Federal Corrupt Practices Act.

1943

War Labor Disputes Act (Public Law 78-89, Smith-Connally Act)

http://legisworks.org/congress/78/publaw-89.pdf Chap. 144, Sec. 9 and 10

A conservative coalition measure, passed over FDR's veto, intended to prevent strikes by permitting the federal government to seize control of industries that were even threatened with a strike during World War II. The CIO and AFL had signed no-strike pledges after Pearl Harbor, but a mineworkers' strike opposed by both labor organizations gave anti-labor forces in Congress an excuse to act. It also included a section prohibiting labor unions from making campaign contributions. It was this Act that led the CIO to create the first political action committee.

1947

An Act To amend the National Labor Relations Act. . . (Public Law 80-101, Taft-Hartley Act)

http://legisworks.org/congress/80/publaw-101.pdf Chap. 120, Sec. 304

Another conservative coalition measure, passed over President Harry Truman's veto, that permanently restricted organized labor's ability to organize and to strike; it also made the Smith-Connally ban on union contributions permanent and added a ban on political expenditures by both unions and corporations.

1948

U.S. v. Congress of Industrial Organizations, 335 U.S. 106

https://supreme.justia.com/cases/federal/us/335/106/case.html

The CIO tested the constitutionality of the Taft-Hartley Act's prohibition against labor union political spending by endorsing a congressional candidate in its in-house publication. The U.S. government indicted the CIO, but the district court dismissed the indictment, saying the act violated the First Amendment. The government appealed to the Supreme Court, where the CIO again challenged the act's constitutionality. The Supreme Court affirmed the lower court's decision, saying the in-house editorial did not violate the Taft-Hartley Act, but it left the act intact.

1957

U.S. v. United Auto Workers, 352 U.S. 567

https://supreme.justia.com/cases/federal/us/352/567/case.html

The U.S. government indicted the UAW for making what would now be called independent expenditures in the 1954 congressional elections. A district court, relying on U.S. v. CIO, dismissed the indictment, and the government appealed to the Supreme Court. The Supreme Court agreed that the expenditures were prohibited under the Taft-Hartley Act, but refrained from ruling on the act's constitutionality. Instead, it remanded the case—sent it back down to the district court—to clarify "the concrete factual setting" of the expenditures. This decision is best known for Justice Felix Frankfurter's lengthy (and historically inaccurate) take on the history of campaign finance law.

1961

International Association of Machinists v. Street, 367 U.S. 740
https://supreme.justia.com/cases/federal/us/367/740/

Railroad employees in Georgia raised a First Amendment challenge to a union shop agreement, saying that the dues they paid to the union were used to finance the campaigns of candidates they did not support. The Supreme Court upheld the constitutionality of the union shop agreement, but did order the union to refund the portion of dues that paid for political activities.

1963

Railway Clerks v. Allen, 373 U.S. 113
https://supreme.justia.com/cases/federal/us/373/113/

Railroad employees in North Carolina sued to enjoin enforcement of a union shop contract, saying that the dues they paid to the union were used to finance the campaigns of candidates they did not support. The Supreme Court directed the union to refund the portion of dues that paid for political activities.

1966

Presidential Election Campaign Fund Act of 1966 (Public Law 89-809, Title III) 80 Stat, 1554
http://babel.hathitrust.org/cgi/pt?id=uc1.b4312568;view=1up; seq=833

The first presidential public funding law, which created the income tax checkoff. There was so much opposition to it in Congress, from both parties, that it never went into effect; the checkoff was postponed in 1967.

1971

Federal Election Campaign Act of 1971 (Public Law 92-225) www. gpo.gov/fdsys/pkg/STATUTE-86/pdf/STATUTE-86-Pg3.pdf

Replaced the Federal Corrupt Practices Act: repealed contribution and spending limits, but did impose limits on media spending; strengthened disclosure requirements; kept enforcement for House and Senate elections in the hands of the Clerk of the House and the Secretary of the Senate, but added the comptroller general to monitor compliance in presidential elections; explicitly legalized the PAC form that organized labor had been using since the 1940s.

1971

Revenue Act of 1971 (Public Law 92-178)

www.gpo.gov/fdsys/pkg/STATUTE-85/pdf/STATUTE-85-Pg497.pdf

Title VII of this act provided tax incentives for small contributions; Title VIII established the Presidential Election Campaign Fund, to be financed by a tax checkoff beginning in 1973.

1972

Pipefitters v. U.S., 407 U.S. 385

https://supreme.justia.com/cases/federal/us/407/385/

The U.S. government indicted the PAC of a Pipefitters Union local for violating the Taft-Hartley Act's prohibitions against union campaign contributions. The PAC, like most labor PACs, made contributions from a fund made up of voluntary donations from union members, but was maintained with union funds and run by union officers. The government said the PAC was a subterfuge for making illegal union contributions, and won its case in the federal district and circuit courts. The union appealed to the Supreme Court, and the AFL-CIO convinced Congress to legalize the PAC form in the 1971 FECA. The Supreme Court upheld the 1971 law and added that the Taft-Hartley Act had not clearly either permitted or prohibited the PAC form.

1974

Federal Election Campaign Act Amendments of 1974 (Public Law 93-443)

www.gpo.gov/fdsys/pkg/STATUTE-88/pdf/STATUTE-88-Pg1263.pdf

Passed to respond to Watergate, these amendments: imposed new campaign contribution and expenditure limits, stricter than those in the FCPA; further strengthened disclosure requirements; established a presidential public funding program, financed by activating the income tax checkoff in the Revenue Act of 1971; created the Federal Election Commission to enforce the new law and administer the public funding program.

1975

Buckley v. Valeo, 519 F.2d 821 (D.C. Circuit Court of Appeals)
http://openjurist.org/519/f2d/821/buckley-v-r-valeo-c
The D.C. Circuit Court of Appeals was the first to hear the challenge to the constitutionality of the 1974 FECA amendments brought by Senator James Buckley et al. Apart from some minor objections, the court upheld the act's constitutionality by a 7–1 vote.

1976

Buckley v. Valeo, 429 U.S. 1
https://supreme.justia.com/cases/federal/us/424/1/
The Supreme Court, on the other hand, largely accepted the challengers' argument that political spending had the same First Amendment protection as political speech, and ruled accordingly. It upheld the most innovative and controversial parts of the law—public funding and the FEC—but struck down limits on all campaign expenditures and all regulation of issue ads.

1976

Federal Election Campaign Act Amendments of 1976 (Public Law 94-283)
www.gpo.gov/fdsys/pkg/STATUTE-90/pdf/STATUTE-90-Pg475.pdf
To comply with the Supreme Court's *Buckley* decision, Congress repealed expenditure limits (except for presidential candidates who accept public funding); repealed all regulations on issue ads; added limits on individual contributions to parties and PACs, and on PAC contributions to parties; revised the method for appointing Federal Election Commissioners; defined solicitable classes for PACs; and restricted the proliferation of labor and corporate PACs.

1977

Abood v. Detroit Board of Education, 431 U.S. 209

https://supreme.justia.com/cases/federal/us/431/209/

The Supreme Court had upheld the constitutionality of union shop contracts in the private sector, but the teachers in this case challenged the practice for government employees. The teachers also raised First Amendment objections to paying dues to finance political activities they opposed. The Supreme Court upheld the union shop for government employees; the union had already changed its policy by refunding that portion of dues that financed political activities the dissenters opposed.

1978

First National Bank of Boston v. Bellotti, 435 U.S. 765

https://supreme.justia.com/cases/federal/us/435/765/

The first Supreme Court decision to grant First Amendment speech rights to corporations; it struck down a Massachusetts state law that prohibited corporations from making expenditures in ballot measure elections.

1979

Federal Election Campaign Act Amendments of 1979 (Public Law 96-187)

www.gpo.gov/fdsys/pkg/STATUTE-93/pdf/STATUTE-93-Pg1339.pdf

Loosened some disclosure regulations and exempted generic party-building activities—get-out-the-vote drives, yard signs, buttons, etc. —from contribution and expenditure limits.

1982

FEC v. National Right to Work Committee, 459 U.S. 197

https://supreme.justia.com/cases/federal/us/459/197/

In 1976, the NRWC, an incorporated, nonprofit voluntary association, solicited contributions to its PAC from 270,000 people. Under the 1976 FECA amendments, which defined whom the different kinds of PACs could and could not solicit, the NRWC could solicit only its officers and members. The FEC sued, saying that the people the group had solicited could not be considered members under any reasonable interpretation of the statute. The Supreme Court agreed. To rule otherwise, the justices said, would "open the door to all but unlimited corporate solicitation" (204).

1986

Tax Reform Act of 1986 (Public Law 99-514)
http://legisworks.org/congress/99/toc-pl-99-514.html
Title I, Subtitle B, Section 112 repealed the tax credit for political contributions.

1986

FEC v. Massachusetts Citizens for Life, 879 U.S. 238
https://supreme.justia.com/cases/federal/us/479/238/
The first Supreme Court decision to limit the coverage of the FECA's ban against corporate contributions and expenditures. Massachusetts Citizens for Life (MCFL) was a 501(c)(4) nonprofit corporation that did not take contributions from for-profit corporations. The case involved an independent expenditure MCFL had made using its treasury funds; because it had not used its PAC, the FEC charged it with violating the FECA. In a 5–4 decision that cut across party and ideological lines, the Supreme Court decided that Congress had intended the Tillman Act to cover only for-profit business corporations, and carved out an exception to the law for incorporated voluntary associations like MCFL. These groups are called "qualified nonprofit corporations," or simply MCFL groups.

1990

Austin v. Michigan Chamber of Commerce, 494 U.S. 652
https://supreme.justia.com/cases/federal/us/494/652/
The Michigan Chamber of Commerce, citing Bellotti and MCFL, challenged the constitutionality of a state law that prohibited corporations from making independent expenditures in candidate elections. Ruling that neither case was a precedent for allowing corporate money into candidate elections, the Supreme Court upheld the law in a 6–3 vote; all the new Reagan appointees—Sandra Day O'Connor, Antonin Scalia, and Anthony Kennedy—dissented. This

was the decision the conservative majority on the Roberts court arranged to overturn in *Citizens United.*

2002

Bipartisan Campaign Reform Act of 2002 (Public Law 107-155, McCain-Feingold Act)

www.gpo.gov/fdsys/pkg/PLAW-107publ155/content-detail. html

The first significant FECA amendment since 1979, the act prohibits national party committees and federal candidates from raising and spending nonfederal money; limits the amount of nonfederal money state and local parties can use to finance generic party activities; extends the FECA to cover some sham issue ads by bringing them under the newly created category of "electioneering communications"; increased the limit on individual contributions to candidates to $2,000 and indexed the new limit for inflation; and raised the individual and party contribution limits for House and Senate candidates facing rivals whose contributions to their own campaigns exceeded certain limits (a provision called the "millionaires' amendment").

2003

McConnell v. FEC, 540 U.S. 93

https://supreme.justia.com/cases/federal/us/540/93/

A challenge to the constitutionality of BCRA. Senate minority leader Mitch McConnell (R-KY) focused his challenge on the prohibition against party soft money and the creation of electioneering communications as a new category of political ads subject to FECA regulation. The Supreme Court upheld both provisions in a 5–4 vote; this was the last time it upheld a campaign finance law.

2007

FEC v. Wisconsin Right to Life, 551 U.S. 449

https://supreme.justia.com/cases/federal/us/551/449/

A challenge to BCRA's electioneering communications provision. Wisconsin Right to Life (WRTL), an incorporated 501(c)(4) that took corporate contributions, wanted to spend treasury funds on ads mentioning Senator Russ Feingold (D-WI). This was illegal under BCRA's electioneering communications provision, which required such ads to be financed with hard money. WRTL wanted an "as applied" exemption from that provision (that is, it did not challenge the provision as unconstitutional on its face) on the grounds that they were genuine issue ads. The Supreme Court granted the exemption in a 5–4 vote; this was the first of a series of anti-reform decisions by the new Roberts court.

2008

Davis v. FEC, 554 U.S. 724

https://supreme.justia.com/cases/federal/us/554/724/

A challenge to BCRA's "millionaires' amendment" brought by Jack Davis, a rich New York Democratic Party candidate for a House seat in an upstate district. The Supreme Court struck down the provision in a 5–4 decision, finding that it burdened rich candidates' ability to "robustly" exercise their First Amendment rights.

2010

Citizens United v. FEC, 558 U.S. 310

https://supreme.justia.com/cases/federal/us/558/08-205/

Citizens United is a 501(c)(4) that, like WRTL, took some corporate money, and sought an as-applied exemption from what remained of BCRA's electioneering communications provision for a political ad it had produced with treasury funds. The ad in this case was a feature-length film about Hillary Clinton, which the group wanted to make available as a free download on cable television. Although almost no corporate funds were used to produce or distribute the film, the FEC ruled that it was an electioneering communication and that Citizens United could not finance it with treasury money.

Instead of deciding the case in 2009, the Supreme Court asked for new briefs that addressed the constitutionality of corporate political expenditures and challenging the constitutionality of *Austin*. After rehearing the case in 2010, it extended *Bellotti* by ruling that corporations (and unions) had the First Amendment right to make independent expenditures in candidate elections.

2010

SpeechNow v. FEC, 599 F.3d 686

www.fec.gov/law/litigation/speechnow_ac_opinion.pdf

SpeechNow, a 527 group created to make only independent expenditures, sued the FEC to prevent it from enforcing the $5,000 limit on individual contributions to PACs that made such expenditures. Citing *Citizens United*, the federal circuit court for the District of Columbia struck down the limit, opening the way for the super PAC.

2011

Arizona Free Enterprise Club's Freedom Club PAC v. Bennett, 564 U.S. ___

https://supreme.justia.com/cases/federal/us/564/10-238/

A challenge to the matching-fund provision of Arizona's public funding program. Publicly financed candidates facing rich opponents who used their personal wealth to build bigger campaign funds than what the state allotted would get enough additional matching funds to match what was spent by those opponents and independent expenditures made on their behalf. The Supreme Court struck down the provision in a 5–4 decision. Quoting *Davis*, it ruled that preventing rich candidates from outspending their opponents "diminishe[d] the effectiveness" of their speech.

2014

McCutcheon v. FEC, 572 U.S. ___

https://supreme.justia.com/cases/federal/us/572/12-536/

A challenge to the FECA's aggregate limit on the amount anyone could contribute to candidates, parties, and PACs in an election cycle. This limit was in the 1974 FECA amendments, and the Supreme Court upheld it in *Buckley* as a way to prevent people from circumventing the limits on individual donations to a candidate by "contribut[ing] massive amounts of money to ... political committees likely to contribute to that candidate, or huge contributions to the candidate's political party" (424 U.S. 1, 38).

But the *Buckley* court itself opened up the major opportunity for circumvention of contribution limits by striking down limits on independent expenditures. In response Congress imposed limits on individual contributions to parties and PACs and PAC contributions to parties in the 1976 FECA amendments. BCRA increased the limits and indexed them to inflation.

Twenty-eight years later Republican donor Sean McCutcheon argued that the contribution limits added in 1976 meant that the aggregate limit could no longer be justified as an anti-circumvention measure. What it did instead was prevent donors from giving to "too many" candidates, which violated the First Amendment rights of people who could afford to give to many more than the limit allowed. The Supreme Court agreed. In a 5–4 decision it struck down the aggregate limit as an unnecessarily heavy-handed way to prevent *quid pro quo* corruption.

2014

Gabriella Miller Kids First Research Act (Public Law 113-94)
www.gpo.gov/fdsys/pkg/PLAW-113publ94/pdf/PLAW-113publ94.pdf
Repealed public funding of party conventions and redirects Presidential Election Campaign Fund money that would have paid for them to do pediatric research.

2014

Consolidated and Further Continuing Appropriations Act, 2015 (Public Law 113-59)
www.gpo.gov/fdsys/pkg/CPRT-113HPRT91668/pdf/CPRT-113HPRT91668.pdf
This appropriations bill was called "Cromnibus" because it combined a short-term spending bill for Homeland Security, called a "continuing resolution," with the usual omnibus bill for the federal government budget. The final bill included an 800 percent increase in the amount of money that private donors can give to parties.

2016

Friedrichs v. California Teachers Association, 578 U.S. ____
www.supremecourt.gov/opinions/15pdf/14-915_1bn2.pdf
A challenge to the constitutionality of *Abood v. Detroit Board of Education*, which upheld the union shop for government employees but required unions to refund the portion of dues that paid for

political activities that dissenting members opposed. The plaintiffs argued that all union activities were political and that even paying dues to cover the costs of collective bargaining was "compelled political speech." This attempt to move the court further to the right on labor issues by overruling *Abood* probably would have succeeded had Justice Scalia not died; without Justice Scalia the court deadlocked 4–4, keeping the precedent in place.

NOTES

CHAPTER 1

1. *New York Times*/CBS News poll, January 20–25, 2006, questions 51 and 52 (www.nytimes.com/packages/pdf/politics/20060127_poll_results.pdf). For a discussion of what money does and does not buy in politics, see Richard L. Hasen, *Plutocrats United:Campaign Money, the Supreme Court, and the Distortion of American Politics* (New Haven: Yale University Press, 2016), chap. 2.
2. For the *New York Times*/CBS News poll, see https://s3.amazonaws.com/s3.documentcloud.org/documents/695362/april13-nytimes-cbs-poll.pdf, question 14. For the CBS News poll, see www.pollingreport.com/politics.htm.
3. Figures for House and Senate campaign expenditures in this and the next three paragraphs are from the Campaign Finance Institute, "House Campaign Expenditures: Major Party General Election Candidates, 1974–2014 (full cycle) Adjusted for Inflation, 2014 dollars" (www.cfinst.org/pdf/vital/VitalStats_t2c.pdf), and "Senate Campaign Expenditures: Major Party General Election Candidates, 1974–2014 (full cycle, net dollars) Adjusted for Inflation, 2014 mean net dollars" (www.cfinst.org/pdf/vital/VitalStats_t5C.pdf). Figures are for the full two-year election cycle and are given in 2014 dollars.
4. Ibid.
5. Campaign Finance Institute, "Non-Party Independent Expenditures in House and Senate Elections, 1978–2014" (www.cfinst.org/pdf/vital/VitalStats_t14c.pdf). Campaign Finance Institute, "Political Party Contributions, Coordinated and Independent Expenditures for Congressional Candidates, 1976–2014" (www.cfinst.org/pdf/vital/VitalStats_t12c.pdf).
6. Michael Cooper, "Rich Are Different: They Get Elected," *New York Times*, December 5, 2001 (www.nytimes.com/2001/12/05/nyregion/rich-are-different-they-get-elected.html); New York City Campaign Finance Board, "Follow the Money" (www.nyccfb.info/follow-the-money), Campaign Finance Summaries for 2001, 2005, and 2009; Jeanne Cummings, "Self-funders Strike Out Big Time," *Politico*, November 3, 2010 (www.politico.com/news/stories/1110/44677.html).

7. Figures for the funding sources of the 2012 presidential candidates are from the Center for Responsive Politics, www.opensecrets.org/pres12/.

8. Figures for PAC contributions to House and Senate candidates are from the Campaign Finance Institute, www.cfinst.org/pdf/vital/VitalStats_t8.pdf. These figures are for general election candidates only. On the sources of individual contributions, see Paul S. Herrnson, Kelly D. Patterson, and Stephanie Perry Curtis, "Financing the 2012 Congressional Elections," in David B. Magleby, ed., *Financing the 2012 Election* (Washington, DC: Brookings Institution Press, 2014), 163.

9. Figures for 2012 and 2014 donors are from the Center for Responsive Politics, www.opensecrets.org/bigpicture/donordemographics.php?cycle=2012&filter=A, and www.opensecrets.org/bigpicture/donordemographics.php?cycle=2014&filter=A. Figures are for contributions to candidates, parties, and PACs. For the relation between income and contributions, see Kay Lehman Schlozman, Sidney Verba, and Henry E. Brady, *The Unheavenly Chorus: Unequal Political Voice and the Broken Promise of American Democracy* (Princeton: Princeton University Press, 2012), 457–59.

10. Figures for party money are from the Campaign Finance Institute, www.cfinst.org/pdf/vital/VitalStats_t8.pdf. The figures are for general election candidates only. Party committees tend to stay out of primary elections because those are contests between members of the same party.

11. For party activity in the 2012 congressional elections, see Herrnson et al., "Financing the 2012 Elections," 148–54. For party activity in the 2012 presidential election, see Candice J. Nelson, "Financing the 2012 Presidential General Election," in David B. Magleby, ed., *Financing the 2012 Election* (Washington, DC: Brookings Institution Press, 2014), 125, 133–34.

12. For the 1971 FECA, see Jeffrey M. Berry and Jerry Goldman, "Congress and Public Policy: A Study of the Federal Election Campaign Act of 1971," *Harvard Journal of Legislation* 10 (1973): 331–65; and David W. Adamany and George E. Agree, *Political Money: A Strategy for Campaign Financing in America* (Baltimore: Johns Hopkins University Press, 1975), 89–91. For the law before the FECA, see Robert E. Mutch, *Campaigns, Congress, and Courts: The Making of Federal Campaign Finance Law* (New York: Praeger, 1988).

CHAPTER 2

1. See the Chronology for brief descriptions of the few campaign finance cases the Supreme Court heard before *Buckley*.

2. Except where otherwise noted, this account of Watergate was taken from Stanley Cutler, *The Wars of Watergate: The Last Crisis of Richard Nixon* (New York: W.W. Norton, 1990), which is generally regarded as the authoritative account; Keith W. Olson, *Watergate: The Presidential Scandal that Shook America* (Lawrence: University Press of Kansas, 2003), which has a chronology of events as an appendix; and the indispensable firsthand account, *All the President's Men* (New York: Simon and Schuster, 1974), by Carl Bernstein and Bob Woodward, the *Washington Post* reporters who broke the story.

3. The FBI began a serious investigation, but it was politically compromised within days of the arrests. John R. Ehrlichman, one of President Nixon's top aides, told acting FBI director L. Patrick Gray—who had been appointed to replace the recently deceased J. Edgar Hoover—to keep the White House fully informed of the Bureau's investigation. Gray did that and more. He allowed White House aides to sit in on interviews and gave them access to raw data even after learning that the White House had been involved in the very events the Bureau and the Senate Watergate Committee were investigating. Gray withdrew his name for consideration as FBI director when it came out during hearings that he had even destroyed evidence.

4. The FBI's discovery of the slush fund got the attention of the brand-new Office of Federal Elections (OFE), which had just been created in the General Accounting Office to monitor compliance with the FECA. The OFE investigated and concluded that the CRP might have committed as many as eleven violations of the new disclosure law. It did not have the authority to prosecute, so it sent a recommendation for legal action to the Department of Justice; the department ignored it. Bernard Gwertzman, "GAO Report Asks Justice Inquiry into GOP Funds," *New York Times*, August 27, 1972, 1.

5. For historical presidential election data, see The American Presidency project (www.presidency.ucsb.edu/elections.php).

6. Representative Ford (R-MI) was the House minority leader when Congress approved his appointment as vice president in December 1973. He was appointed to replace Vice President Spiro Agnew, who had resigned after pleading no contest to charges of taking bribes and evading taxes while he was governor of Maryland. The Twenty-fifth Amendment, passed after President John F. Kennedy's assassination, required the president to appoint a new vice president, whose nomination had to be approved by both houses of Congress (see www.archives.gov/education/lessons/ford-nixon-letter/). The same amendment required President Ford to appoint his own vice president, and he chose former New York Governor Nelson A. Rockefeller (www.senate.gov/artandhistory/history/common/generic/VP_Nelson_Rockefeller.htm).

7. For disclosure requirements, see the Federal Election Campaign Act of 1971, Sec. 304 and Sec. 309 (www.gpo.gov/fdsys/pkg/STATUTE-86/pdf/STATUTE-86-Pg3.pdf). For a brief description, see CQ Press, *Guide to Congress*, Seventh Edition (Thousand Oaks, CA: Sage Publications, 2013), 1063–64.

8. Robert E. Mutch, *Campaigns, Congress, and Courts: The Making of Federal Campaign Finance Law* (New York: Praeger, 1988), 45–46.

9. For Common Cause's suit, see Robert E. Mutch, *Buying the Vote: A History of Campaign Finance Reform* (New York: Oxford University Press, 2014), 133–34.

10. Herbert E. Alexander, *Financing the 1972 Election* (Lexington, MA: Lexington Books, 1976), 279, 280.

11. Common Cause got the information about constituent mail when it gained access to Congress's mailing records as part of a 1973 suit about the congressional frank (March 31, 1987, interview with Ken Guido).

12. The phrase "oversee and enforce" was in Senate Report 93-310, the Rules Committee report on S. 372, 2; the final vote is at *Congressional Record*, July 30, 1973, 26613.

13. The Senate passed the bill 60–16, the House by 365–24 (*Cong. Rec.* 120, part 26, Oct. 8, 1974, 34392, 35148–49 [93–2]).

14. For a summary of the 1974 amendments, see Anthony Corrado, Thomas E. Mann, Daniel R. Ortiz, Trevor Potter, and Frank J. Sorauf, *Campaign Finance Reform: A Sourcebook* (Washington, DC: Brookings Institution Press, 1997), 53–55.

15. The New York Conservative Party is one of several minor parties active in New York State. Like the Liberal Party, the Conservatives usually nominate someone who is also the nominee of either the Republican or Democratic Party. In the 1970 election, however, Buckley did not get a major party nomination and ran against a Democrat, a Republican-Liberal, and the candidates of three small left-wing parties.

16. The Secretary of the Senate and the Clerk of the House were defendants because the 1974 law made them *ex officio*, non-voting, members of the FEC. They kept those positions until 1993, when the federal circuit court for the District of Columbia ruled that Congress had violated the constitutional separation of powers by placing its agents in an independent agency (*FEC v. NRA Political Victory Fund*, 6 F.3d 821).

17. For President Ford's signing statement, see www.presidency.ucsb.edu/ws/?pid=4464.

18. April 22, 1987, interview with Robert H. Bork, who was solicitor general in the Nixon and Ford administrations.

19. *Buckley v. Valeo*, Brief of the Appellants, 39, 47.

20. Ibid., 41, 42.

21. Ibid., 55–67.

22. *Buckley v. Valeo*, 519 F.2d 821, paragraphs 7, 8, 9.

23. Ibid., paragraphs 9, 49.

24. Ibid., paragraph 225.

25. Ibid., paragraph 42.

26. *Buckley v. Valeo*, 424 U.S. 1, 20, 21.

27. Ibid., 26. In this instance, the Supreme Court agreed that a law serving a compelling public interest did justify an incidental infringement upon First Amendment rights.

28. Ibid., 39.

29. For independent expenditures before the FECA, see Mutch, *Buying the Vote*, 104–106.

30. *Buckley v. Valeo*, 424 U.S. 1, 47.

31. The court's list of "magic" words and phrases is at *Buckley v. Valeo*, 424 U.S. 1, 44 n52.

32. *Buckley v. Valeo*, 424 U.S. 1, Brief for Appellees Center for Public Financing . . ., 67–74; *Buckley v. Valeo*, 519 F.2d 821, paragraphs 18–26. The cost of presidential elections had in fact increased very much very quickly: the 1968 and 1972 campaigns were the most expensive in history at the time. Costs had been trending down since the previous high of $13 million in 1936, a trend that continued through the 1950s. The trendline began to go up again in the 1960s, and the $14.9 million spent in 1968 and the $19.4 million spent in 1972 (in 1936 dollars) set two consecutive new records. Louise Overacker, "Campaign Funds in the Presidential Election of 1936," *American Political Science Review*

31 (1937): 479; Herbert E. Alexander, *Financing the 1968 Election* (Lexington, MA: Heath Lexington, 1971), 117, 119; Alexander, *Financing the 1972 Election*, 294, 405, 406.

33. *Buckley v. Valeo*, 424 U.S. 1, 57.
34. Ibid., Brief for Appellees Center for the Public Financing of Elections, Common Cause, League of Women Voters et al., 81.
35. *Buckley v. Valeo*, 424 U.S. 1, 49–50.
36. *Buckley v. Valeo*, 424 U.S. 1, 27.
37. Ibid., 67.
38. *Buckley v. Valeo* oral argument transcript, 24.
39. Ibid., 262.
40. Ibid., 244; Blackmun's dissent is at 290.
41. Ibid., 264, 265.

CHAPTER 3

1. Herbert E. Alexander and Anthony Corrado, *Financing the 1992 Election* (Armonk, NY: M. E. Sharpe, 1995), 11.
2. *Wall Street Journal*, March 24, 1904, 1; House Committee on Election of President, Vice President, and Representatives in Congress hearing, *Contributions to Political Committees in Presidential and Other Campaigns*, March 12, 1906 (59–1), 40.
3. "Toward a More Responsible Two-Party System," *American Political Science Review* 44, no. 3, Part 2 (1950): 75.
4. United Press, "Bill Provides U.S. Funds for Politics," *Washington Post*, February 21, 1956, 1.
5. This section is based on Robert E. Mutch, *Campaigns, Congress, and Courts: The Making of Federal Campaign Finance Law* (New York: Praeger, 1988), 37–40.
6. This was the Revenue Act of 1971.
7. On the 1971 federal tax incentives, see David Rosenberg, *Broadening the Base: The Case for a New Federal Tax Credit for Political Contributions* (Washington, DC: American Enterprise Institute, 2002), 7–8 (http://classic.followthemoney.org/press/Reports/200201014.pdf); Thomas Cmar, *Toward a Small Donor Democracy: The Past and Future of Incentives for Small Political Contributions* (Washington, DC: U.S. PIRG Education Fund, 2004), 12–20 (www.uspirg.org/sites/pirg/files/reports/Toward_A_Small_Donor_Democracy_USPIRG.pdf).
8. Joint Committee on Taxation, *General Explanation of the Tax Reform Act of 1986* (Washington, DC: Government Printing Office, 1987), 88 (https://archive.org/stream/generalexplanati00jcs1087/generalexplanati00jcs1087_djvu.txt).
9. The Miller Center has the text and a recording of Roosevelt's speech, http://millercenter.org/president/fdroosevelt/speeches/speech-3305.
10. Louise Overacker, "Campaign Funds in the Presidential Election of 1936," *American Political Science Review* 31, no. 3 (1937): 479–80; "Convention Book Lauds Roosevelt," *New York Times*, June 21, 1936, 29.
11. C. P. Trussell, "To Probe Ads in Book Issued by Democrats," *Baltimore Sun*, October 23, 1936, 2; Alexander Heard, *The Costs of Democracy* (Chapel Hill: University of North Carolina Press, 1960), 249.

12. Herbert E. Alexander, *Financing the 1964 Election* (Princeton: Citizens' Research Foundation, 1966), 39–41, 99–100.

13. Herbert E. Alexander and Brian A. Haggerty, *Financing the 1984 Election* (Lexington, MA: Lexington Books, 1987), 290; Campaign Finance Institute, *How to Revive and Improve Public Funding for Presidential Nomination Politics* (Washington, DC: 2003), 67–68.

14. Alexander and Haggerty, *Financing the 1984 Election*, 291–94; Alexander and Corrado, *Financing the 1992 Election*, 100, 105–106; John C. Green and Diana Kingsbury, "Financing the 2008 Presidential Nomination Campaigns," in David B. Magleby and Anthony Corrado, eds., *Financing the 2008 Election* (Washington, DC: Brookings Institution Press, 2011), 118–19. The share paid by private donors dropped to 73 percent in 2012 because a supplemental federal grant for security reduced the need for more private money. See John C. Green, Michael E. Kohler, and Ian P. Schwarber, "Financing the Presidential Nomination Campaigns," in David B. Magleby, ed., *Financing the 2012 Election* (Washington, DC: Brookings Institution Press, 2014), 111.

15. Ben Pershing, "House Votes to End Public Funding for Presidential Campaigns," *Washington Post*, December 1, 2011 (www.washingtonpost.com/blogs/2chambers/post/house-votes-to-end-public-funding-for-presidential-campaigns/2011/12/01/gIQAc8SaHO_blog.html); Matt Fuller, "Cantor's Pediatric Research Bill Has Democrats Fuming," *Roll Call*, December 10, 2013 (http://blogs.rollcall.com/218/the-surprise-bill-that-has-democrats-and-republicans-at-each-others-throats/?dcz=); Associated Press, "Senate Sends Obama Childhood Cancer Research Bill," *New York Times*, March 11, 2014 (www.nytimes.com/aponline/2014/03/11/us/politics/ap-us-congress-pediatric-research.html).

16. Kenneth P. Vogel, "The Man Behind the Political Cash Grab," *Politico*, December 12, 2014 (www.politico.com/story/2014/12/democratic-lawyer-crafted-campaign-finance-deal-113549). The spending bill was called "Cromnibus" because it combined a short-term spending bill for Homeland Security, called a "continuing resolution," with the usual omnibus bill for the federal government budget.

17. The problem for a new party is that "money that arrives in December doesn't buy much television time in October." Steven J. Rosenstone, *Third Parties in America: Citizen Response to Major Party Failure*, 2nd ed. (Princeton: Princeton University Press, 1996), 272.

18. For a detailed account of the arguments about Anderson's eligibility see Mutch, *Campaigns*, 145–49.

19. Alexander and Corrado, *Financing the 1992 Election*, 128, 130; Rosenstone, *Third Parties*, 231. It cost Perot almost seven times as much money to get those votes: in 1992 dollars, Roosevelt's campaign would have cost about $10 million. For Roosevelt's campaign receipts, see Louise Overacker, *Money in Elections* (New York: Macmillan, 1932), 143–44.

20. For Perot's 1996 campaign, see Alexander and Corrado, *Financing the 1992 Election*, 134; Rosenstone, *Third Parties*, 271; Herbert E. Alexander, "Spending in the 1996 Elections," in John C. Green, ed., *Financing the 1996 Election* (Armonk, NY: M.E. Sharpe, 1999), 21–22; Joe Wesley and Clyde Wilcox, "Financing the 1996 Presidential Nominations," in John C. Green,

ed., *Financing the 1996 Election* (Armonk, NY: M.E. Sharpe, 1999), 57–58; Anthony Corrado, "Financing the 1996 Presidential General Election," in John C. Green, ed., *Financing the 1996 Election* (Armonk, NY: M.E. Sharpe, 1999), 67–68.

21. Candice J. Nelson, "Spending in the 2000 Elections," in David B. Magleby, ed., *Financing the 2000 Election* (Washington, DC: Brookings Institution Press, 2002), 28.

22. Alexander and Corrado, *Financing the 1992 Election*, 11–12; Ruth S. Jones and Warren Miller, "Financing Campaigns," *Western Political Quarterly* 38 (1985): 195–97.

23. Campaign Finance Institute, *How to Revive and Improve Public Funding*, 106.

24. Federal Election Commission, "Presidential Fund Income Tax Checkoff Chart" (www.fec.gov/press/bkgnd/presidential_fund.shtml).

25. Ibid.

26. Ibid.

27. The other three candidates were Senator Henry Jackson of Washington, a dark-horse candidate who was well respected but lacked the prominence needed for a serious national campaign; and Rep. Shirley Chisholm of New York (the first African-American woman to be elected to Congress); and Rep. Wilbur Mills of Arkansas, who weren't even dark horses. For the 1972 campaign, see Hunter S. Thompson, *Fear and Loathing on the Campaign Trail '72* (San Francisco: Straight Arrow Books, 1973).

28. For the public funds received by 1976 Democratic primary candidates, see the FEC's chart at www.fec.gov/press/bkgnd/AllPublicFunds.xls.

29. Herbert E. Alexander, *Financing the 1980 Election* (Lexington, MA: Lexington Books, 1983), 163. For the public funds Reagan received in 1976 and 1980, see the FEC's chart at www.fec.gov/press/bkgnd/AllPublicFunds.xls.
Public funding was not the only factor increasing the number of candidates. Another factor was the parties' decision to nominate presidential candidates in primaries. Increasing the number and importance of presidential primaries changed nomination politics by making individual campaign organizations more important than the strength of candidates' relationships inside the party organizations. It is difficult to disentangle the effects of the two factors. For an early analysis of the change in nomination politics, see Byron E. Shafer, *Bifurcated Politics: Evolution and Reform in the National Party Convention* (New York: Russell Sage Foundation, 1988), esp. chap. 3.

30. Jonathan Van Fleet, "Lawrence Lessig Compares the Number of Fundraisers Between Presidents Reagan and Obama," *PolitiFact New Hampshire*, January 20, 2015 (www.politifact.com/new-hampshire/statements/2015/jan/20/lawrence-lessig/lawrence-lessig-compares-number-fundraisers-betwee/).

31. Stephen R. Weissman and Ruth A. Hassan, *Public Opinion Polls Concerning Public Financing of Federal Elections, 1972–2000* (Washington, DC: Campaign Finance Institute, 2005), 16 (www.cfinst.org/president/pdf/PublicFunding_Surveys.pdf); Mutch, *Campaigns*, 134.

32. Herbert E. Alexander, "Spending in the 1996 Elections," in John C. Green, ed., *Financing the 1996 Election* (Armonk, NY: M.E. Sharpe, 1999), 33–34.

33. Weissman and Hassan, *Public Opinion Polls*, 13, 25.

34. David W. Moore, "Public Dissatisfied with Campaign Finance Laws, Supports Limits on Contributions," Gallup News Service, August 3, 2001; Weissman and Hassan, *Public Opinion Polls*, 3.

35. Lydia Saad, "Americans Prefer Presidential Candidates to Forgo Public Funding," Gallup News Service, April 27, 2007 (www.gallup.com/poll/27394/Americans-Prefer-Presidential-Candidates-Forgo-Public-Funding.aspx?utm_source=); Lydia Saad, "Half in U.S. Support Publicly Financed Federal Campaigns," *Gallup News Service*, June 24, 2013 (www.gallup.com/poll/163208/half-support-publicly-financed-federal-campaigns.aspx). There were partisan and regional differences in the responses: 60 percent of Democrats said they would vote for it, compared to only 41 percent of Republicans; and only 42 percent of Southern respondents said they would vote for it.

36. For a list of state tax incentives as of 2013, see Vermont Legislature, "Tax refunds, credits and deductions for political contributions," December 2012 (http://legislature.vermont.gov/assets/Documents/2016/WorkGroups/House%20Government%20Operations/Bills/H.21/H.21~Rep.%20Maida%20Townsend~Credits,%20refunds%20poslital%20contributions~3-18-2015.pdf).

37. Minnesota Senate, "Minnesota's Campaign Finance Law" (www.senate.leg.state.mn.us/departments/scr/treatise/campfin.htm#_1_3).

38. Campaign Finance Institute press release, "Minnesota's $50 Political Contribution Refunds Ended on July 1," July 8, 2009 (www.cfinst.org/press/PReleases/09-07-08/CFI_s_Comments_on_Minnesota_s_50_Political_Contribution_Refunds.aspx).

39. Ibid.; Cynthia Dizikes, "Land of 10,000 small donors," *Minneapolis Post*, July 9, 2009 (www.minnpost.com/politics-policy/2009/07/land-10000-small-donors-minnesota-leads-modest-campaign-contributions); Rachel E. Stassen-Berger, "Hot Dish Politics: Political Refund Program Returns," *Minneapolis StarTribune*, July 27, 2013 (www.startribune.com/hot-dish-politics-political-refund-program-returns/217250571/); Heather J. Carlson, "Drazkowski Leads Charge to Get Rid of Campaign Refund Program," *Rochester Post-Bulletin*, May 11, 2015 (www.postbulletin.com/news/politics/drazkowski-leads-charge-to-get-rid-of-campaign-refund-program/article_5cc8652b-b96f-586f-97e2-954e71cd2052.html); "Legislative Roundup," May 19, 2015 (http://www.twincities.com/politics/ci_28142920/legislature-roundup-buffer-strips-transportation-public-safety-and).

40. See Michael G. Miller, *Subsidizing Democracy: How Public Funding Changes Elections and How It Can Work in the Future* (Ithaca, NY: Cornell University Press, 2013), 8–15, for an excellent introduction to state public funding programs. Much of this and following sections on those state programs was based on Miller's book.

41. *Arizona Free Enterprise Club v. Bennett*, 131 S.Ct. 2806 (2011), 2818.

42. Howard Fischer, "Lawmakers Reject Election Changes, Alter Speed Limit," *Arizona Daily Star*, April 3, 2015 (http://tucson.com/news/local/govt-and-politics/lawmakers-reject-election-changes-alter-speed-limit/article_6ffb4569-2a0b-55a4-9e8e-db26bfd50a1e.html); Susan Haigh, "Election Reform Advocates Blast Plan to Halt Public Money," *Connecticut Post*,

November 17, 2015 (www.ctpost.com/news/article/Election-reform-advocates-blast-proposal-to-halt-6638298.php); "Maine 'Clean Elections' Initiative, Question 1 (2015)," *Ballotpedia* (https://ballotpedia.org/Maine_%22Clean_Elections%22_Initiative,_Question_1_(2015).

43. For a quick overview of state programs, see National Conference of State Legislatures, "State Public Financing Options, 2015-2016 Election Cycle" (www.ncsl.org/Portals/1/documents/legismgt/elect/StatePublicFinancing OptionsChart2015.pdf).

44. Steven M. Levin, *Public Campaign Financing in Wisconsin Showing Its Age* (Los Angeles: Center for Governmental Studies, 2008) www.policyarchive.org/collections/cgs/index?section=5&id=8788; Miller, *Subsidizing Democracy*, 22–23. There was about $2 million left in the program's fund when it was repealed, which the legislature used to help finance its new voter ID law. See Dena Braun, "JFC Votes to Eliminate Public Financing of Campaigns," *Mediatrackers*, May 25, 2011 (http://mediatrackers.org/wisconsin/2011/05/25/jfc-votes-to-eliminate-public-financing-of-campaigns).

45. Herbert E. Alexander, Lori Cox Han, Nina Weiler, and Jeff Whitten, *Public Financing of Local Elections* (Los Angeles: Citizens Research Foundation, 1999), 11–25, 43–63 (http://cfinst.org/pdf/HEA/001_publicfinancingoflocal.pdf); J. B. Wogan, "Seattle Voters Reject Public Financing of Council Elections," *Governing*, November 26, 2013 (http://cfinst.org/pdf/HEA/001_publicfinancingoflocal.pdf).

46. Bob Young, "'Democracy Vouchers' Win in Seattle; First in Country," *Seattle Times*, November 4, 2015 (www.seattletimes.com/seattle-news/politics/democracy-vouchers/).

47. Molly Milligan, *Public Campaign Financing in Albuquerque* (Los Angeles: Center for Governmental Studies, 2011), www.policyarchive.org/collections/cgs/index?section=5&id=96100; New Mexico State legislature, 2003 House Bill 0420 (www.nmlegis.gov/Sessions/03%20Regular/FinalVersions/house/HB0420.pdf); City of Tucson, "Campaign Finance Administration Rules and Regulations," October 2014 (www.tucsonaz.gov/files/clerks/Rules_Regs_2014.pdf); *Public Campaign Financing in Portland: Should "Voter-Owned Elections" Survive?* (Los Angeles: Center for Governmental Studies, 2011) www.policyarchive.org/collections/cgs/index?section=5&id=95885; Brad Schmidt, "City Hall: Portland's Publicly Funded Campaign System Ends Without Reaching Aspirations," *The Oregonian*, November 3, 2010 (www.oregonlive.com/portland/index.ssf/2010/11/city_hall_portlands_publicly_f.hml).

48. Alexander et al., *Public Financing of Local Elections*, 27–42.

49. For a history and description of New York's program, see Angela Migally and Susan Liss, *Small Donor Matching Funds: The NYC Election Experience* (New York: Brennan Center for Justice, 2010), www.brennancenter.org/sites/default/files/legacy/Small%20Donor%20Matching%20Funds-The%20 NYC%20Election%20Experience.pdf.

50. See Elizabeth Genn, Sundeep Iyer, Michael J. Malbin, and Brendan Glavin, *Donor Diversity Through Public Matching Funds* (**New York**: Brennan Center for Justice and Campaign Finance Institute, 2012).

51. NYC Campaign Finance Board, *2013 Post-Election Report* (2014), 7 www.nyc-cfb.info/PDF/per/2013_PER/2013_PER.pdf.

52. NYC Campaign Finance Board, Campaign Finance Summary, 2001, 2005, 2009 Citywide Elections (www.nyccfb.info/VSApps/WebForm_Finance_Summary.aspx?as_election_cycle=2013&sm=press_12&sm=press_12).   For vote totals in the 2001, 2005, and 2009 general elections, see Board of Elections in the City of New York, Election Results Summary (http://vote.nyc.ny.us/html/results/results.shtml). The Campaign Finance Board does not list Bloomberg as a candidate in 2001, but the amount he spent on his campaign that year was reported in Michael Cooper, "Rich Are Different: They Get Elected," *New York Times*, December 5, 2001 (www.nytimes.com/2001/12/05/nyregion/rich-are-different-they-get-elected.html).

53. Anthony Corrado, *Paying for Presidents* (New York: Twentieth Century Fund, 1993), 19–25; Federal Elections Commission, "Presidential Fund Income Tax Checkoff Status, 1992-2013" (www.fec.gov/press/bkgnd/pres_cf/PresidentialFundStatus_September2012.pdf); Paul Houston, Norman Kempster, and Greg Miller, "Checkoff Change," *Los Angeles Times*, August 30, 1993 (http://articles.latimes.com/1993-08-30/news/mn-29440_1_federal-lection-commission).

54. Jacob S. Hacker and Paul Pierson, "After the 'Master Theory': Downs, Schattschneider, and the Return of Policy-Focused Analysis" (www.maxpo.eu/Downloads/Paper_Pierson.pdf), 22.

55. For independent expenditures in 1980s presidential campaigns see Alexander, *Financing the 1980 Election*, 141–42, 302–303, 328; Alexander and Haggerty, *Financing the 1984 Election*, 186, 358–59; Herbert E. Alexander and Monica Bauer, *Financing the 1988 Election* (Boulder, CO: Westview Press, 1991), 85. For the 1996 and 200 elections, see Corrado, "Financing the 1996 Presidential General Election," 92–93; Nelson, "Spending in the 2000 Elections," 44.

56. John C. Green and Nathan Bigelow, "The 2000 Presidential Nominations: The Costs of Innovation," in David B. Magleby, ed., *Financing the 2000 Election* Washington, DC: Brookings Institution Press, 2002), 58–61, 70.

57. John C. Green, "Financing the 2004 Presidential Nominating Campaigns," in David B. Magleby, Anthony Corrado, and Kelly D. Patterson, eds., *Financing the 2004 Election* (Washington, DC: Brookings Institution Press, 2006), 103–106.

58. Anthony Corrado, "Financing the 2008 Presidential General Election," in David B. Magleby and Anthony Corrado, eds., *Financing the 2008 Election* (Washington, DC: Brookings Institution Press, 2011), 130; David B. Magleby, "The 2012 Election as a Team Sport," in David B. Magleby, ed., *Financing the 2012 Election* (Washington, DC: Brookings Institution Press, 2014), 3–4.

CHAPTER 4

1. Perry Belmont, "Publicity of Election Expenses," *North American Review*, February 1905, 185.

2. *Wall Street Journal*, November 25, 1908, 1. For a detailed account of how the first disclosure law was passed, see Robert E. Mutch, *Buying the Vote: A History of Campaign Finance Reform* (New York: Oxford University Press, 2014), 58–75.

3. Committees with more than $50,000 in contributions or expenditures must file electronically, using software supplied free of charge by the FEC. Reports

filed electronically are available online almost as soon as they are received, and the information in them is automatically entered into the FEC's database. Smaller committees can submit paper reports. IT staff must manually enter information from paper reports into the database, but scanned copies of those reports must be made publicly available within forty-eight hours of receipt. Federal Election Commission, "Thirty-Year Report," September 2005, 10–12 (www.fec.gov/info/publications/30year.pdf); Federal Election Commission, "Office of Compliance Overview—Enforcement Hearing January 2, 2009," 1–3 (www.fec.gov/em/enfpro/complistatsfy05-08.pdf).

4. The next two tables are based on data from the Center for Responsive Politics, "2012 Presidential Race" (www.opensecrets.org/pres12/).

5. Committee on Election of President, Vice President and Representatives in Congress, *Hearing to Provide Additional Publicity for Campaign Contributions*, February 21, 1924 (68–1), 12. Senate candidates filed their reports with the Secretary of the Senate after the Seventeenth Amendment, which was added to the Constitution in 1913, required all senators to be chosen by popular vote. Presidential candidates had to file with the Clerk of the House, which they continued to do through 1968.

6. For a brief description of the 1971 FECA, see Anthony Corrado et al., *Campaign Finance Reform: A Sourcebook* (Washington, DC: Brookings Institution, 1997), 52.

7. Alexander Heard, *The Costs of Democracy* (Chapel Hill: University of North Carolina Press, 1960), 465. For early proposals to create an independent agency, see Robert E. Mutch, *Campaigns, Congress, and Courts: The Making of Federal Campaign Finance Law* (New York: Praeger, 1988), 40–42. The addition of the comptroller general was a compromise between Republicans and Democrats. Republicans wanted to take enforcement authority away from the Clerk and the Secretary, who reported to the majority Democrats, and give it to an independent agency. Democrats preferred to keep it in the hands of their own employees. The compromise was arranged by Rep. Wayne Hays (D-OH), a vocal opponent of reform, so it cannot be seen as an attempt to strengthen the law.

8. *Buckley v. Valeo*, 519 F.2d 821, 197, 211.

9. *Buckley v. Valeo*, 424. U.S. 1, 138.

10. Michael M. Franz, "The Devil We Know? Evaluating the Federal Election Commission as Enforcer," *Election Law Journal* 8, no. 3 (2009): 170–71 (www.bowdoin.edu/~mfranz/Franz_ELJ09_ILL.pdf). There have been exceptions. Ann Ravel, who was appointed to the FEC in 2013, was nominated by President Obama, not by Congress.

11. For agency capture, see Malcolm K. Sparrow, *The Regulatory Craft: Controlling Risks, Solving Problems, and Managing Compliance* (Washington, DC: Brookings Institution, 2000), 34–37.

12. Bradley A. Smith and Stephen M. Hoersting, "A Toothless Anaconda: Innovation, Impotence, and Overenforcement at the federal Election Commission," *Election Law Journal* 1, no. 2 (2002)" 160–61; Franz, "The Devil We Know?" 170.

13. Jennifer Hedwig and Katherine Shaw, "Through a Glass, Darkly: The Rhetoric and Reality of Campaign Finance Disclosure," *Georgetown Law*

Journal 102 (2014): 1484 (http://georgetownlawjournal.org/files/2014/06/HeerwigShaw-Through.pdf).

14. See FEC, *Campaign Guide for Congressional Candidates and Committees* (2014), 63, 74, 76–77 (www.fec.gov/pdf/candgui.pdf).

15. Matea Gold, "The FEC Just Made It Easier for Super PAC Donors to Hide Their Identities,: *Washington Post*, March 7, 2016 (https://www.washington-post.com/news/post-politics/wp/2016/03/07/the-fec-just-made-it-easier-for-super-pac-donors-to-hide-their-identities/).

16. For FEC enforcement procedures, see Federal Election Commission, *OGC Enforcement Manual*, June 2013 (www.fec.gov/agenda/2013/mtgdoc_13-21-b.pdf), and Federal Election Commission, *Guidebook for Complainants and Respondents on the FEC Enforcement Process*, May 2012 (www.fec.gov/em/respondent_guide.pdf).

17. Scott E. Thomas and Jeffrey H. Bowman, "Obstacles to Effective Enforcement of the Federal Election Campaign Act," *Administrative Law Review* 52, no. 2 (2000): 607 (www.fec.gov/members/former_members/thomas/thomasar-ticle1.htm); Franz, "The Devil We Know?" 186.

18. Bradley A. Smith, "Why Campaign Finance Reform Never Works," *Wall Street Journal*, March 19, 1997; Walter Pincus, "Lott and McConnell Also Have Holds on Holbrooke: Appointment to Election Panel at Stake," *Washington Post*, July 7, 1999, A4.

19. Helen Dewar, "Senate Agrees to End Impasse on Nominees; Deal Clears Way for Judges, Many Others," *Washington Post*, May 24, 2000, A35.

20. "President Bush at Recess," *New York Times*, January 9, 2006 (www.nytimes.com/2006/01/09/opinion/09mon1.html?_r=0).

21. Michael A. Fletcher, "Will the Different Voices make a Difference?" *Washington Post*, June 18, 2007 (www.washingtonpost.com/wp-dyn/content/article/2007/06/17/AR2007061701083.html); Matthew Mosk, "No Quorum on Election Board as Nominees Stall in Congress," *Washington Post*, December 22, 2007 (www.washingtonpost.com/wp-dyn/content/article/2007/12/21/AR2007122102299.html); Associated Press, "Nominee for FEC Withdraws," *New York Times*, May 17, 2008 (www.nytimes.com/2008/05/17/washing-ton/17fec.html?_r=0).

22. Eric Lichtblau, "FEC Can't Curb Election Abuse, Commission Chief Says," *New York Times*, May 2, 2015 (www.nytimes.com/2015/05/03/us/politics/fec-cant-curb-2016-election-abuse-commission-chief-says.html).

23. Matthew S. Petersen, Caroline C. Hunter, and Lee E. Goodman, "Dissension at the Federal Election Commission," *New York Times*, May 8, 2015 (www.nytimes.com/2015/05/08/opinion/dissension-at-the-federal-election-commission.html).

24. Franz, "The Devil We Know?" 167–87, 176.

25. Michael M. Franz, "The Federal Election Commission as Regulator: The Changing Evaluations of Advisory Opinions," *U.C. Irvine Law Review* 3, no. 735 (2013): 750, 755, 762; Public Citizen press release, "Roiled in Partisan Deadlock, Federal Election Commission Is Failing," January 2013 (www.cit-izen.org/documents/fec-deadlock-statement-and-chart-january-2013.pdf); R. Sam Garrett, "Deadlocked Votes Among Members of the Federal Election Commission (FEC): Overview and Potential Considerations for Congress,"

Congressional Research Service, August 26, 2009 (www.bradblog.com/wp-content/uploads/CRS_FEC_Deadlocks.pdf); Franz, "Federal Election Commission as Regulator," 757.

26. *Citizens United v. FEC*, 130 S. Ct. 876 (2010), 895, 896.
27. *Buckley v. Valeo*, 424 U.S. 1 (1976), Brief of the Appellants, 171.
28. *Buckley v. Valeo*, 424 U.S. 1 (1976), Brief of the Appellants, 187–88.
29. Ibid., 173.
30. Raymond J. La Raja, "Political Participation and Civic Courage: The Negative Effect of Transparency on Making Campaign Contributions," 19 (http://papers.ssrn.com/sol3/papers.cfm?abstract_id=2202405).
31. Dick M. Carpenter II, David M. Primo, Pavel Tendetnik, and Sandy Ho, "Campaign Finance Disclosure Has Costs," *Roll Call*, November 26, 2012 (www.rollcall.com/news/carpenter_primo_tendetnik_and_ho_campaign_finance_disclosure_has_costs-219370-1.html?pg=1&dczone=opinion).
32. Dan Eggen, "To Shield Donors, Chamber Gets More Political," *Washington Post*, May 31, 2012, A13.
33. "Liberals vs. the IRS: Even the left doesn't want the tax man regulating speech," *Wall Street Journal*, February 24, 2014. The "left" referred to was the ACLU, which came out against the disclosure bill. See also Bradley A. Smith, "Connecting the Dots in the IRS Scandal," *Wall Street Journal*, February 27, 2014.
34. Daniel Fisher, "Inside the Koch Empire: How the Brothers Plan to Reshape America," *Forbes*, December 24, 2012 (www.forbes.com/sites/danielfisher/2012/12/05/inside-the-koch-empire-how-the-brothers-plan-to-reshape-america/).

CHAPTER 5

1. For a detailed account of the rise of labor and corporate PACs, see Robert E. Mutch, *Campaigns, Congress, and Courts: The Making of Federal Campaign Finance Law* (New York: Praeger, 1988), 152–74.
2. Formally called the War Labor Disputes Act, the law is known as Smith-Connally after its sponsors, Rep. Howard Smith (D-VA) and Senator Tom Connally (D-TX). See Raymond J. La Raja, *Small Change: Money, Political Parties, and Campaign Finance Reform* (Ann Arbor: University of Michigan Press, 2008), 63–64.
3. Formally called the Labor-Management Relations Act, the law is known as Taft-Hartley after its sponsors, Senator Robert A. Taft (R-OH) and Fred A. Hartley Jr. (R-NJ).
4. For an excellent account of such programs just before the 1971 FECA took effect, see Walter Pincus, "Silent Spenders in Politics—They Really Give at the Office," *New York Magazine*, January 31, 1972, 37–45.
5. On the double-envelope method, see Larry J. Sabato, *PAC Power: Inside the World of Political Action Committees* (New York: W.W. Norton, 1984), 6–7. On the IRS prosecutions, see Morton Mintz, "Contributions Crackdown," *Washington Post*, June 28, 1970, G1.
6. On the early corporate PACs, see Edward Handler and John R. Muller, *Business in Politics: Campaign Strategies of Corporate Political Action Committees* (Lexington, MA: D.C. Heath, 1982).

7. Bernadette A. Budde, "The Practical Role of Corporate PACs in the Political Process," *Arizona Law Review* 22, no. 2 (1980): 558.

8. Anthony Corrado, "Money and Politics: A History of Federal Campaign Finance Law," in Anthony Corrado et al., ed., *The New Campaign Finance Sourcebook* (Washington, DC: Brookings Institution, 2005), 31.

9. For the figures in this paragraph, see Herbert E. Alexander and Brian A. Haggerty, *Financing the 1984 Election* (Lexington, MA: Lexington Books, 1987), 109 and 111.

10. Sabato, *PAC Power,* 161–63. Polls conducted by pro-business groups, however, tended to produce different results. And more detailed surveys revealed that while large majorities of respondents saw big corporate and labor PACs as a bad influence, smaller majorities thought the opposite about environmental and women's PACs.

11. Martin Schram, "Askew to Reject Funds From PACs," *Washington Post,* February 10, 1983; Alexander and Haggerty, *Financing the 1984 Election,* 269–70.

12. Bernard Weinraub, "Mondale Directs Disputed Groups to End Operation," *New York Times,* April 26, 1984 (www.nytimes.com/1984/04/26/us/mondale-directs-disputed-groups-to-end-operation.html).

13. Dan Balz, "Clinton, Tsongas, Wilder Spar on New Hampshire TV," *Washington Post,* November 2, 1991 (www.washingtonpost.com/archive/politics/1991/11/02/clinton-tsongas-wilder-spar-on-new-hampshire-tv/d344e478-2e35-4834-85df-752dc488abfc/); Jeffrey Birnbaum, "A Tax Break for Legislators, Whether 'On the Job' or 'Working.'" *Washington Post,* November 6, 2007 (www.washingtonpost.com/wp-dyn/content/article/2007/11/05/AR2007110501588.html).

14. Quoted in Sabato, *PAC Power,* 101.

15. *Pipefitters v. United States,* 407 U.S. 385 (1972), 386.

16. Campaign Finance Institute, "How PACs Distributed Their Contributions to Congressional Candidates" (www.cfinst.org/pdf/vital/VitalStats_t11.pdf).

17. Federal Election Commission, "Summary of PAC Activity 1990–2010," www.fec.gov/press/bkgnd/cf_summary_info/2010pac_fullsum/4sumhistory2010.pdf; Center for Responsive Politics, "Labor Sector: PAC Contributions to Federal Candidates" (www.opensecrets.org/pacs/sector.php?txt=P01&cycle=2014); David B. Magleby and Anthony Corrado, eds., *Financing the 2008 Election* (Washington, DC: Brookings Institution Press, 2011), 147. (Independent spending in the 2012 election was dominated by Super PACs.)

18. For a brief explanation of these PAC strategies, see David B. Magleby, ed., *Financing the 2012 Election* (Washington, DC: Brookings Institution Press, 2014), 156–57 (www.opensecrets.org/pacs/lookup2.php?cycle=2012&strID=C00457291).

19. Federal Election Commission press release, "Top 50 Non-Connected PACs by Receipts January 1, 2015–June 30, 2015," www.fec.gov/press/summaries/2016/tables/pac/PAC7a_2015_6m.pdf.

20. Center for Responsive Politics, "MoveOn.org" (www.opensecrets.org/pacs/lookup2.php?strID=C00341396&cycle=2012); "Tea Party Express/Our Country Deserves" (www.opensecrets.org/outsidespending/detail.php?cmte=C00454074&cycle=2012).

21. Center for Responsive Politics, "Democracy for America" (www.opense-crets.org/pacs/lookup2.php?cycle=201210&strID=C00370007); Center for Responsive Politics, "Conservative StrikeForce" (www.opensecrets.org/pacs/lookup2.php?cycle=2012&strID=C00457291).

22. On leadership PACs generally, see Ross K. Baker, *The New Fat Cats: Members of Congress as Political Benefactors* (New York: Twentieth Century Fund, 1989).

23. Richard L. Berke, "Incumbents Turn to Personal PACs," *New York Times*, June 16, 1989 (www.nytimes.com/1989/06/16/us/incumbents-turn- to-personal-pac-s.html).

24. Marcus Stern and Jennifer LaFleur, "Leadership PACs Provide a Ticket to Luxury Lawmaking," *Washington Post*, September 27, 2009 (www.washing-tonpost.com/wp-dyn/content/article/2009/09/26/AR2009092602083.html).

25. See, for example, David S. Broder, "Campaign Finance Flimflam," *Washington Post*, December 5, 1993, C7.

26. Gerald F. Seib, "GOP Presidential Hopefuls Use Leadership PACs to Get Early Start Without Tossing Hats in Ring," *Wall Street Journal*, April 5, 1994, A20; Mary Jacoby, "Where Dole Got His Boost: PAC He Set Up to Aid GOP Candidates May Have Skirted Rules," *Baltimore Sun*, December 17, 1995 (http://articles.baltimoresun.com/1995-12-17/news/1995351011_1_campaign-america-des-moines-convention-straw-poll).

27. Center for Responsive Politics, "Hope Fund" (http://www.opensecrets.org/pacs/lookup2.php?strID=C00409052&cycle=2008), "HillPAC" (http://www.opensecrets.org/pacs/lookup2.php?strID=C00363994&cycle=2008); Alex Seitz-Wald, "Mitt Romney's Money Man," *Salon*, June 21, 2012 (www.salon.com/2012/06/21/mitt_romneys_money_man/).

CHAPTER 6

1. *SpeechNow v. FEC*, 599 F.3d 686 (2010). The case was brought by SpeechNow, a PAC created to make only independent expenditures. The PAC might have been created primarily to bring the case, as it made few independent expenditures. It spent $135,000 against Senator Russ Feingold (D-WI) in 2010, but has raised and spent nothing since then. Center for Responsive Politics, "SpeechNow.org," www.opensecrets.org/pacs/lookup2.php?strID=C00488783.

2. The same argument SpeechNow made in 2010 had been made thirty years ear-lier by the National Conservative Political Action Committee (NCPAC), one of the first independent spending groups. NCPAC lost its case in 1980, but the same argument won in the very different political climate of 2010. For a brief account of the 1980 case, see Robert E. Mutch, *Buying the Vote: A History of Campaign Finance Reform* (New York: Oxford University Press, 2014), 285, 305.

3. The FEC made its announcement in two advisory opinions: AO 2010-09, to the Club for Growth (saos.fec.gov/aodocs/AO%202010-09.pdf), and AO 2010–11, to a super PAC created to support Democratic congressional candi-dates. (saos.fec.gov/aodocs/AO%202010-11.pdf).

4. Federal Election Commission press release, "PAC Table 3a: Independent Expenditure-Only Committees Campaign Activity from January 1, 2011–December 31, 2012" (http://www.fec.gov/press/summaries/2012/tables/pac/PAC3a_2012_24m.pdf).

5. Kenneth P. Vogel, *Big Money: 2.5 Billion Dollars, One Suspicious Vehicle, and a Pimp—on the Trail of the Ultra-Rich Hijacking American Politics* (New York: Public Affairs, 2014), 34–35, 47–52; Thomas Catan and Brody Mullins, "Karl Rove–Backed Groups Raised $325 Million in 2012 Cycle," *Wall Street Journal*, November 14, 2013 (http://blogs.wsj.com/washwire/2013/11/14/karl-rove-backed-groups-raised-325-million-in-2012-cycle/?dsk=y).

6. Center for Responsive Politics, "National Defense PAC" (www.opensecrets.org/pacs/lookup2.php?strID=C00359992&cycle=2014).

7. Federal Election Commission, "*Carey v. FEC* Case Summary" (www.fec.gov/law/litigation/carey.shtml#dc). *Carey* PAC is another name for a hybrid PAC.

8. Which does not mean there has been no attempt at all. See the FEC's case summary for *Stop This Insanity Inc. v. FEC*. (www.fec.gov/law/litigation/StopthisInsanity.shtml).

9. *Investigation of Presidential, Vice Presidential, and Senatorial Campaign Expenditures, 1944*, Senate Report 101 (79–1), 6.

10. Ibid., 8.

11. *Federal Election Reform*, Hearings before the Senate Rules and Administration Committee June 28, 1967 (90–1), 13.

12. Public Law 94–283, Section 104(c)(3), www.govtrack.us/congress/bills/94/s3065/text.

13. 52 USC Sec. 30125(a)1 and (e)1 (http://uscode.house.gov/browse/prelim@title52/subtitle3/chapter301/subchapter1&edition=prelim).

14. Melanie Mason, "New GOP 'Super PAC' Tests Limits of Campaign Finance Laws," *Los Angeles Times*, May 17, 2011 (http://articles.latimes.com/2011/may/17/news/la-pn-gop-super-pac-20110517); Dan Eggen, "Political Groups, Now Free of Limits, Spending Heavily Ahead of 2012," May 22, 2011, A5 (www.washingtonpost.com/politics/political-groups-now-free-of-limits-spending-heavily-ahead-of-2012/2011/05/20/AF9ZKc8G_print.html).

15. AO 2011–12, June 30, 2011 (saos.fec.gov/aodocs/AO%202011-12%20(Majority%20PAC%20dated%206-30-11).pdf). It is worth noting that, at a time when the FEC was often stymied by partisan deadlocks, the vote on this question was unanimous.

16. Ralph Z. Hallow, "Republican Super PAC Gets FEC Go-ahead," *Washington Times*, June 30, 2011 (www.washingtontimes.com/news/2011/jun/30/republican-super-pac-gets-fec-go-ahead/?page=all).

17. Federal Election Commission, "Coordinated Communications and Independent Expenditures Brochure," updated January 2015, 2–3 (www.fec.gov/pages/brochures/indexp.shtml); for a non-bureaucratic description of the rules, see Daniel P. Tokaji and Renata E. B. Strause, *The New Soft Money: Outside Spending in Congressional Elections* (Columbus: Ohio State University Moritz College of Law, 2014), 21–23 (http://moritzlaw.osu.edu/thenewsoftmoney/).

18. Larry Sabato, *PAC Power: Inside the World of Political Action Committees* (New York: W.W. Norton, 1984), 184.

19. *FEC v. Colorado Republican Federal Campaign Committee*, 533 U.S. 431 (2001), 442.

20. Matea Gold, "Undisclosed Spending a Democratic Tactic, Too," *Los Angeles Times*, April 30, 2011; Dan Eggen and Chris Cilizza, "Romney Supporters Start 'Super PAC' for Donations," *Washington Post*, June 24, 2011, A4; Jim Rutenberg, "Groups Form to Aid Democrats with Anonymous Money," *New York Times*, April 29, 2011 (www.nytimes.com/2011/04/30/us/politics/30donate.html).

21. Michael D. Shear, "Deputy Press Secretary Leaving White House," *New York Times*, February 16, 2011 (http://thecaucus.blogs.nytimes.com/2011/02/16/deputy-press-secretary-leaving-white-house/); Jim Rutenberg, "Romney to Get Some Welcome Help," *New York Times*, June 23, 2011 (http://thecaucus.blogs.nytimes.com/2011/06/23/romney-to-get-some-welcome-help/).

22. Richard Briffault, "Coordination Reconsidered," *Columbia Law Review Sidebar* 113 (2013): 89; Ryan is quoted in David B. Magleby and Jay Goodliffe, "Interest Groups," in David B. Magleby, ed., *Financing the 2012 Election* (Washington, DC: Brookings Institution, 2014), 242.

23. Bradley A Smith, "Super PACs and the Role of 'Coordination' in Campaign Finance Law," *Willamette Law Review* 49 (2013): 606.

24. Ibid., 632.

25. Briffault, "Coordination Reconsidered," 97; Rep. Price introduced the Empowering Citizens Act in 2013 and again in 2015 (www.govtrack.us/congress/bills/114/hr424).

26. Matea Gold and Tom Hamburger, "Must-have Accessory for House Candidates in 2014: The Personalized Super PAC," *Washington Post*, July 18, 2014 (www.washingtonpost.com/politics/one-candidate-super-pac-now-a-must-have-to-count-especially-in-lesser-house-races/2014/07/17/aaa2fcd6-0dcd-11e4-8c9a-923ecc0c7d23_story.html). For similar PACs in the 2012 congressional elections, see Dan Eggen, "Super PACs Are Often a Friends and Family Plan," *Washington Post*, June 11, 2012, A1. The Center for Responsive Politics listed fifty-one super PACs (omitting those that raised less than $1,000) as supporting or opposing House and Senate candidates in 2012, and ninety-one in 2014. Matea Gold, "Guy Cecil in Talks to Join Pro-Clinton Super PAC, Reducing Jim Messina's Role," *Washington Post*, May 1, 2015 (www.washingtonpost.com/news/post-politics/wp/2015/05/01/guy-cecil-in-talks-to-join-pro-clinton-super-pac-reducing-jim-messinas-role/).

27. Marty Cohen, David Karol, Hans Noel, and John Zaller, "The Invisible Primary in Presidential Nominations, 1980–2004," in William G. Mayer, ed., *The Making of the Presidential Candidates 2008* (Lanham, MD: Rowman & Littlefield, 2008), 1–38.

28. Code of Federal Regulations, Chapter 11, Section 100.72 Testing the waters (www.gpo.gov/fdsys/pkg/CFR-2010-title11-vol1/xml/CFR-2010-title11-vol1-sec100-72.xml); Shailagh Murray and Matthew Mosk, "Before Running, Candidates Must Explore: Committees Let Them Begin Raising Money," *Washington Post*, January 18, 2007, A3 (www.washingtonpost.com/archive/politics/2007/01/18/before-running-candidates-must-explore-span-class-bankheadcommittees-let-them-begin-raising-moneyspan/7046f4f6-5a79-4cd0-8462-4d36f3341822/); Mark Leibovich, "Today's Version of 'I Will Run'

Is Way More Than 3 Little Words," *New York Times*, February 10, 2007 (http://www.nytimes.com/2007/02/10/us/politics/10announce.html?_r=0).

29. Shailagh Murray and Chris Cilizza, "Obama Jumps into Presidential Fray: Senator Forms Exploratory Committee," *Washington Post*, January 18, 2007, A1; Dan Balz, "McCain Prepares for '08 Bid with Appeal to Right," *Washington Post*, November 17, 2006, A7 (www.washingtonpost.com/wp-dyn/content/article/2006/11/16/AR2006111601592.html); James Gerstenzang, "Romney Takes 1st Step for Presidential Bid," *Los Angeles Times*, January 4, 2007, A7 (http://articles.latimes.com/2007/jan/04/nation/na-romney4); Sewell Chan, "Giuliani Is Definitely Interested," *New York Times*, February 6, 2007 (http://www.nytimes.com/2007/02/06/us/politics/06cnd-rudy.html); Adam Nagourney and Jeff Zeleny, "Obama Formally Enters Presidential Race," *New York Times*, February 11, 2007 (http://www.nytimes.com/2007/02/11/us/politics/11obama.html); Adam Nagourney, "Romney Declares '08 Candidacy in Michigan," *New York Times*, February 13, 2007 (http://www.nytimes.com/2007/02/13/us/politics/13cnd-romney.html); Jonathan Weisman, "Romney Jumps into Fray for 2012," *Wall Street Journal*, April 13, 2011, A5 (www.wsj.com/articles/SB10001424052748704529204576257343590577276).

30. Brad Knickerbocker, "Hillary Clinton Makes It Official: 'I'm Hitting the Road to Earn Your Vote,'" *Christian Science Monitor*, April 12, 2015 (www.csmonitor.com/USA/Politics/2015/0412/Hillary-Clinton-makes-it-official-I-m-hitting-the-road-to-earn-your-vote.-video); Michael Barbaro and Jonathan Martin, "Jeb Bush Announces White House Bid," *New York Times*, June 15, 2015 (www.nytimes.com/2015/06/16/us/politics/jeb-bush-presidential-campaign.html).

31. Matea Gold, "Election 2014: A New Level of Collaboration Between Candidates and Big-Money Allies," *Washington Post*, November 4, 2014 (www.washingtonpost.com/politics/election-2014-a-new-level-of-collaboration-between-candidates-and-big-money-allies/2014/11/03/ec2bda9a-636f-11e4-836c-3bc4f26eb67_story.html); Thomas Beaumont, "Jeb Bush Prepares to Give Traditional Campaign a Makeover," Associated Press, April 21, 2015 (http://bigstory.ap.org/article/409837aa09ee405493ad-64a94b8c2c3d/bush-preparing-delegate-many-campaign-tasks-super-pac).

32. Trevor Potter, "How Stephen Colbert Schooled Americans in Campaign Finance," *Time*, December 16, 2014 (http://time.com/3600116/stephen-colbert-report-finale-super-pac/).

33. Chad Livengood, "Armed with His Delaware-Based 'Anonymous Shell Corporation,' Colbert Seeks 'Massive' Donations," *Dialogue Delaware*, October 7, 2011 (http://blogs.delawareonline.com/dialoguedelaware/2011/10/07/armed-with-his-anonymous-delaware-shell-corporation-colbert-seeks-massive-donations/?nclick_check=1).

34. *The Colbert Report*, September 29, 2011 (http://thecolbertreport.cc.com/videos/3yzu4u/colbert-super-pac---trevor-potter---stephen-s-shell-corporation). See also Richard Briffault, "Super PACs," *Minnesota Law Review* 96 (2012): 1673–74.

35. Livengood, "Armed with His Delaware-Based 'Anonymous Shell Corporation.'" For a detailed report on the Colbert super PAC's receipts and

expenditures, see Melissa Yeager, "It's Been 4 Years Since Stephen Colbert Created a Super PAC—Where Did All That Money Go?" *Sunlight Foundation*, September 30, 2015 (http://sunlightfoundation.com/blog/2015/09/30/its-been-four-years-since-stephen-colbert-created-a-super-pac-where-did-all-that-money-go/).

36. "Under New Management!," the Definitely Not Coordinating with Stephen Colbert Super PAC press release, January 12, 2012 (http://www.colbertsuperpac.com/archive/).

37. *The Colbert Report*, January 12, 2012 (http://thecolbertreport.cc.com/videos/av6bvx/colbert-super-pac---coordination-resolution-with-jon-stewart); *The Daily Show*, January 17, 2012 (http://thedailyshow.cc.com/videos/3pwzi5/colbert-super-pac---not-coordinating-with-stephen-colbert).

38. Susan Saulny, "A Defiant Cain Suspends His Bid for Presidency," *New York Times*, December 3, 2011 (www.nytimes.com/2011/12/04/us/politics/herman-cain-suspends-his-presidential-campaign.html); Padmananda Rama, "Herman Cain Gets 'a Colbert Bump' in South Carolina," *NPR*, January 21, 2012 (www.npr.org/sections/itsallpolitics/2012/01/21/145583425/herman-cain-gets-a-colbert-bump-in-south-carolina).

39. HuffPost Pollster, "2016 National Republican Primary" (http://elections.huffingtonpost.com/pollster/2016-national-gop-primary) and "2016 National Democratic Primary" (http://elections.huffingtonpost.com/pollster/2016-national-democratic-primary).

40. Mark Murray, "Nearly 70% of Ad Dollars in 2016 Race Come From Outside Groups," *NBC News*, January 12, 2016 (www.nbcnews.com/politics/first-read/nearly-70-ad-dollars-2016-race-come-outside-groups-n494876).

41. Ibid.; Amber Phillips, "5 Times Ted Cruz Went to War with the Republican Establishment," *Washington Post*, December 22, 2015 (https://www.washingtonpost.com/news/the-fix/wp/2015/12/22/5-times-ted-cruz-went-to-war-with-the-republican-establishment/); Murray, "Nearly 70% of Ad Dollars"; CNN, 2016 election center (www.cnn.com/election/primaries/states/ia).

42. Will Tucker, "$100 Million Floods into Presidential Super PACs in Second Half of 2015," *OpenSecretsblog*, February 1, 2016 (www.opensecrets.org/news/2016/02/100-million-floods-into-presidential-super-pacs-in-second-half-of-2015/).

CHAPTER 7

1. Adam Bonica, Nolan McCarty, Keith T. Poole, and Howard Rosenthal, "Why Hasn't Democracy Slowed Rising Inequality?" *Journal of Economic Perspectives* 27, no. 3 (Summer 2013), Figure 5 (http://pubs.aeaweb.org/doi/pdfplus/10.1257/jep.27.3.103).

2. Nicholas Confessore, Sarah Cohen, and Karen Nourish, "The Families Funding the 2016 Presidential Election," *New York Times*, October 10, 2015 (www.nytimes.com/interactive/2015/10/11/us/politics/2016-presidential-election-super-pac-donors.html?ref=politics); Kenneth P. Vogel and Isaac Arnsdorf, "The POLITICO 100: Billionaires dominate 2016," *Politico*, February 8, 2016 (www.politico.com/story/2016/02/100-billionaires-2016-campaign-finance-218862).

3. Campaign Finance Institute, "New CFI Table Arrays the Sources of Candidates' Early Money," press release, August 24, 2015 (www.cfinst. org/Press/PReleases/15-08-24/Presidential_Fundraising_New_CFI_Table_Arrays_the_Sources_of_Candidates'_Early_Money.aspx); Kenneth P. Vogel and Isaac Arnsdorf, "The POLITICO 100: Billionaires Dominate 2016," *Politico*, February 8, 2016 (www.politico.com/story/2016/02/100-billionaires-2016-campaign-finance-218862).

4. John C. Green, John E. Kohler, and Ian P. Schwarber, "Financing the 2012 Presidential Nomination Campaigns," in David B. Magleby, ed., *Financing the 2012 Election* (Washington, DC: Brookings Institution Press, 2014), 100–107. After Gingrich dropped out of the race in May, the Adelsons became the biggest donors to Mitt Romney's super PAC, Restore Our Future, giving it a whopping $30 million. Center for Responsive Politics, "Restore Our Future" (www.opensecrets.org/pacs/indexpend.php?strID=C00490045&cycle=2012).

5. See the RNC's report on the 2012 election, "Growth and Opportunity Project" (http://goproject.gop.com/rnc_growth_opportunity_book_2013.pdf), 72.

6. Center for Responsive Politics, "Jeb Bush" (www.opensecrets.org/pres16/candidate.php?id=N00037006); Bob Biersack, Viveca Novak, and Will Tucker, "A Few New Faces—But Not Many—Among Megadonors to Presidential Super PACs," *OpenSecretsBlog*, August 1, 2015 (www.opensecrets.org/news/2015/08/a-few-new-faces-but-not-many-among-megadonors-to-presidential-super-pacs/).

7. Matea Gold and Tom Hamburger, "The Lament of the Not Quite Rich Enough," *Washington Post*, March 25, 2015 (www.washingtonpost.com/politics/in-2016-campaign-the-lament-of-the-not-quite-rich-enough/2015/03/24/f0a38b18-cdb4-11e4-8a46-b1dc9be5a8ff_story.html).

8. Center for Responsive Politics, "Super PACs Rule the Airwaves in GOP Primaries" (www.opensecrets.org/news/2015/12/super-pacs-rule-the-airwaves-in-gop-primaries-wesleyan-media-project-and-crp-document-the-onslaught/); The Wesleyan Media Project, "Super PACs Dominate Airwaves" (http://mediaproject.wesleyan.edu/releases/super-pacs-dominate- airwaves/).

9. Michael C. Bender, "Bush Team Sets Bold Fundraising Goal: $100 Million in Three Months," *Bloomberg.com*, January 9, 2015 (www.bloomberg.com/politics/articles/2015-01-09/bush-team-sets-bold-fundraising-goal-100-million-in-three-months).

10. Ben White, "Jeb Bush's Eye-Popping Event: $100k per Ticket," *Politico*, February 10, 2015 (www.politico.com//story/2015/02/jeb-bush-fundraiser-100k-per-ticket-115086.html); Matea Gold, "Awash in Cash, Bush Asks Donors Not to Give More Than $1 Million—For Now," *Washington Post*, March 5, 2015 (www.washingtonpost.com/politics/awash-in-cash-bush-asks-donors-to-limit-gifts-to-1-million--for-now/2015/03/04/0b8d3fc6-c1c8-11e4-9271-610273846239_story.html).

11. Matt Flegenheimer and Maggie Haberman, "Trailing in Polls, Jeb Bush Cuts Staff and Salaries, Vowing Focus on Early States," *New York Times*, October 23, 2015 (www.nytimes.com/politics/first-draft/2015/10/23/trailing-in-polls-jeb-bush-cuts-staff-and-salaries-vowing-focus-on-early-states/?action=click&contentCollection=Politics&module=RelatedCoverage&region=Marginalia&pgtype=article).

12. For Trump's fundraising numbers, see Center for Responsive Politics, "Donald Trump" (www.opensecrets.org/pres16/candidate.php?cycle=2016 &id=N00023864&type=f). For his ad spending, see Wesleyan Media Project, "Super PACs Dominate Airwaves" (http://mediaproject.wesleyan.edu/ releases/super-pacs-dominate-airwaves/). For Ted Cruz's fundraising numbers, see Center for Responsive Politics, "Ted Cruz" (www.opensecrets.org/ pres16/candidate.php?id=N00033085). For Republican poll rankings, see HuffPost Pollster, "2016 National Republican Primary" (http://elections. huffingtonpost.com/pollster/2016-national-gop-primary).

13. For conservative views on the GOP "crackup," see "The Republican Crack-Up," *Wall Street Journal*, October 8, 2015 (www.wsj.com/articles/ the-republican-crack-up-1444347391), and Jonah Goldberg, "This Time the Conservative Crackup Is Real," *Los Angeles Times*, January 26, 2016 (www. latimes.com/opinion/op-ed/la-oe-0126-goldberg-conservative-crackup-20160126-column.html).

14. Peter Stone, "Koch Donors Divided Over Failure to Stop Donald Trump," *Guardian*, March 16, 2016 (www.theguardian.com/us-news/2016/mar/ 15/koch-brothers-republican-donors-disappointed-donald-trump-attacks?CMP=share_btn_tw); Nicholas Confessore and Rachel Shore, "Donald Trump Is Finally Uniting Top Republican Donors— Against Him," *New York Times*, March 20, 2016 (www.nytimes.com/2016/03/21/us/poli-tics/donald-trump-republican-donors.html?ref=politics).

15. For Clinton's fundraising numbers, see Center for Responsive Politics, "Hillary Clinton" (www.opensecrets.org/pres16/candidate.php?id=N00000019).

16. Center for Responsive Politics, "Bernie Sanders" (www.opensecrets.org/ pres16/candidate.php?id=N00000528); Maggie Haberman, "Bernie Sanders Campaign Says It Is Outpacing Obama's Record for Donations," *New York Times*, December 20, 2015 (www.nytimes.com/politics/first-draft/2015/12/ 20/sanderss-campaign-says-its-outpacing-obamas-record-for-donations/); Daniel Strauss and Isaac Arnsdorf, "Sanders Far Outpaced Clinton in February Fundraising," *Politico*, March 20, 2016 (www.politico.com/story/ 2016/03/bernie-sanders-fundraising-hillary-clinton-221024).

17. CNN, 2016 election center (www.cnn.com/election/primaries/states/ia).

18. The Kochs earlier said they would spend almost $900 million; see Nicholas Confessore, "Koch Brothers' Budget of $889 Million Is on par with Both Parties' Spending," *New York Times*, January 26, 2015 (www.nytimes. com/2015/01/27/us/politics/kochs-plan-to-spend-900-million-on-2016-campaign.html). Charles Koch gave the lower figure in October, saying "our latest budget is going to be lower because people aren't contributing"; see Kai Ryssdal's October 21 *Marketplace* interview with Koch at www.marketplace. org/topics/business/corner-office/full-interview-charles-koch.

19. Jane Mayer, "Covert Operations," *New Yorker*, August 30, 2010 (www.newy-orker.com/magazine/2010/08/30/covert-operations); Daniel Fisher, "Inside the Koch Empire: How the Brothers Plan to Reshape America," *Forbes*, December 24, 2012 (www.forbes.com/sites/danielfisher/2012/12/05/ inside-the-koch-empire-how-the-brothers-plan-to-reshape-america/). The Kochs have been big GOP donors since the late 1980s, and David contrib-uted more than $1.5 million to the party's soft money accounts from 1992 to

2002. See Center for Responsive Politics, Donor Lookup, www.opensecrets. org/indivs/. The Koch Industries PAC is one of the biggest corporate PACs, and has been active since the 1990s. Federal Election Commission, Campaign Finance Statistics, Political Action Committees (PAC) data Summary Tables (www.fec.gov/press/campaign_finance_statistics.shtml).

20. Kenneth P. Vogel, "How the Koch Network Rivals the GOP," *Politico,* December 30, 2015 (www.politico.com/story/2015/12/koch-brothers-network-gop-david-charles-217124).

21. David Herszenhorn and Sheryl Gay Stolberg, "Health Plan Opponents Make Voices Heard," *New York Times,* August 3, 2009 (www.nytimes.com/2009/08/04/health/policy/04townhalls.html); Andrew Goldman, "The Billionaire's Party," *New York,* July 25, 2010 (http://nymag.com/news/features/67285/); Center for Responsive Politics, "Americans for Prosperity" (www.opensecrets.org/outsidespending/recips.php?cycle=2010&cmte=Americans%20for%20Prosperity); Theda Skocpol and Vanessa Williamson, *The Tea Party and the Remaking of Republican Conservatism* (New York: Oxford University Press, 2012), 84.

22. Kenneth P. Vogel, *Big Money: 2.5 Million Dollars, One Suspicious Vehicle and a Pimp—on the Trail of the Ultra-Rich Hijacking American Politics* (New York: Public Affairs, 2014), 119.

23. Matea Gold, "Koch-Backed Political Coalition, Designed to Shield Donors, Raised $400 Million in 2012," *Washington Post,* January 5, 2014 (www.washingtonpost.com/politics/koch-backed-political-network-built-to-shield-donors-raised-400-million-in-2012-elections/2014/01/05/9e7cfd9a-719b-11e3-9389-09ef9944065e_story.html).

24. Peter Henderson, "Kochs Help Republicans Catch Up on Technology," *Reuters,* May 17, 2012 (www.reuters.com/article/2012/05/17/us-usa-politics-kochs-idUSBRE84G0E820120517); Vogel, *Big Money,* 126–27.

25. The information in those huge databases is only as valuable as the people who use it, though. Past research has shown that potential voters see the volunteers who knock on their doors as representatives of the candidates they support and judge the candidates accordingly. With this research in mind, two political scientists analyzed a survey of pro-Obama volunteers in 2012 and concluded that "typical Obama campaign workers were far different demographically and ideologically than the undecided and Democratic voters whom they were targeting in swing states." Ryan D. Enos and Eitan D. Hersh, "Party Activists as Campaign Advertisers: the Ground Campaign as a Principal-Agent problem," *American Political Science Review* 109, no. 2 (May 2015): 264.

26. David M. Drucker, "Top GOP Data Firms Partner Ahead of Elections," *Washington Examiner,* August 28, 2014 (www.washingtonexaminer.com/top-gop-data-firms-partner-ahead-of-elections/article/2552557).

27. Jon Ward, "The Koch Brothers and the Republican Party Go to War—With Each Other," *Yahoo! Politics,* June 11, 2015 (www.yahoo.com/politics/the-koch-brothers-and-the-republican-party-go-to-121193159491.html).

28. Ibid.; Vogel, "How the Koch Network Rivals the GOP." The Kochs and the RNC were equally wary of Donald Trump, though. The Kochs did not invite him to their summer 2015 meeting and refused to sell him any of

the i360 voter data. Kenneth P. Vogel and Cate Martel, "The Kochs Freeze out Trump," *Politico*, July 29, 2015 www.politico.com/story/2015/07/kochs-freeze-out-trump-120752).

29. Gabriel Sherman, "Republican Billionaires Just Can't Seem to Buy This Election," *New York Magazine*, December 13, 2015 (http://nymag.com/daily/intelligencer/2015/12/gop-billionaires-cant-seem-to-buy-this-election.html).

30. Peter Overby, "A Political Family, Funding and Running on Both Sides of the Aisle," *NPR*, September 1, 2014 (www.wnyc.org/story/a-political-family-funding-and-running-on-both-sides-of-the-aisle/); ESAFund (http://endingspendingfund.com/); Center for Responsive Politics, "Ending Spending Action Fund." (www.opensecrets.org/pacs/lookup2.php?strID=C00489856); Sam Stein, "The New Anti-Sanders Super PAC is Funded by Anti-Clinton Donors," *HuffPost Politics*, January 31, 2016 (www.huffingtonpost.com/entry/esa-fund-anti-sanders-super-pac_us_56ae76cae4b0010e80ea89fa?4nsl9pb9=); Center for Responsive Politics, "Our Principles PAC" (www.opensecrets.org/outsidespending/detail.php?cmte=C00603621&cycle=2016).

31. Center for Responsive Politics, "American Unity PAC" (www.opensecrets.org/pacs/lookup2.php?strID=C00523589); Peter Stone, "Inside the Big-Moneyed Network Rallying Around Marco Rubio," *HuffPost Politics*, November 98, 2015 (www.huffingtonpost.com/entry/paul-singer-marco-rubio_5640ca23e4b0411d3071b673).

32. Center for Responsive Politics, "Donor Lookup: Mercer, Robert" (www.opensecrets.org/indivs/search.php?name=mercer%2C+robert&cycle=All&sort=R&state=&zip=&employ=&cand=&submit=Submit); Center for Responsive Politics, "Vendor: Cambridge Analytica" (www.opensecrets.org/expends/vendor.php?year=2014&vendor=Cambridge+Analytica); Frances Stead Sellers, "Cruz Campaign Paid $750,000 to 'Psychographic Profiling' Company," *Washington Post*, October 19, 2015 (www.washingtonpost.com/politics/cruz-campaign-paid-750000-to-psychographic-profiling-company/2015/10/19/6c83e508-743f-11e5-9cbb-790369643cf9_story.html).

33. Center for Responsive Politics, Donor Lookup (www.opensecrets.org/indivs/).

34. Rebecca Ballhaus, "Carl Icahn to Invest $150 Million in Super PAC," *Wall Street Journal*, October 21, 2015 (www.wsj.com/articles/carl-icahn-to-invest-150-million-in-super-pac-1445441825).

35. This section on the Democracy Alliance is based mainly on: Vogel, *Big Money*, 55–76; Thomas B. Edsall, "Rich Liberals Vow to Fund Think Tanks; Aim Is to Compete with Conservatives," *Washington Post*, August 7, 2005 (www.washingtonpost.com/wp-dyn/content/article/2005/08/06/AR2005080600848.html); Jim VandeHei and Chris Cilizza, "A New Alliance of Democrats Spreads Funding," *Washington Post*, July 17, 2006 (www.washingtonpost.com/wp-dyn/content/article/2006/07/16/AR2006071600882_pf.html); and Matea Gold, "Rich Liberal Donors Throw Weight Behind Obama Agenda," *Los Angeles Times*, May 4, 2014 (http://articles.latimes.com/2013/may/04/nation/la-na-donor-network-20130504).

36. The Democracy Alliance may be secretive, but it does have a website: www. democracyalliance.org.

37. Kenneth P. Vogel, "Secret Effort to Sell Hillary to Rich Liberals," *Politico*, June 2, 2015 (www.politico.com/story/2015/06/secret-effort-to-sell-hillary-clinton-to-rich-liberals-118528); Vogel and Arnsdorf, "The POLITICO 100."

38. Center for Responsive Politics, "NextGen Climate Action" (www.opense-crets.org/pacs/lookup2.php?strID=C00547349); Andrew Restuccia and Elana Schor, "Steyer's Group Shutters Climate Policy Arm as Political Efforts Ramp Up." *Politico*, April 1, 2015 (www.politico.com/story/2015/04/tom-steyer-nonprofit-shuts-down-climate-program-116584); Maggie Haberman, "Tom Steyer Joins Forces with Group Pushing Hispanic Candidates," *New York Times*, January 15, 2016 (www.nytimes.com/poli-tics/first-draft/2016/01/15/tom-steyer-joins-forces-with-group-pushing-hispanic-candidates/).

39. Center for Responsive Politics, "Independence USA PAC" (www.opensecrets. org/pacs/lookup2.php?strID=C00532705). Bloomberg briefly considered spending $1 billion to finance his own independent presidential candidacy, but decided against it for fear it would help Trump. Maggie Haberman and Alexander Burns, "Michael Bloomberg Says He Won't Run for President," *New York Times*, March 7, 2016 (www.nytimes.com/2016/03/08/us/politics/michael-bloomberg-not-running-for-president.html).

CHAPTER 8

1. This paragraph and the next three are based on Anthony Corrado et al., eds., *Campaign Finance Reform: A Sourcebook* (Washington, DC: Brookings Institution Press, 1997), 168–73, and Anthony Corrado et al., eds., *Inside the Campaign Finance Battle* (Washington, DC: Brookings Institution Press, 2003), 19–23.

2. Herbert E. Alexander and Anthony Corrado, *Financing the 1992 Election* (Armonk, NY: M.E. Sharpe, 1995), 157; Federal Election Commission press release, "1995-96 Non-Federal Accounts of National Party Committees, January 1, 1995–December 31, 1996" (www.fec.gov/finance/demsoft. htm); Federal Election Commission press release, "1999-2000 Non-Federal Accounts of National Party Committees, January 1, 1999–December 31, 2000" (www.fec.gov/press/press2001/051501partyfund/nonfeddem2000. html): Robert G. Boatright, Michael J. Malbin, Mark J. Rowell, and Clyde Wilcox, "Interest Groups and Advocacy Organizations After BCRA," in Michael J. Malbin, ed., *The Election After Reform: Money, Politics, and the Bipartisan Campaign Reform Act* (Lanham, MD: Rowman and Littlefield, 2006), 114.

3. This paragraph and the next two are based on Herbert E. Alexander, *Financing the 1980 Election* (Lexington, MA: Heath Lexington, 1983), 302, 327; Elizabeth Drew, *Politics and Money: The New Road to Corruption* (New York: Macmillan, 1983), 104–108; and Robert E. Mutch, *Campaigns, Congress, and Courts: The Making of Federal Campaign Finance Law* (New York: Praeger, 1988), 111–13.

4. Robert Jackson, "FEC Fails to Enforce Laws, Should be Abolished, Common Cause Says," *Los Angeles Times*, September 8, 1989, 19; Herbert E. Alexander

and Monica Bauer, *Financing the 1988 Election* (Boulder, CO: Westview Press, 1991), 37, 81; Charles R. Babcock, "Big Donations Again a Campaign Staple; Not Since 1972 Have Presidential Races Seen Such Money," *Washington Post*, November 27, 1988, A20; Xandra Kayden, "Campaign Cash Now Sluicing to State Parties," *Los Angeles Times*, May 14, 1989, 3.

5. Alexander and Corrado, *1992 Election*, 159–66.

6. *Buckley v. Valeo*, 424 U.S. 1, 45.

7. Thomas E. Mann, "The Rise of Soft Money," in Anthony Corrado et al., eds., *Inside the Campaign Finance Battle* (Washington, DC: Brookings Institution Press, 2003), 23–26; Anthony Corrado, "Financing the 1996 General Election," in John C. Green, ed., *Financing the 1996 Election* (Armonk, NY: M.E. Sharpe, 1999), 80.

8. Campaign Finance Institute, "Hard and Soft Money Raised by National Party Committees, 1992–2012" (www.cfinst.org/pdf/vital/VitalStats_t13.pdf).

9. Citizens Research Foundation, *New Realities, New Thinking: Report of the Task Force on Campaign Finance Reform* (Los Angeles: Citizens Research Foundation, 1997); Norman J. Ornstein et al., eds, *Five Ideas for Practical Campaign Reform* (Washington, DC: Brookings Institution Press, 1997); Committee for Economic Development, *Investing in the People's Business; A Business Proposal for Campaign Finance Reform* (New York: Committee for Economic Development, 1999).

10. Robert E. Mutch, "The Reinvigorated Reform Debate," in John C. Green, ed., *Financing the 1996 Election* (Armonk, NY: M.E. Sharpe, 1999), 229–32.

11. Senate Committee on Governmental Affairs, *Investigation of Illegal and Improper Activities in Connection with the 1996 Federal Election Campaign*, Senate Report 105–167 (105–2), vol. 3, 4469, 4499.

12. For a summary of BCRA, see Anthony Corrado, "The Regulatory Environment: Uncertainty in the Wake of Change," in David B. Magleby, Anthony Corrado, and Kelly B. Patterson, eds., *Financing the 2004 Election* (Washington, DC: Brookings Institution Press, 2006), 32–43; see also Federal Election Commission, "Major Provisions of the Bipartisan Campaign Reform Act of 2002" (www.fec.gov/press/bkgnd/bcra_overview.shtml). The electioneering communication provision originated in a 1998 amendment to the McCain-Feingold bill sponsored by Senators Olympia Snowe (R-ME) and James M. Jeffords (R-VT); the amendment was a compromise to bridge partisan differences over an anti-labor amendment sponsored by Senators Trent Lott (R-MI) and Mitch McConnell (R-KY). Mutch, "Reinvigorated Reform Debate," 231–32. *McConnell v. FEC*, 540 U.S. 93 (2003).

13. The gift tax, passed in 1932, kicked in for amounts of more than $3,000. After 1932, rich donors tended to write smaller checks to a larger number of committees to avoid paying gift taxes. Some big donors went to great lengths to avoid the gift tax: Richard Mellon Scaife made his $1 million 1972 contribution (actually $990,000) in $3,000 checks to 330 Nixon fundraising committees. Morton Mintz, "Politics, Gifts, and Taxes: Politics of Gift Giving," *Washington Post*, December 25, 1972, C1.

14. Donald B. Tobin, "Anonymous Speech and Section 527 of the Internal Revenue Code," *Georgia Law Review* 37 (2003): 620–23 (http://digitalcommons.law.umaryland.edu/cgi/viewcontent.cgi?article=2482&context=fac_

pubs); Richard Briffault, "The 527 Problem ... and the *Buckley* Problem," *George Washington Law Review* 73 (2005): 1708–709 (http://lsr.nellco.org/columbia_pllt/0596/).

15. Tobin, "Anonymous Speech," 623–35; Briffault, "527 Problem," 1710–11.

16. Briffault, "527 Problem," 1711–12; American Bar Association, "Comments of the Individual Members of the Exempt Organizations Committee's Task Force on Section 501(c)(4) and Politics," May 25, 2004, 24–26, 32 (www.americanbar.org/content/dam/aba/migrated/tax/pubpolicy/2004/040525exo.authcheckdam.pdf); Ellen P. Aprill, "Regulating the Political Speech of Noncharitable Exempt Organizations after *Citizens United*," *Election Law Journal* 10 (2011): 363–405, 385–86 (www1.law.nyu.edu/ncpl/resources/documents/EAprillpaperFormatted.pdf); Tobin, "Anonymous Speech," 628–30.

17. Briffault, "527 Problem," 1712–23, 1725–26; Aprill, "Regulating Political Speech," 389–90.

18. Boatright et al., "Interest Groups," 113; John C. Green, "Financing the 2004 Presidential Nomination Campaigns," in David B. Magleby, Anthony Corrado, and Kelly B. Patterson, eds., *Financing the 2004 Election* (Washington, DC: Brookings Institution Press, 2006), 110–11; on 527s in the 2004 election more generally, see Allan J. Cigler, "Interest Groups and Financing the 2004 Election," in Magleby et al., *Financing the 2004 Election*, 229–34.

19. David B. Magleby, "Adaptation and Innovation in the Financing of the 2008 Election," in David B. Magleby and Anthony Corrado, eds., *Financing the 2008 Election* (Washington, DC: Brookings Institution Press, 2011), 19; see also Stephen R. Weissman and Ruth Hassan, "BCRA and the 527 Groups," in Michael J. Malbin, ed., *The Election After Reform: Money, Politics, and the Bipartisan Campaign Reform Act* (Lanham, MD: Roman and Littlefield, 2006), 79–82.

20. Norquist is quoted in Weissman and Hassan, "BCRA and the 527 Groups," 229.

21. Center for Responsive Politics, "Top 50 Federally Focused Organizations" (www.opensecrets.org/527s/527cmtes.php?level=C&cycle=2004); Cigler, "Interest Groups and Financing the 2004 Election," 224–29; Raymond J. La Raja, *Small Change: Money, Political Parties, and Campaign Finance Reform* (Ann Arbor: University of Michigan Press, 2008), 212–13.

22. Center for Responsive Politics, "Top Individual Contributors to Federally Focused 527 Organizations, 2004 Election Cycle" (www.opensecrets.org/527s/527indivs.php?cycle=2004).

23. Thomas B. Edsall, "Democrats' Financing Plan Challenged; Watchdog Groups File Complaint with FEC Over Party's 'Soft Money' Network," *Washington Post*, January 16, 2004, A4; Associated Press, "FEC Assessed a Record $6.2 Million in Penalties in 2006," *Washington Post*, December 29, 2006, A6; Federal Election Commission press release, "Club for Growth Agrees to Pay $350,000 Penalty for Failing to Register as a Political Committee," September 5, 2007 (www.fec.gov/press/press2007/20070905cfg.shtml).

24. Center for Responsive Politics, "Top 50 Federally Focused Organizations" (www.opensecrets.org/527s/527cmtes.php?level=C&cycle=2004); Weissman and Hassan, "BCRA and the 527 Groups," 104–105 (www.cfinst.org/pdf/books-reports/EAR/EAR_ch5.pdf).

25. Stephen R. Weissman and Kara D. Ryan, "Soft Money in the 2006 Election and the Outlook for 2008: The Changing Nonprofits Landscape," Campaign Finance Institute, 2008 (http://cfinst.org/books_reports/pdf/NP_SoftMoney_06-08.pdf).

26. Aprill, "Regulating the Political Speech of Noncharitable Exempt Organizations After *Citizens United*," 375–76.

27. Ibid., 381.

28. *FEC v. Wisconsin Right to Life*, 551 U.S. 449 (2007) (www.law.cornell.edu/supct/html/06-969.ZS.html).

29. Ibid., 451

30. This paragraph and the next are based on Campaign Finance Institute press release, "Soft Money Political Spending by 501(c) Nonprofits Tripled in 2008 Election" (www.cfinst.org/press/preleases/09-02-25/Soft_Money_Political_Spending_by_Nonprofits_Tripled_in_2008.aspx).

31. CFR §1040.20(c)(9) (www.gpo.gov/fdsys/pkg/CFR-2008-title11-vol1/xml/CFR-2008-title11-vol1-sec104-20.xml).

32. See Corrado, "Regulatory Environment in 2012," 67–68. The FEC deadlocked on a complaint about the new regulation in 2010. The three Republican commissioners interpreted it to mean that groups had to report only donors who had given to finance specific ads.

33. "*Van Hollen v. FEC* Case Summary" (www.fec.gov/law/litigation/van_hollen.shtml); *Citizens United v. FEC*, 130 S. Ct. 876 (2010).

34. For a general overview of 501(c)(4) social welfare groups, see John Francis Reilly, Carter C. Hull, and Barbara A. Braig Allen, "IRC 501(c)(4) Organizations" (www.irs.gov/pub/irs-tege/eotopici03.pdf); for the political activities of social welfare groups, see Erika K. Lunder and L. Paige Whitaker, "501(c)(4) Organizations and Campaign Activity: Analysis Under Tax and Campaign Finance Laws" Congressional Research Service Report, January 29, 2009, 1.

35. For a brief description of the case, see Lisa McElroy, "*Citizens United v. FEC* in plain English," *SCOTUSblog*, January 22, 2010 (www.scotusblog.com/2010/01/citizens-united-v-fec-in-plain-english/).

36. To comply with the Supreme Court's decision in *FEC v. Massachusetts for Life* (1986), the FEC made an exception to the FECA ban for some nonprofit corporations. It exempted incorporated voluntary associations that did not accept business or labor contributions or have shareholders, and were formed to promote political ideas. This exception became irrelevant when the court exempted all corporations from the ban in *Citizens United*.

37. Treasury Inspector General for Tax Administration (TIGTA), "Inappropriate Criteria Were Used to Identify Tax-Exempt Applications for Review," U.S. Department of the Treasury report 2103-10-053, 2013, 3, 43; Center for Responsible Politics, "Total Outside Spending by Election Cycle, Excluding Party Committees" (www.opensecrets.org/outsidespending/cycle_tots.php); Campaign Finance Institute, "Soft Money Political Spending by 501(c) Nonprofits Tripled in 2008 Election" (www.cfinst.org/press/preleases/09-02-25/Soft_Money_Political_Spending_by_Nonprofits_Tripled_in_2008.aspx); Center for Responsible Politics, "Outside Spending" (www.opensecrets.org/outsidespending/fes_summ.php?cycle=2012).

38. Center for Responsive Politics, "Outside Spending by Disclosure, Excluding Party Committees" (www.opensecrets.org/outsidespending/disclosure.php).

39. Jonathan Martin and Nicholas Confessore, "Nonprofit Masks Source of Ads backing Rubio," *New York Times*, October 11, 2015 (www.nytimes.com/2015/10/12/us/politics/nonprofit-masks-dark-money-ads-backing-marco-rubio.html).

40. Max Ehrenfreund, "IRS Reportedly Targeted Tea Party Groups, Other Conservative Nonprofits," *Washington Post*, May 13, 2013 (https://www.highbeam.com/doc/1P2-34646715.html); David Grant, "Tea Party Investigation: Is the Problem the IRS or the Tax Code?" *Christian Science Monitor*, May 15, 2013, 11 (http://www.csmonitor.com/USA/Politics/2013/0515/Tea-party-investigation-Is-the-problem-the-IRS-or-the-tax-code-video).

41. TIGTA, "Inappropriate Criteria," 17.

42. Donald B. Tobin, "The 2013 IRS Crisis: Where Do We Go From Here?" *Tax Notes*, March 2014, 1122 (http://taxprof.typepad.com/files/tobin-142-tax-notes-1120.pdf).

43. American Bar Association, "Comments . . . on Section 501(c)(4) and Politics," 2, 4; Lunder and Whitaker, "501(c)(4) Organizations and Campaign Activity," 2.

44. Quoted in Bruce R. Hopkins, *The Law of Tax-Exempt Organizations*, 10th ed. (New York: Wiley, 2011), 426n. See also Briffault, "527 Problem," 1709.

45. American Bar Association, "Comments . . . on Section 501(c)(4) and Politics," 35–36, 39–40, 44.

46. Lunder and Whitaker, "501(c)(4) Organizations and Campaign Activity," May 17, 2013, 6; Joseph Tanfani, "IRS Plans to Curb Secret Campaign Cash; the Rules Would Set Clearer Limits for Nonprofits That Have Played a Greater Role in Recent Elections," *Los Angeles Times*, November 27, 2013, A1; John McKinnon, "IRS Plans for Nonprofits Spur Strong Public Reaction," *Wall Street Journal*, March 1, 2014, A4.

47. Katy O'Donnell, "White House Surrenders on 'Dark Money' Regulation," *Politico*, December 18, 2015 (www.politico.com/story/2015/12/white-house-dark-money-216956). For a glimpse into how weak IRS rules are, see Robert Maguire, "How Crossroads GPS Beat the IRS and Became a Social Welfare Group," *OpenSecrets.org* (www.opensecrets.org/news/2016/02/how-crossroads-gps-beat-the-irs-and-became-a-social-welfare-group/).

CHAPTER 9

1. The 2010 polls were by the Pew Research Center for the People & the Press (http://people-press.org/files/legacy-pdf/589.pdf) and the *Washington Post*–ABC News poll (www.washingtonpost.com/wp-dyn/content/article/2010/02/17/AR2010021701151.html?hpid=topnews). For the 2015 poll, see Greg Stohr, "Bloomberg Poll: Americans Want Supreme Court to Turn Off Political Spending Spigot," *Bloomberg.com*, September 28, 2015 (www.bloomberg.com/politics/articles/2015-09-28/bloomberg-poll-

americans-want-supreme-court-to-turn-off-political-spending-spigot?
cmpid=BBD092815_POL).

2. "Ban on Trust Gifts," *Washington Post*, September 2, 1912, 1; Duncan Norton-Taylor, "How to Give Money to Politicians," *Fortune*, May 1956, 113. For the 1972 corporate contributions, see the Watergate Committee Report (*The Final Report of the Select Committee on Presidential Campaign Activities*, S. Rept. 93–981), 445–92. Watergate testimony actually provides some evidence that the Tillman Act was at least partly successful: the biggest contributions, the ones for $100,000 made by the Gulf, Phillips, and Ashland oil companies, were less than half the size, in constant dollars, of the contributions the insurance companies made in 1904.

3. For corporate political contribution programs before the PAC explosion of the late 1970s, see Walter Pincus, "Silent Spenders in Politics—They Really Give at the Office," *New York Magazine*, January 31, 1972, 37–45.

4. For a detailed account of the events described in this section, see Robert E. Mutch, *Buying the Vote: A History of Campaign Finance Reform* (New York: Oxford University Press, 2014), 85–86, 101–107.

5. Alexander Heard, *The Costs of Democracy* (Chapel Hill: University of North Carolina Press, 1960), 169.

6. See the Chronology for brief descriptions of the Smith-Connally and Taft-Hartley acts.

7. After the *Machinists* case, the Supreme Court handed down similar rulings in *Railway Clerks v. Allen* (1963) and *Abood v. Detroit Board of Education* (1977). See the Chronology for brief descriptions of these cases. In states that have "right to work" laws, employees who are covered by a union contract do not have to share the costs of negotiating it.

8. For a more detailed account of the *Pipefitters* case in the courts and in Congress, see Mutch, *Buying the Vote*, 120–22.

9. Joseph A. Loftus, "Ballot May Pose Threat to Labor," *New York Times*, November 3, 1968, 48; Morris Kaplan, "SIU and 8 Aides Indicted in Plot," *New York Times*, July 1, 1970, 55; Damon Stetson, "Labor's Council Assails Mitchell," *New York Times*, August 5, 1970, 24; Damon Stetson, "Head of ILGWU Sees Threat by U.S. to Union's Political Role," *New York Times*, May 14, 1971, 45.

10. *First National Bank of Boston v. Attorney General*, 359 N.E.2d 1262 (1977), 1275.

11. *First National Bank of Boston v. Bellotti*, 435 U.S. 765, 777, 784.

12. On *First National Bank of Boston v. Bellotti*, 435 U.S. 765 (1978), see Mutch, "Before and After *Bellotti*: The Corporate Contributions Cases," *Election Law Journal* 5 (2006): 308–12.

13. This section deals with responses to *Citizens United* from various points of view. For a sample of these responses see: Heather Gerken, "The Real Problem with *Citizens United*," *The American Prospect*, January 22, 2010 (https://prospect.org/article/real-problem-citizens-united); Bradley A. Smith, "Newsflash: First Amendment Upheld," *Wall Street Journal*, January 22, 2010 (www.wsj.com/articles/SB1000142405274870450970457501911217293162 0); Nathaniel Persily, "The Floodgates Were Already Open," *Slate*, January 25, 2010 (www.slate.com/articles/news_and_politics/jurisprudence/2010/01/the_floodgates_were_already_open.html); Richard L. Hasen, "What

the Court Did—and Why," *The American Interest*, July 1, 2011 (www.the-american-interest.com/2010/07/01/what-the-court-didand-why/).

14. For the cases Justice Kennedy cited, and his conclusion from them, see *Citizens United*, 130 S.Ct. 876, 899–900.

15. The two quotations from Justice Stevens are at *Citizens United*, 130 S.Ct. 876, 930 and 948.

16. The FEC stopped enforcing its regulations prohibiting corporations and unions from making electioneering communications or any express advocacy immediately after the Supreme Court handed down its *Citizens United* decision in January 2010. But it waited almost five years before changing the regulations themselves: see "Final Rules on Independent Expenditures and Electioneering Communications by Corporations and Labor Organizations," *FEC Record*, November 2014, 1–3 (www.fec.gov/pages/fecrecord/2014/november/finalrulescliesecs.shtml).

17. For this paragraph and the next, Morton J. Horwitz, *The Transformation of American Law, 1870-1960* (New York: Oxford University Press, 1992), 73, 105–106. For the Supreme Court's Fifth Amendment ruling, see *Hale v. Henkel* 201 U.S. 370 (1906), http://uscivilliberties.org/cases/3897-hale-v-henkel-201-us-370-1906.html. The court recognized that corporations were legal persons entitled to the equal protection of law under the Fourteenth Amendment in *Santa Clara v. Southern Pacific Railroad*, 118 U.S. 394 (1886). Some modern critics believe this decision began the trend in constitutional thought that ended with *Citizens United*'s expanded grant of First Amendment speech rights to corporations. An early example of this criticism was Justice William Rehnquist's dissent in *Bellotti*, 435 U.S. 765, 822 (http://caselaw.lp.findlaw.com/scripts/getcase.pl?court=US&vol=435&invol=765). For a modern example aimed at *Citizens United*, see Pamela S. Karlan, "Me, Inc." *Boston Review*, July/August 2011 (http://bostonreview.net/pamela-karlan-corporate-personhood). See also Ruth H. Bloch and Naomi Lamoreaux, "Property v. Liberty: The Supreme Court's Radical Break with Its Historical Treatment of Corporations," in *Perspectives on History*, July 2014 (http://historians.org/publications-and-directories/perspectives-on-history/historians-weigh-in-on-hobby-lobby/property-v-liberty).

18. *Citizens United*, 130 S.Ct. 876, 900, 904, 908.

19. For a clip of President Obama's comment about *Citizens United*, see www.youtube.com/watch?v=8v-rJb8G15I.

20. Adam Bonica, "Avenues of Influence: On the Political Expenditures of Corporations and Their Directors and Executives," June 20, 2014, app. (http://papers.ssrn.com/sol3/papers.cfm?abstract_id=2313232). The rise of dark money groups is one reason why Senate Democrats publicly called on the Securities and Exchange Commission to require corporations to disclose their political spending to investors. "SEC Nominees Face Pressure from Senate Democrats to Back Political Spending Disclosure Rule," *Thomson Reuters Tax & Accounting News*, October 22, 2015 (https://tax.thomson-reuters.com/media-resources/news-media-resources/checkpoint-news/daily-newsstand/sec-nominees-face-pressure-from-senate-democrats-to-back-political-spending-disclosure-rule/).

21. David B. Magleby and Jay Goodliffe, "Interest Groups," in David B. Magleby, ed., *Financing the 2012 Election* (Washington, DC: Brookings Institution Press, 2014), 233.

22. Jackie Crosby, "Target Apologizes for Giving to Group Backing Emmer," *Minneapolis Star-Tribune*, August 5, 2010 (www.startribune.com/business/100051999.html).

23. Barry Hirsch and David Macpherson, "Union Membership and Coverage Database" (www.unionstats.com).

24. Josh Eidelson, "'Wisconsin Is the Model': Grover Norquist's Tea Party Scheme to Crush His Union Enemies," *Salon*, March 8, 2014 (www.salon.com/2014/03/08/wisconsin_is_the_model_grover_norquists_tea_party_scheme_to_crush_his_union_enemies/).

25. Thomas B. Edsall, "Republicans Sure Love to Hate Unions," *New York Times*, November 18, 2014 (www.nytimes.com/2014/11/19/opinion/republicans-sure-love-to-hate-unions.html).

26. *Citizens United*, 130 S.Ct. 876, 947–48.

27. Federal Election Commission, *Federal Election Commission Record*, December 1989, 5 (www.fec.gov/pdf/record/1989/december1989.pdf); Federal Election Commission, *Foreign Nationals Brochure*, July 2003, 2–3 (www.fec.gov/pages/brochures/foreign_nat_brochure.pdf).

28. Court Orders for January 9, 2012, 11–275 (www.supremecourt.gov/orders/courtorders/010912zor.pdf); Robin Bravender, "SCOTUS Upholds Foreign-Money Ban," *Politico*, January 9, 2012 (www.politico.com/news/stories/0112/71239.html). This was not a universally popular decision. Pro-reform groups welcomed it as narrowing, if not closing, the loophole in *Citizens United*; reform opponents criticized it for not living up to the principles set forth in that decision.

29. Meredith McGehee, "Foreign Money and U.S. Elections," The Arena, *Politico*, October 13, 2012 (www.politico.com/arena/perm/Meredith_McGehee_ACDB8164-727B-4813-9969-2D0ECEB787B9.html).

30. This paragraph and the next are based on Michelle Colin and Lucas Iberico Lozada, "FEC Decision May Allow More Foreign Money in U.S. Votes, Critics Say," *Reuters*, April 24, 2015 (www.reuters.com/article/2015/04/24/us-usa-election-fec-idUSKBN0NF1V420150424); and Ciara Torres-Spelliscy, "How a Pornographer Tried to Win a U.S. Election," *BrennanCenter.org* (www.brennancenter.org/blog/how-foreign-pornographer-tried-win-us-election).

31. For 1992, see Herbert E. Alexander and Anthony Corrado, *Financing the 1992 Election* (Armonk, NY: M.E. Sharpe, 1995), 157. For 1996 and 2000, see Federal Election Commission press releases: "1995-96 Non-Federal Accounts of National Party Committees, January 1, 1995–December 31, 1996" (www.fec.gov/finance/demsoft.htm); "1999-2000 Non-Federal Accounts of National Party Committees, January 1, 1999–December 31, 2000" (www.fec.gov/press/press2001/051501partyfund/nonfeddem2000.html). For 2012 figures, see Center for Responsive Politics, "Business-Labor-Ideology Split in PAC & Individual Donations to Candidates" (www.opensecrets.org/bigpicture/blio.php?cycle=2012).

32. Lee Drutman, *The Business of America Is Lobbying: How Corporations Became Politicized and How Politics Became More Corporate* (New York: Oxford University Press, 2015), 16, 94. Political scientists Stephen Ansolabehere, James M. Snyder Jr., and Mickey Tripathi found "a strong association between expenditures on lobbying and campaign contributions": "Are PAC Contributions and Lobbying Linked? New Evidence from the 1995 Lobby Disclosure Act," August 2000, 13–14 (http://economics.mit.edu/files/1209).

33. This paragraph and the next are based on Benjamin C. Waterhouse, *Lobbying America: The Politics of Business from Nixon to NAFTA* (Princeton: Princeton University Press, 2014), 25–27.

34. Anne E. Kornblut, "Lobbyist Accepts Plea Deal," *New York Times*, January 4, 2006 (www.nytimes.com/2006/01/04/politics/04abramoff.html).

35. Craig Holman, "The Tension Between Lobbying and Campaign Finance Laws: Rolling Back Gains Made Under the Honest Leadership and Open Government Act of 2007," *Election Law Journal* 13 (2014): 45–53. This law was supposed to go into effect for the 2008 election, but a partisan stalemate in Congress over appointments to the FEC prevented that agency from writing the regulations to implement it; see Anthony Corrado, "The Regulatory Environment of the 2008 Election," in David B. Magleby and Anthony Corrado, eds. *Financing the 2008 Election* (Washington, DC: Brookings Institution Press, 2014), 76–77. See also Federal Election Commission, "FAQ on Lobbyist Bundling" (www.fec.gov/law/lobbybundlingfaq.shtml).

36. Holman, "The Tension Between Lobbying and Campaign Finance Laws," 61; Eric Lipton, "A Loophole Allows Lawmakers to Reel in Trips and Donations," *New York Times*, January 19, 2014 (www.nytimes.com/2014/01/20/us/politics/a-loophole-allows-lawmakers-to-reel-in-trips-and-donations.html).

CHAPTER 10

1. Greg Stroh, "Bloomberg Poll: Americans Want Supreme Court to Turn off Political Spending Spigot," *Bloomberg.com*, September 28, 2015 (www.bloomberg.com/politics/articles/2015-09-28/bloomberg-poll-americans-want-supreme-court-to-turn-off-political-spending-spigot?cmpid=BBD092815_POL). This response was especially striking because the question did not mention the decision by name: it asked respondents' opinion of a Supreme Court ruling that "corporations and unions may spend unlimited amounts on political causes." Sarah Dutton, Jennifer De Pinto, Anthony Savant, and Fred Backus, "Poll: Americans Say Money Has Too Much Influence in Campaigns," *CBSNews.com* (www.cbsnews.com/news/poll-americans-say-money-has-too-much-influence-in-campaigns/).

2. "Unity Statement of Principles: Solutions to the Undue Influence of Money in Politics" (www.pfaw.org/sites/default/files/UnityStatementSigners0114.pdf).

3. Some of the newly disillusioned are conservative Republicans who have formed new reform groups. The best-known ones are Issue One, which organized a 100-member "ReFormers Caucus" made up of Republican and Democratic former governors and members of Congress to come up with solutions; and Take Back Our Republic, which is more conservative.

4. "Honest Elections, 1967," *Washington Post*, April 5, 1967, A18. Metcalf tried again in 1975: R. W. Apple, "Federal Elections Panel Making a Delayed Start," *New York Times*, May 20, 1975, L77. For the recent revival, see: Bruce Ackerman, "Crediting the Voters: A New Beginning for Campaign Finance," *American Prospect*, March 21, 1993, 71–90, and Bruce Ackerman and Ian Ayres, *Voting with Dollars: A New Paradigm for Campaign Finance* (New Haven: Yale University Press, 2002); Richard L. Hasen, "Clipping Coupons for Democracy: An Egalitarian/Public Choice Defense of Campaign Finance Vouchers," *California Law Review* 84 (1996): 1–59, and Richard L. Hasen, *Plutocrats United: Campaign Money, the Supreme Court, and the Distortion of American Elections* (New Haven: Yale University Press, 2016); Lawrence Lessig, *Republic, Lost: How Money Corrupts Congress—and a Plan to Stop It* (New York: Twelve, 2011). See also Edward B. Foley, "Equal Dollars per Voter: A Constitutional Principle of Campaign Finance," *Columbia Law Review* 94 (1994): 1204–57; Government by the People Act of 2015 (www.congress.gov/bill/114th-congress/house-bill/20).

5. See Robert E. Mutch, *Buying the Vote: A History of Campaign Finance Reform* (New York: Oxford University Press, 2014), for the parties' small-donor programs from the late nineteenth to the early twenty-first centuries.

6. UPI, "GOP Chief Wants Contribution Law Eased for Parties," *Washington Post*, November 21, 1981, A3. For the big contributions in 1972, and the Nixon campaign's attempt to keep them secret, see Mutch, *Buying the Vote*, 132–34.

7. On the post-BCRA period, see Linda Feldman, "In Politics, the Rise of Small Donors," *Christian Science Monitor*, June 28, 2004 (www.csmonitor.com/2004/0628/p01s01-uspo.html).

8. NYC Campaign Finance Board, *2013 Post-Election Report* (2014), 41 (www.nyccfb.info/sites/default/files/pressfiles/2013_PER.pdf).

9. Kenneth P. Vogel, "How the Koch Network Rivals the GOP," *Politico*, December 30, 2015 (www.politico.com/story/2015/12/koch-brothers-network-gop-david-charles-217124).

10. "The Federal Election Administration Act Introduced by Senator Tom Udall" (www.scribd.com/doc/301502991/Federal-Election-Administration-Act-Summary). See also the Restoring Integrity to America's Elections Act, introduced by Representative Derek Kilmer (D-Washington) on June 25, 2015 (www.govtrack.us/congress/bills/114/hr2931).

11. *Van Hollen v. FEC*, USCA Case #15-5016, slip opinion, 17, 25, 28 (www.fec.gov/law/litigation/van_hollen_ac155016_opinion.pdf).

12. On judicialization, see Ran Hirsch, "The Judicialization of Politics," in Robert E. Goodin ed., *The Oxford Handbook of Political Science* (New York: Oxford University Press, 2013), published online at www.oxfordhandbooks.com/view/10.1093/oxfordhb/9780199604456.001.0001/oxfordhb-9780199604456-e-013. On the conservatism of the Roberts court, see William A. Landes and

Richard A. Posner, "Rational Judicial Behavior: A Statistical Study," *Journal of Legal Analysis* 1 (2009): 782–83. Anthony Kennedy is the tenth most conservative justice.

13. On asymmetrical polarization, see Adam Bonica, Nolan McCarty, Keith T. Poole, and Howard Rosenthal, "Why Hasn't Democracy Slowed Rising Inequality?" *Journal of Economic Perspectives* 27 (Summer 2013): 103-24.

14. Richard L. Hasen, *The Voting Wars: From Florida 2000 to the Next Election Meltdown* (New Haven: Yale University Press, 2012), chap. 2.

15. Pew Research Center, "Political Polarization in the American Public," June 2014 (http://www.people-press.org/2014/06/12/political-polarization-in-the-american-public/).

16. Martin Gilens and Benjamin I. Page, "Testing Theories of American Politics: Elites, Interest Groups, and Average Citizens," *Perspectives on Politics* 12 (Sept. 2014): 573.

GLOSSARY

501(c) groups The Internal Revenue Service exempts groups formed under this section of the tax code from paying taxes on their income as long as that income is used only for the "exempt purposes" covered under its subsections, and not for the benefit of private persons or for any profit-making activities. These groups disclose the identities of their donors only to the IRS, which does not make them public.

501(c)(3) Groups formed under this subsection are generally called charities, although they also include religious, educational, and scientific activities; contributions to them are tax-deductible. Some of the best-known charities are Doctors Without Borders USA, the American Red Cross, the Salvation Army, Save the Children, and the Carnegie Institute for Science. Groups formed under this subsection may not engage in political activity.

501(c)(4) Organizations formed under this subsection, called "social welfare groups," are dedicated to the "common good and general welfare of the people of the community"; contributions to them are not tax-deductible. Some of the best-known social welfare groups are the American Association of Retired People, the National Rifle Association, and the National Association for the Advancement of Colored People. Groups formed under this subsection are permitted to lobby because promoting legislation is one way to achieve their exempt purpose.

Social welfare groups may make electioneering communications and independent expenditures as long as this political activity is not their primary purpose. The IRS, however, has no way to tell whether a group is primarily engaged in its exempt purpose or in political activities. Most of these groups are nonprofit corporations, and since *Citizens United* they have been widely used to make political expenditures.

501(c)(5) Labor unions are the best-known groups formed under this section of the tax code. To qualify for tax exemption under this section, an organization must be dedicated to improving the "conditions of those engaged in the pursuits of labor." These organizations are typically supported in large part by membership dues, which may be deductible as a business expense. These groups, too, may lobby for legislation related to their exempt function and can participate in elections as long as they do not make that their primary activity.

501(c)(6) Chambers of commerce, boards of trade, real estate boards, and "business leagues" generally fall under this section. Business leagues tend to be membership organizations, and member dues may be deductible as a business expense. Business leagues also may lobby for legislation related to their exempt function and may participate in elections as long as they do not make that their primary activity.

527s Congress added section 527 to the Internal Revenue Code in 1975 to clarify the tax status of political organizations—party committees, candidate committees, and PACs. These organizations are not taxed on the income they receive from contributions, and those contributions are not subject to the gift tax. Republican and Democratic Party committees, candidate committees, and PACs registered with the IRS as 527 groups and with the FEC as political committees.

In the 1990s the IRS was persuaded that issue ads, which *Buckley v. Valeo* had said were not political, were political enough for the groups making them to register as 527s. With issue ads classified as political by the IRS and as nonpolitical by the FEC, groups formed to do issue advocacy benefited from section 527's tax exemption while not having to register with or disclose their donors to the FEC. After the McCain-Feingold Act banned soft money, 527 groups became the major vehicle for raising and spending non-FECA money.

Aggregate contribution limit The 1974 FECA amendments imposed a limit on how much a donor could contribute to candidates and an aggregate limit on the total amount an individual could contribute in a calendar year. The Supreme Court upheld both limits in *Buckley v. Valeo* (1976) but struck down the aggregate limit in *McCutcheon v. FEC* (2014).

Bipartisan Campaign Reform Act of 2002 Also known as the McCain-Feingold Act, after its sponsors, Senators John McCain (R-AZ) and Russ Feingold (D-WI). See Chronology for a brief description.

Bundling Soliciting many individual contributions and presenting them to a candidate as one large "bundle." The people who do this are called "bundlers."

Carey committee The FEC's term for a hybrid PAC. The reference is to *Carey v. FEC*, 791 F. Supp. 2d 121 (D.D.C. 2011), the district court case that permitted nonconnected PACs to become hybrid PACs.

Code of Federal Regulations Contains all the regulations issued by the departments and agencies of the federal government (www.ecfr.gov/cgi-bin/ECFR?page=browse).

Connected PAC A political action committee sponsored by an organization, such as a corporation or labor union. Also called a "separate segregated fund."

Conservative coalition The ad hoc coalition of Republicans and Southern Democrats in Congress who voted together from the 1930s through the 1970s to oppose the New Deal and later civil rights, welfare, and labor legislation. The coalition's importance here is that it was strong enough to overcome presidential vetoes to pass the Smith-Connally Act and the Taft-Hartley Act, which had significant campaign finance provisions.

Contribution limits For the 2015–16 election cycle, individuals may contribute no more than $2,700 per election (the primary and the general each count as one election); $5,000 per year to a (non-super) PAC; $10,000 per year to state and local party committees; $33,400 per year to a national party committee; $100,400 per year to a national party committee's convention account; $100,400 per year to a national party's headquarters account; and $100,400 to a national party's account for election contests and other legal expenses. The limits on contributions to candidates and national party committees are indexed for inflation at the beginning of each election cycle. For these and other limits, see FEC, "Contribution Limits for 2015–2016 Federal Elections" (www.fec.gov/info/contriblimitschart1516.pdf).

Coordination What candidates and the committees that make independent expenditures to support them are legally prohibited from doing. Independent expenditures are legally required to be made without the authorization or participation of the candidates they support.

Democratic Congressional Campaign Committee The Democratic Party's fundraising committee for House candidates.

Democratic Senatorial Campaign Committee The Democratic Party's fundraising committee for Senate candidates.

Disclosure The legal requirement for political committees to disclose the identities of their donors. Disclosure laws usually require committees to identify only those donors who make contributions that exceed a threshold amount. The threshold amount in the FECA is $200, a figure that is not adjusted for inflation. Most states set their thresholds much lower, most of them in the single and double digits. The first federal disclosure law was passed in 1910, and some form of disclosure has been a requirement for federal candidates and national party committees ever since.

Election cycle The two-year cycle made up of the even-numbered election year and the odd-numbered year preceding it.

Electioneering communication BCRA created this category of political ads to bring sham issue ads under FECA regulation. The category covers any ad that mentions a clearly identified federal candidate and is publicly distributed by radio or TV within thirty days of a primary election or sixty days of a general election. Such ads must be financed with hard money and their financing must be reported to the FEC. The Supreme Court weakened this provision in *FEC v. Wisconsin Right to Life.*

Expenditure limits Ceilings on how much candidates, parties, PACs, and individuals can spend in an election campaign. Some kind of expenditure limit was in federal campaign finance law from 1911 to 1972. Congress reinstated limits in the 1974 FECA amendments, but the Supreme Court struck them down in *Buckley v. Valeo* as violations of the First Amendment. The only expenditure limits the Supreme Court allowed were those that candidates agreed to as a condition for receiving federal subsidies for their campaigns. Such limits are part of the various kinds of state and local public funding programs.

Exploratory committee Formally called a "testing the waters fund," this is a committee formed by someone who wants to explore the possibility of running for a federal office. An exploratory committee must raise its funds in compliance with FECA limits and prohibitions, but does not have to file disclosure reports. If the person decides not to run, the exploratory committee is disbanded without having to disclose its finances. But if the person does decide to run, the exploratory committee becomes a candidate committee; the candidate committee is considered to have begun with the formation of the exploratory committee and must disclose the financing of its exploratory activities.

Express advocacy Political advertisements that expressly advocate the election or defeat of clearly identified candidates for federal office. The Supreme Court struck down limits on these expenditures, but they do have to be financed with hard money.

FCPA See Federal Corrupt Practices Act of 1925.

FECA See Federal Election Campaign Act.

Federal Corrupt Practices Act of 1925 The predecessor of the Federal Election Campaign Act. The name was first applied to federal campaign finance laws that had been passed since 1907 when they were recodified and partly revised in 1925.

Federal Election Campaign Act The FECA of 1971 took effect on April 7, 1972. Like the Federal Corrupt Practices Act of 1925, it was a recodification and partial revision of existing law. It strengthened disclosure requirements but repealed contribution limits and kept limits only on expenditures for media advertisements. See Chronology for 1974, 1976, and 1979 amendments.

General election Held to elect candidates to government office (see PRIMARY ELECTION).

Gift tax A tax on gifts of more than $3,000 passed by Congress in 1932 to prevent people from evading the estate tax by making transfers of property before death. The IRS treated campaign contributions as taxable gifts until Congress exempted them from that tax in 1975 (see 527S).

Hard money The colloquial term for money raised under FECA limits on the size of contributions and prohibitions against contributions from corporations and labor unions.

Hybrid PAC A hybrid PAC combines a nonconnected PAC with a super PAC. It has two bank accounts: one for hard money raised by the nonconnected PAC; and a second one for the super PAC, which *Citizens United* and *SpeechNow* allow to raise money without being bound by those limits and restrictions. The hybrid PAC is also called a *Carey* PAC.

Income tax checkoff The way the Presidential Election Campaign Fund is financed; taxpayers have the option of checking a box on their income tax forms that sends $3 of their payment to the fund.

Independent expenditures Defined by the Supreme Court in *Buckley v. Valeo* as express advocacy expenditures made on behalf of a candidate, but "made totally independently of the candidate and his campaign" (424 U.S. 1, 47). Until *Citizens United* these expenditures had to be financed with money raised under the original FECA limits and prohibitions; they can now be financed with contributions of unlimited size from individuals, corporations, and labor unions. PACs that make only independent expenditures are called super PACs.

Independent-expenditure-only political committee The FEC's official term for a super PAC.

Invisible primary What political scientists call the jockeying for place among presidential hopefuls in the odd-numbered year before the state primaries and caucuses are held. The "winner" of the invisible primary has usually been the candidate who has the most endorsements from the leaders of his or her party, the biggest campaign fund, and the highest ranking in public opinion polls; this candidate has almost always won most of the primaries and the party nomination. That pattern did not hold for the GOP in the 2015–16 cycle.

Issue advocacy Advertisements about public policy issues, which the Supreme Court has defined as nonpolitical. Issue ads can remain nonpolitical even if they mention clearly identified federal candidates, but not if they expressly advocate the election or defeat of those candidates. There are no limits on how much can be spent on such ads, they do not have to be financed with hard money, and they do not have to be reported to the FEC.

Joint fundraising committee A committee formed to raise campaign funds for several candidates and party committees. The advantage of a joint committee is that it allows donors to write one check covering the legally allowable amounts they can give to the candidates and the party committees.

Leadership PAC Politicians form leadership PACs to raise money for their own non-campaign activities and contribute to the campaigns of other politicians.

Magic words The label given to the kinds of words and phrases the Supreme Court said in *Buckley v. Valeo* need to be in a political advertisement to classify it as "express advocacy." The court's suggestions—" 'vote for,' 'elect,' 'support,' 'cast your ballot for,' 'Smith for Congress,' 'vote against,' 'defeat,' 'reject' "—appear in footnote 52.

Matching funds Government subsidies for small contributions in public funding programs. Under the presidential public funding program candidates in presidential primaries received one-to-one matches for contributions of up to $250; New York City's public funding program provides six-to-one matches for contributions of up to $175.

McCain-Feingold Act See Bipartisan Campaign Reform Act of 2000.

MCFL group or corporation Another name for qualified nonprofit corporation.

Midterm election Congressional election held in the even-numbered years between presidential elections.

Millionaires' amendment A provision in the 2002 McCain-Feingold Act that lifted the individual and party contribution limits for candidates facing rich opponents who financed their own campaigns. The Supreme Court struck it down in *Davis v. FEC*.

National Republican Congressional Committee The Republican Party's fundraising committee for House candidates.

National Republican Senatorial Committee The Republican Party's fundraising committee for Senate candidates.

Nonconnected PAC A political action committee that is not sponsored by a corporation, labor union, trade association, or other organization.

Political action committee The term "political action committee" and its acronym PAC are popular terms, not legal ones found in legislation or FEC regulations. Under the FECA, a PAC is a political committee that is neither a party committee nor an authorized candidate committee.

Presidential Election Campaign Fund The money used to subsidize presidential primary and general election campaigns. It is financed by taxpayers who voluntarily check the box on their federal income tax returns to send $3 of their payment to the fund.

Primary election Held to elect the people who will be a party's candidates for government office.

Public funding Federal, state, and local government programs to subsidize the campaigns of candidates for elective office.

Qualified nonprofit corporation An incorporated voluntary association that was exempted from the FECA ban against corporate express advocacy independent expenditures because it was formed to promote political ideas, did not have shareholders, and did not accept business or labor contributions. The FEC created this category to comply with the Supreme Court's decision in *FEC v. Massachusetts for Life* (1986), but it became irrelevant when the court exempted all corporations from the FECA ban in *Citizens United*.

Quid pro quo corruption The term *quid pro quo* means an exchange of one thing for another thing; as the description of a kind of corruption it is hard to see it as anything but bribery. The Supreme Court said in *Buckley* that preventing the fact or appearance of *quid pro quo* corruption is the only constitutionally permissible justification for regulating campaign funds.

Separate segregated fund This is the legal term for a connected PAC, indicating that it is separate from its sponsoring organization and its treasury is segregated from that of its sponsor.

Sham issue ads Issue ads that mention candidates in clearly positive or negative ways but escape regulation because they do not use any of the magic words.

Social welfare group See 501(C)(4), above.

Soft money General term for money raised outside FECA regulations.

Super PAC Popular term for what the FEC calls an independent-expenditure-only political committee.

Super Tuesday The day on which several states hold their presidential primaries or caucuses; the date and the number of states changes from election to election. The first Super Tuesday was on March 8, 1988. Eleven southern and border states, all controlled by Democrats, agreed to hold their primaries on that day, hoping that the South would be able to counter the more liberal voters in northern states. Super Tuesdays in succeeding elections included fewer southern states and more states from the North and West. The biggest so far was on February 5, 2008, when twenty-four states participated.

Tax incentives Tax deductions and/or credits offered to encourage taxpayers to make small contributions.

Testing the waters fund The legal name for an exploratory committee.

FURTHER READING

Cain, Bruce. *Democracy More or Less: America's Political Reform Quandary.* New York: Cambridge University Press, 2015.

Hasen, Richard L. *Plutocrats United: Campaign Money, the Supreme Court, and the Distortion of American Politics.* New Haven: Yale University Press, 2016.

Hohenstein, Kurt. *Coining Corruption: The Making of the American Campaign Finance System.* DeKalb: Northern Illinois University Press, 2007.

Kushner, Timothy K. *Capitalism v. Democracy: Money in Politics and the Free Market Constitution.* Stanford, CA: Stanford Law Books, 2014.

La Raja, Raymond J. *Small Change: Money, Political Parties and Campaign Finance Reform.* Ann Arbor: University of Michigan Press, 2008.

La Raja, Raymond J., and Brian F. Schaffner. *Campaign Finance and Political Polarization: When Purists Prevail.* Ann Arbor: University of Michigan Press, 2015.

Lessig, Lawrence. *Republic, Lost: How Money Corrupts Congress and a Plan to Stop It.* New York: Twelve, 2011.

Magleby, David B., ed. *Financing the 2012 Election.* Washington, DC: Brookings Institution Press, 2014.

Magleby, David B., and Anthony Corrado, eds. *Financing the 2008 Election.* Washington, DC: Brookings Institution Press, 2011.

Magleby, David B., Anthony Corrado, and Kelly D. Patterson, eds. *Financing the 2004 Election.* Washington, DC: Brookings Institution Press, 2006.

Malbin, Michael J., ed. *The Election After Reform: Money, Politics, and the Bipartisan Campaign Reform Act.* Lanham, MD: Rowman and Littlefield, 2006.

Mayer, Jane. *Dark Money: The Hidden History of the Billionaires Behind the Rise of the Radical Right.* New York: Random House, 2016.

Mutch, Robert E. *Buying the Vote: A History of Campaign Finance Reform.* New York: Oxford University Press, 2014.

Post, Robert C. *Citizens Divided: Campaign Finance Reform and the Constitution.* Cambridge, MA: Harvard University Press, 2014.

Teachout, Zephyr. *Corruption in America: From Benjamin Franklin's Snuff Box to Citizens United.* Cambridge, MA: Harvard University Press, 2014.

Vogel, Kenneth P. *Big Money: 2.5 Billion Dollars, One Suspicious Vehicle, and a Pimp—on the Trail of the Ultra-Rich Hijacking American Politics.* New York: Public Affairs, 2014.

Youn, Monica, ed. *Money, Politics, and the Constitution: Beyond* Citizens United. New York: Century Foundation Press, 2011.

For campaign finance data and analysis, consult these websites:

Federal Election Commission
www.fec.gov

Campaign Finance Institute
www.cfinst.org

CampaignMoney.com
www.campaignmoney.com

Center for Responsive Politics
www.opensecrets.org

INDEX

Abramoff, Jack, 2, 136
Abood v. Detroit Board of Education
(1977). *See* under Supreme Court
Adelson, Sheldon, 91, 101, 114, 182n4
AFL-CIO, 127, 154
Agnew, Vice President Spiro, 165n6
Alito, Justice Samuel, 113, 146
American Federation of Labor, 62, 63,
125–26, 142–43, 151
Americans for Prosperity, 96–97, 133
Anderson, Representative John
(R-IL), 33–34
*Arizona Free Enterprise Club's Freedom
Club PAC v. Bennett* (2011). *See*
under Supreme Court
*Austin v. Michigan Chamber of
Commerce* (1990). *See* under
Supreme Court

BCRA. *See* Bipartisan Campaign
Reform Act
Belmont, Perry, 46
Bipartisan Campaign Reform Act, 80,
108, 110, 112–15, 140, 158, 159,
198, 199
Blackmun, Justice Harry, 23
Bloomberg, Michael, 5, 43, 102,
172n52, 186n39
Bork, Solicitor General Robert H.,
12, 166n18

Briffault, Richard, 83
Buckley, Senator James, xvi,
16, 166n15
Buckley v. Valeo (1976). *See* under
Supreme Court
bundling, 92, 94, 136, 198
Burger, Chief Justice Warren,
13, 23–24
Burroughs v. United States (1934). *See*
under Supreme Court
Bush, Governor Jeb, 85, 87–88, 92, 93
Bush, President George W., 44, 45, 96,
113, 146
Business Roundtable, 132

Campaign Finance Institute, 36, 39,
53, 89–90
Campaign Legal Center, 53
Center for Responsive Politics, 53
Clinton, President Bill, 55, 66,
107–08, 116
Clinton, Hillary, 74, 83, 84, 85, 87, 92,
94–95, 101, 159
Colbert, Stephen, 85–87
Common Cause, 13–14, 16
Congress of Industrial Organizations,
61–63, 68, 125–26, 151
congressional elections, 7, 15, 47, 49,
59, 62, 83, 125, 152, 201
cost of, xv, 3–5, 6, 149–50

conservative coalition, 125, 151,
152, 198
contribution limits
before FECA, 7, 151
in 1974 FECA, 1, 8, 15–16, 19,
22–24, 44, 64, 79, 80–81, 123, 155,
160–61, 198
in BCRA, 45, 108, 158
and super PACs, 8–9, 75–76, 81,
85, 160
in state and local laws, 41–42,
105, 141
corporations
before FECA, 7, 30–31, 123–25,
149, 152
in 1972 election, xvi, 14
corporate PACs, 61, 63–65, 66, 69–71
and Supreme Court, 8, 75, 80–81,
121–23, 127–32, 156–57, 159, 192
and outside money, 105–06, 111
nonprofit, 9, 59, 75, 96, 113, 116–17,
130, 143–44, 189n36, 201
foreign, 133–34
Citizens United v. FEC (2010). *See*
under Supreme Court

dark money, 53, 59, 103, 117, 118, 130,
134, 143, 192
Davis v. FEC (2008). *See* under
Supreme Court
Democracy Alliance, 95, 99–101
Durbin, Senator Richard (D-IL), 138
disclosure
in 1908 election, 46
1910 law, 7, 48, 58, 149, 150, 173n5
in 1971 FECA, 8, 13–14, 49,
150–51, 200
and Watergate, 14, 165n4
in 1974 FECA amendments, 8, 15,
22, 154–55
and FEC, 47–48, 51–53,
105–06, 114–15
controversy about, 57–60, 143–44

and 501(c)s, 103, 114–15, 117, 197–98
and 527s, 109–10, 198
and lobbyists, 136
Drutman, Lee, 135

electioneering communication, 108,
110, 113–14, 115, 158, 197, 199
Expenditure limits
before FECA, 7, 149–50, 199
in 1974 FECA, 8, 9, 15–17
in *Buckley v. Valeo*, 1, 19,
22–24, 154–55
in state and local laws, 41–42
express advocacy
in *Buckley v. Valeo*, 20–21, 106–07,
109, 200
in *Citizens United*, 96, 116,
130, 192n16
and dark money, 116–17

FCPA. *See* Federal Corrupt
Practices Act
FEC. *See* Federal Election Commission
FEC v. Massachusetts Citizens for Life
(1986). *See* under Supreme Court
*FEC v. National Right to Work
Committee* (1982). *See* under
Supreme Court
FEC v. Wisconsin Right to Life (2007).
See under Supreme Court
FECA. *See* Federal Election
Campaign Act
Federal Corrupt Practices Act, 14, 63,
150, 151
Federal Election Campaign Act, 9, 44,
52, 55, 80–81, 84, 116, 130, 134
1971 act, 7–8, 13, 46, 49, 64, 67, 76,
127, 153–154, 200
1974 amendments, 8, 10, 15, 17–18,
27, 30, 63, 79, 109, 140, 154
1976 amendments, 75, 79–80,
155, 156
1979 amendments, 104–105, 156

BCRA, 80, 108, 110, 140, 158
Federal Election Commission,
    creation of, 8, 15, 48–51, 166n16
    and public funding, 32, 33–35, 37
    and disclosure, 47–49, 51–54,
        114–15, 144, 172n3, 189n32
    and soft money, 104–08
    enforcement by, 54–55, 61, 69,
        76, 77, 81–82, 104–05, 111–12,
        133–34, 143, 189n36
    appointments to, 55–56
    deadlocks on, 53, 56–57, 134n35
First National Bank of Boston v. Bellotti
    (1978). *See* under Supreme Court
Ford, President Gerald R., 13, 14,
    16–17, 37, 165n6
foreign money, 108, 133–34
Friedrichs v. California Teachers
    Association (2016). *See* under
    Supreme Court

Gore, Vice President Al Jr. (D-TN), 45
Gore, Senator Al Sr. (D-TN), 79

Heard, Alexander, 49, 124
hard money, 44, 92, 94, 95, 104, 107,
    108, 109, 110, 113, 130, 142, 159,
    199, 200, 201

independent expenditures
    before FECA, 78–79
    in 1974 FECA, 15, 20, 79
    in 1980s, 44, 67–68, 82
    by corporations, 59, 121–23, 125,
        131–32, 157–58
    by labor unions, 70, 125, 132
    by ideological PACs, 71–72
    and super PACs, 71, 75–76, 160,
        177nn1–2,
    by 501(c)s, 116–17, 134, 144, 157
Internal Revenue Code, 109–10,
    117–20, 197–98
Internal Revenue Service

and tax incentives, 30
    and convention funds, 31–32
    and 527s, 109–10, 198, 200
    and 501(c)s, 59, 96, 103, 116–20,
        130, 134, 197–98
International Association of Machinists
    v. Street (1961). *See* under
    Supreme Court
issue advocacy, 200–01
    in *Buckley*, 20–21, 155
    and outside money, 23, 106–10, 113,
        116, 130, 158, 198

Kennedy, Senator Edward
    M. (D-MA), 15, 29
Kennedy, Justice Anthony M., 57,
    129, 131, 157, 196
Kerry, Senator John (D-MA), 45
Koch brothers' network, 94, 95–98, 142
Koch, Charles, 60, 142
Koch, David, 96, 99

labor unions, 76, 101, 107, 111, 112,
    132–33, 137, 145, 197
    before FECA, 7, 61–63, 68, 79,
        124–26, 151–52
    labor PACs, 61–63, 66, 68–69, 70,
        125–27, 134–35, 176n10
    and 1971 FECA, 127
    and Supreme Court, 68–69, 125–27,
        132, 152–53, 154, 156, 161–62
League of Women Voters, 16
Lewis, Peter, 100, 111
limited liability company, 53
Long, Senator Russell (D-LA), 27–29,
    43, 139

Mercer, Robert, 99
Metcalf, Senator Lee (D-MT), 139
McConnell v. FEC (2003). *See* under
    Supreme Court
McCutcheon v. FEC (2014). *See* under
    Supreme Court

Neuberger, Senator Richard
L. (D-OR), 27
Nixon, President Richard M., xvi,
11–14, 29, 35, 36, 146

Obama, President Barack
in 2008 election, 45, 66, 70, 72, 74,
84, 96, 100, 101, 112
in 2012 election, 6, 37, 48, 83, 96,
100, 184n25
and campaign finance, 120, 131
and FEC, 173n10
O'Connor, Justice Sandra Day, 157

PACs. *See* political action committees
Page, Clerk of the House William
Tyler, 49
Pipefitters v. United States (1972). *See*
under Supreme Court
political action committees, 4, 6, 26,
42, 61–74, 125, 152, 198, 201
CIO-PAC, 61–63, 68, 125,
126, 151–52
connected PACs, 61, 68–71
nonconnected PACs, 61, 71–74
super PACs, 9, 23, 51, 61, 71, 75–88,
90–91, 92, 94–95, 98–99, 101–102,
117, 130, 136, 142, 146, 200, 202
hybrid PACs, 77–78
Potter, Trevor, 85–87
Powell, Justice Lewis, 127–28
presidential elections, 8, 25–27, 43–45
1904, 7, 124
1908, 46, 140
1936, 30–31, 62, 124–25
1940, 7, 31, 78, 125
1972, xvi, 8, 10–14, 18, 22, 36, 140
1976, 6, 27, 35, 36–37, 104
1980, 30, 33–34, 35, 37, 44, 61, 66,
82, 89, 96, 103–105
1984, 37, 65, 66, 105
1988, 106
1992, 34, 66, 106
1996, 34, 35, 44, 73–74, 106–08

2000, 26, 34–35, 38, 44–45, 100,
107, 110
2004, 35, 44–45, 100, 110, 111, 112,
114, 116, 117
2008, 8, 45, 66, 70, 74, 92, 96, 100,
101, 111–12, 114, 116, 117
2012, 6, 25, 26, 37, 45, 47–48, 53,
71–72, 74, 76, 82–83, 95, 96, 97,
100, 117, 135
2016, 61, 85, 87–88, 89–90, 91–97,
98–99, 101–02, 143
Price, Representative David (D-NC), 83
Primo, David M., 59
public funding, 9, 15, 16, 25–45,
137–38, 139, 157, 201
presidential, 6, 8, 16, 17, 22, 25–38,
43–45, 47, 103, 138, 153, 154–55,
161, 200, 201
state and local, 38–43, 137, 138–39,
160, 201
vouchers, 41, 139
tax incentives, 25, 29, 30, 39, 141,
154, 157, 170n36, 202

quid pro quo corruption, 2–3, 19–20,
22, 75, 83, 128, 202

Ravel, FEC Commissioner Ann,
56, 173
Railway Clerks v. Allen (1963). *See*
under Supreme Court
Richards, Richard, 140
Ricketts, J. Joe, 98
Roberts, Chief Justice John G., 113
Rockefeller, Vice President
Nelson, 165n6
Romney, Governor, Mitt, 6, 48, 53, 72,
74, 83, 84–85, 90–91, 98
Rove, Karl, 76–77, 98
Rubio, Senator Marco (R-FL), 99, 117
Ryan, Paul S., 83

Sanders, Senator Bernie (D-VT), 87, 95
Scaife, Richard Mellon, 14, 187n13

Scalia, Justice Antonin, 131, 146, 147, 157, 162
Scott, Senator Hugh (R-PA), 15, 29
Singer, Paul, 98–99
small donors, xv, 90
    before FECA, 46, 140
    and public funding, 25–26, 29–30, 35–36, 154, 201, 202
    state and local laws, 25, 38–43, 139, 141
    and disclosure, 58–59
Smith, Bradley A., 55, 83
Smith-Connally Act, 62–63, 125, 151–52, 198
soft money
    party soft money, 23, 44, 61, 103–08, 131, 134–35, 183n19
    and BCRA, 80, 108, 140, 158
    and tax-exempt groups, 109–11, 112–14, 118, 130
Soros, George, 95, 100, 111
Stevens, Justice John Paul, 129, 133
Stewart, Jon, 86–87
Stewart, Justice Potter, 23
Steyer, Thomas Fahr, 101–02
Stone, W. Clement, 14
Sunlight Foundation, 53
super PACs. See under political action committees
Supreme Court, xvi, 3, 10, 13, 18, 40, 44, 46, 50, 57, 67, 79–80, 82, 144–47
    United States v. Newberry (1921), 150
    Burroughs v. United States (1934), 150
    United States v. Congress of Industrial Organizations (1948), 152
    United States v. United Auto Workers (1957), 152–53
    International Association of Machinists v. Street (1961), 125–26, 153
    Railway Clerks v. Allen (1963), 1963), 153

Pipefitters v. United States (1972), 68, 126–27
Buckley v. Valeo (1976), xvi, 1–2, 8, 9, 10, 16–24, 51, 58, 75, 78–80, 106–107, 109, 122, 128, 129–30, 146, 147, 155, 160, 198, 199, 200, 201, 202
Abood v. Detroit Board of Education (1977), 156
First National Bank of Boston v. Bellotti (1978), 127–29, 156
FEC v. National Right to Work Committee (1982), 156–57
FEC v. Massachusetts Citizens for Life (1986), 157
Austin v. Michigan Chamber of Commerce (1990), 157–58
McConnell v. FEC (2003), 108, 158
FEC v. Wisconsin Right to Life (2007), 112–14, 158–59, 199
Davis v. FEC (2008), 159
Citizens United v. FEC (2010), 8, 85, 95, 96, 116–17, 121–22, 129–34, 144, 146, 159
Arizona Free Enterprise Club's Freedom Club PAC v. Bennett (2011), 160
McCutcheon v. FEC (2014), 160–61, 198
Friedrichs v. California Teachers Association (2016), 161–62

Taft, President William Howard, 46
tax-exempt groups
    501(c)(3) charities, 197
    501(c)(4) social welfare groups, xvi, 23, 76–77, 86, 92, 96, 113, 115–18, 134, 157, 158, 159, 197, 202
    501(c)(5) labor groups, 112, 116, 197
    501(c)(6) business groups, 112, 116, 134, 198
    527 political groups, 108–12, 114, 119, 120, 160, 198, 200

tax incentives. *See* under public
   funding
Tea Party, 72, 88, 96, 133
Thomas, Justice Clarence, 146
Tillman Act, 7, 8, 10, 31, 62, 64, 65,
   122–29, 149, 157, 191
Trump, Donald, 87–88, 93–94, 98–99,
   184n28, 186n39

Udall, Senator Tom (D-NM), 143
*United States v. Congress of Industrial
   Organizations* (1948). *See* under
   Supreme Court
United States v. Newberry (1921). *See*
   under Supreme Court

*United States v. United Auto
   Workers* (1957). *See* under
   Supreme Court
U.S. Chamber of Commerce, 59, 60,
   114, 127

Van Hollen, Representative Chris
   (D-MD), 115
von Spakovsky, Hans, 55–56
vouchers. *See* under public funding

Watergate, xvi, 8, 10–14, 22, 25, 27,
   29, 35, 37, 49, 63–64, 123, 140,
   164, 191
White, Justice Byron, 23, 24